Prentice Hall LITERATURE

PENGUIN EDITION

Unit Two
Resources

The American Experience

PEARSON

Upper Saddle River, New Jersey
Boston, Massachusetts
Chandler, Arizona
Glenview, Illinois

Copyright© by Pearson Education, Inc., or its affiliates. All Rights Reserved. Printed in the United States of America. This publication is protected by copyright, and permission should be obtained from the publisher prior to any prohibited reproduction, storage in a retrieval system, or transmission in any form or by any means, electronic, mechanical, photocopying, recording, or likewise. The publisher hereby grants permission to reproduce these pages, in part or in whole, for classroom use only, the number not to exceed the number of students in each class. Notice of copyright must appear on all copies. For information regarding permissions, write to Pearson School Rights & Permissions, One Lake Street, Upper Saddle River, New Jersey 07458.

Pearson® is a trademark, in the U.S. and/or other countries, of Pearson plc or its affiliates.
Prentice Hall® is a trademark, in the U.S. and/or in other countries, of Pearson Education, Inc., or its affiliates.

ISBN–13: 978-0-13-366463-8
ISBN–10:   0-13-366463-5

3 4 5 6 7 8 9 10 V036 12 11 10

CONTENTS

For information about the Unit Resources, a Pronunciation Guide, and a Form for Analyzing Primary Source Documents, see the opening pages of your Unit One Resources.

"The Devil and Tom Walker" by Washington Irving

Commission of Meriwether Lewis by Thomas Jefferson

Crossing the Great Divide by Meriwether Lewis

"The Tide Rises, The Tide Falls" and *from* The Song of Hiawatha by Henry Wadsworth Longfellow

"Thanatopsis" by William Cullen Bryant

"Old Ironsides" by Oliver Wendell Holmes

"The Minister's Black Veil" by Nathaniel Hawthorne

"The Fall of the House of Usher" and "The Raven" by Edgar Allan Poe

"The Fall of the House of Usher" by Edgar Allan Poe

"Where Is Here?" by Joyce Carol Oates

Name _____

Starting Date _____ Ending Date _____

Concept Map Unit 2
A Growing Nation: Literature of the American Renaissance (1800–1870)

Three Essential Questions serve as lenses through which to view the literature—

How does literature shape or reflect society?

What is the relationship between place and literature?

What makes American literature American?

Reflected in these selections:

Reflected in these selections:

Reflected in these selections:

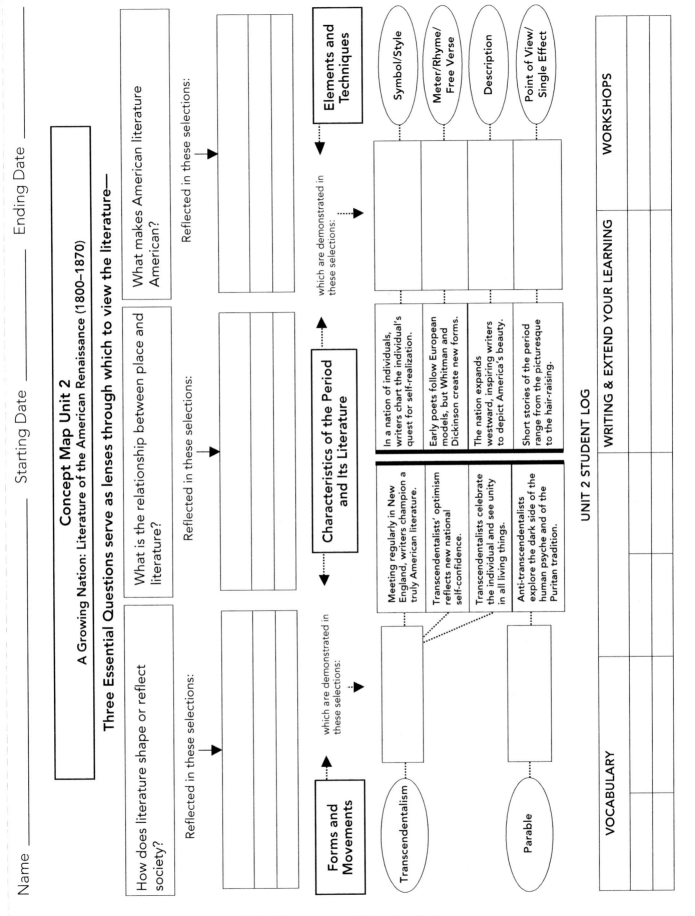

Elements and Techniques

- Symbol/Style
- Meter/Rhyme/ Free Verse
- Description
- Point of View/ Single Effect

which are demonstrated in these selections:

Characteristics of the Period and Its Literature

- In a nation of individuals, writers chart the individual's quest for self-realization.
- Early poets follow European models, but Whitman and Dickinson create new forms.
- The nation expands westward, inspiring writers to depict America's beauty.
- Short stories of the period range from the picturesque to the hair-raising.

- Meeting regularly in New England, writers champion a truly American literature.
- Transcendentalists' optimism reflects new national self-confidence.
- Transcendentalists celebrate the individual and see unity in all living things.
- Anti-transcendentalists explore the dark side of the human psyche and of the Puritan tradition.

which are demonstrated in these selections:

Forms and Movements

- Transcendentalism
- Parable

UNIT 2 STUDENT LOG

VOCABULARY

WRITING & EXTEND YOUR LEARNING

WORKSHOPS

Unit 2 Introduction
Names and Terms to Know

A. DIRECTIONS: *Write a brief sentence explaining each of the following names and terms. You will find all of the information you need in the Unit 2 Introduction in your textbook.*

1. Louisiana Purchase: _____

   _____

2. Andrew Jackson: _____

   _____

3. Trail of Tears: _____

   _____

4. Henry Wadsworth Longfellow: _____

   _____

5. "barbaric yawp": _____

   _____

6. Seneca Falls Convention _____

   _____

B. DIRECTIONS: *Use the hints below to help you answer each question.*

1. How did new technology change life in the United States during the American Renaissance?
   [Hints: What types of new technology developed during the 19th century? How did this new technology improve American life?]

   _____

   _____

   _____

2. What was the relationship between geographic expansion and Indian removal?
   [Hints: What did easterners do as the United States acquired more western territory? How did this activity affect the Indian peoples? What was Indian removal?]

   _____

   _____

   _____

3. How did Transcendentalism figure in the American Renaissance?
   [Hints: Who were the Transcendentalists? What ideals did they express?]

   _____

   _____

   _____

Unit 2 Resources: A Growing Nation
2

Name _____ Date _____

Unit 2 Introduction

Essential Question 1: What is the relationship between place and literature?

A. DIRECTIONS: *Answer the questions about the first Essential Question in the Introduction about the relationship between place and literature. All the information you need is in the Unit 2 Introduction in your textbook.*

1. *Discoveries Through Exploration*

    a. As they moved westward, Americans were impressed with _____
    _____

    b. What were some examples of natural wonders found by American settlers?
    _____

2. *Attitudes Toward the Land*

    a. What opportunities did American settlers find as they moved to new parts of the
    country? _____
    _____

    b. What nonmaterial feelings did the American landscape inspire? _____
    _____

3. *Attitudes Toward Nature Expressed in the Literature*

    a. Describe the settings for the "new American mythology." _____
    _____

    b. American masters of literature during this period included _____
    _____

    c. Give examples of other artists who reflected Americans' appreciation of nature.
    _____

B. DIRECTIONS: *Answer the questions that include the Essential Question Vocabulary words.*

    1. Name a person who inspires you with *awe*. _____
    _____

    2. What kind of language would you expect to hear from someone with a sense of *grandeur*?
    _____

    3. Would a company's board be pleased to learn that there had been an *expansion* in the market for their product? Explain.
    _____

Name _____ Date _____

Unit 2 Introduction

Essential Question 2: How does literature shape or reflect society?

A. DIRECTIONS: *On the lines provided, answer the questions about the second Essential Question in the Introduction about the relationship between the writer and society. All the information you need is in the Unit 2 Introduction in your textbook.*

1. *Social and Political Forces of the Period*

   a. Give examples of new technology in 19th-century America. _____
   _____

   b. The effects of the new technology were _____
   _____

   c. What were an example of the growth of democracy during this time? _____
   _____

   d. The spread of democracy did not include these groups: _____
   e. Slavery divided the country because _____
   _____

2. *What Americans Read*

   a. Popular writings in this period included _____
   _____

   b. What two British writers were extremely popular during this time?
   _____

3. *What American Writers Wanted to Achieve*

   a. Describe the "social vision" expressed by American writers of this period.
   _____

   b. Which American writers expressed a "romantic vision"? _____
   _____

   c. The "transcendental vision" argued that _____
   _____

B. DIRECTIONS: *Complete the sentence stems based on the Essential Question Vocabulary words.*

1. A *personal* narrative is one that reveals _____.
2. The vacation was *fantastic* because _____.
3. When someone is *self-reliant,* he or she handles problems _____.

Unit 2 Introduction

Essential Question 3: What makes American literature American?

A. DIRECTIONS: *On the lines provided, answer the questions about the third Essential Question in the Introduction about what makes American literature American. All the information you need is in the Unit 2 Introduction in your textbook.*

1. *American Styles of Speaking and Writing*

   a. American English was characterized by _____

   _____

   b. Give examples of colloquial expressions. _____

   _____

   c. In what way did Walt Whitman represent the American voice? _____

   _____

2. *American Literary Character Types*

   a. Examples of the "frontiersman" character can be found in _____

   _____

   b. Examples of the "romantic hero" in American Renaissance writing include

   _____

   c. Describe the "Transcendental seeker." _____

   _____

3. *American Literary Themes*

   a. What does "Westering" mean? _____
   b. What feelings did "bright Romanticism" express? _____

   _____

   c. Writing that exemplifies "dark Romanticism" had a different viewpoint, which was that

   _____

   d. Why was self-reliance an important value during the American Renaissance? _____

   _____

B. DIRECTIONS: *Answer the following questions based on the Essential Question Vocabulary words.*

   1. How does *technology* bring people together? _____

   _____

   2. Name one of the basic *rights* protected by the Constitution. _____

   _____

   3. What attitude are most people likely to have during periods of *prosperity?* _____

   _____

Name _____ Date _____

Unit 2 Introduction
Following-Through Activities

A. CHECK YOUR COMPREHENSION *Use this chart to complete the Check Your Comprehension activity in the Unit 2 Introduction. In the middle column, fill in two key concepts related to each Essential Question. In the right column, list a key author connected with each concept. One concept-author pairing has been done for Place and Literature.*

ESSENTIAL QUESTION	KEY CONCEPT	KEY AUTHOR
Place and Literature	kinship with nature _____	Thoreau 2._____
American Literature	1._____ 2._____	1._____ 2._____
Writer and Society	1._____ 2._____	1._____ 2._____

B. EXTEND YOUR LEARNING: *Use this graphic organizer to help plan your research for the Extend Your Learning activity.*

What invention are you researching?	_____
What aspects of American life did the invention change?	_____ _____ _____
What ripple effects did the invention cause?	_____ _____ _____ _____
Whom did the invention benefit most?	_____ _____ _____ _____
Whom did the invention harm?	_____ _____ _____ _____ _____
Technical/scientific vocabulary to use:	_____ _____ _____

Vocabulary Warm-up Word Lists

Study these words from the selection. Then, complete the activities.

Word List A

consequence [KAHN suh kwents] *n.* result; effect
  As a <u>consequence</u> of your carelessness, we have no more water.

elapsed [ee LAPST] *v.* passed; went by
  Five minutes <u>elapsed</u> before they returned.

indifference [in DIF uhr uhnts] *n.* not caring; lack of interest
  They showed <u>indifference</u> and paid no attention to the screaming fans.

meager [MEE ger] *adj.* very thin; inadequate
  Such a <u>meager</u> salary for this tough job is unfair.

notorious [noh TOR ee us] *adj.* having a bad reputation; infamous
  That government was <u>notorious</u> for corruption and injustice.

prior [PRY er] *adj.* previous; coming before
  Her <u>prior</u> service in the military helped her get the job.

prone [PROHN] *adj.* inclined (to)
  Because he did everything so fast, he was <u>prone</u> to having accidents.

zeal [ZEEL] *n.* great enthusiasm; passion
  The candidate wanted campaign workers with plenty of <u>zeal</u>.

Word List B

contradiction [kahn truh DIK shun] *n.* something opposite; denial
  This evidence is a <u>contradiction</u> of what we thought was true.

disclosed [dis KLOHZD] *v.* showed; revealed
  The witness finally <u>disclosed</u> the fact that he had not been there.

precaution [pree KAW shun] *n.* care taken in advance
  We took every <u>precaution</u> to avoid running out of supplies.

prevalent [PRE vuh lent] *adj.* widely existing; most common
  The <u>prevalent</u> attitude around here is that the mayor is doing a good job.

squeamish [SKWEEM ish] *adj.* easily nauseated or offended
  If you are <u>squeamish</u>, you may want to avoid this graphic documentary.

steadfastly [STED fast lee] *adv.* with firmness; without changing
  The soldier remained at his post <u>steadfastly</u> throughout the night.

strenuous [STREN yoo us] *adj.* demanding great effort or energy
  Before <u>strenuous</u> exercise, be sure to warm up and stretch.

uppermost [UP uhr mohst] *adj.* highest; first
  Protecting ourselves from danger was <u>uppermost</u> in our minds.

"The Devil and Tom Walker" by Washington Irving
Vocabulary Warm-up Exercises

Exercise A *Fill in the blanks, using each word from Word List A only once.*

Even though organized recycling has been around for a number of years, many people still show nothing but [1] _____ to it. So, in order to inject some renewed [2] _____ into this important movement, our community has just held a "Pay Attention to Recycling" campaign. People who had been making only a [3] _____ effort to recycle bottles, cans, and paper were bombarded with ads, fliers, door-to-door visits, and even legal pressure. Businesses that were [4] _____ for waste and individuals who were [5] _____ to just throwing things away did seem to respond positively. [6] _____ to the campaign, the recycling center was seldom busy; after the campaign, it was bustling. As a [7] _____, before one month had [8] _____, our community was a cleaner and more environmentally friendly place.

Exercise B *Decide whether each statement is true or false. Circle T or F, and explain your answer.*

1. If two statements agree, one of them is clearly a <u>contradiction</u>.
   T / F _____

2. If winning is <u>uppermost</u> in your mind, you are a fierce competitor.
   T / F _____

3. A nurse who stays at a patient's side all night does her job <u>steadfastly</u>.
   T / F _____

4. If you have no problem eating squishy, slimy things, you are not <u>squeamish</u>.
   T / F _____

5. Buckling your seatbelt is a <u>precaution</u> that can save your life.
   T / F _____

6. If a sport is too <u>strenuous</u> for you, you play it easily every day.
   T / F _____

7. If, in a mystery novel, a letter <u>disclosed</u> the truth, then the letter kept the truth hidden.
   T / F _____

8. If a disease is <u>prevalent</u> among a group of people, no one has it.
   T / F _____

"The Devil and Tom Walker" by Washington Irving
Reading Warm-up A

Read the following passage. Pay special attention to the underlined words. Then, read it again, and complete the activities. Use a separate sheet of paper for your written answers.

Salmagundi, or The Whim-Whams and Opinions of Launcelot Langstaff, was a collection of satires produced in twenty pamphlets during 1807–08. The writers were Washington Irving, his brother William, and the novelist James Kirke Paulding. These young men wrote with great zeal and enthusiasm under a variety of names, including Will Wizard and Anthony Evergreen. They took on the tastes, attitudes, and behavior of New York society. Their targets ranged from politics to fashion, from the notorious and celebrated to the merely harmless and obscure.

The pieces in *Salmagundi* were full of whimsy and satire, and they were prone to caricature, tending to exaggerate their portraits. They often created humor by pretending to have learning that they obviously did not really possess, claiming "serious truths conveyed in every paper." *Salmagundi* offered sophisticated and genuinely funny writing in post-colonial America, when elegance was scarce and the production of really fine humorous writing was also still quite meager.

The writers of *Salmagundi* never seemed to articulate any detailed political or aesthetic principles. As a consequence, the overall effect of the satires was very scattered and random. In fact, it was just like a salmagundi—a mixed salad of chicken, veal, anchovies, onions, and oil and lemon dressing. Some critics see this attitude as particularly American—practical, on-the-spot satire, dealing with whatever came to mind. It was the approach of a society that was still unsure of itself. It was the stance of a nation still trying to establish its identity with such a short time having elapsed since the Revolution.

What *Salmagundi* did have was vitality. It projected the high spirit that assumes the worst crime is indifference, not caring at all. Before this display of extravagant humor—that is, prior to *Salmagundi*—Washington Irving was a young law student, fond of theater and music. After *Salmagundi,* he was a writer.

1. Circle the word that means the same as zeal. Name something that you do with **zeal**.

2. Underline the words that help explain notorious. Name something for which a person can be **notorious**.

3. Circle the words that mean prone. Use **prone** in a sentence of your own.

4. Underline the word that helps explain meager. Name something of which you can have a **meager** supply.

5. Circle the words that identify the consequence of not articulating principles. Describe one possible **consequence** of winning the lottery.

6. Underline the words that tell what elapsed. How many hours have **elapsed** since your last English class?

7. Circle the words that explain indifference. Name something toward which you feel **indifference**.

8. Underline the word that means the same as prior. Name something you do **prior** to having lunch.

"The Devil and Tom Walker" by Washington Irving
Reading Warm-up B

Read the following passage. Pay special attention to the underlined words. Then, read it again, and complete the activities. Use a separate sheet of paper for your written answers.

The mythology of the American wilderness has engaged scholars for decades. What role did the great expanse of nature, especially the forest, play in the American imagination? One fact has been <u>disclosed</u> by the many analyses of the literature and history of eighteenth-century and nineteenth-century America. These studies reveal that the wilderness was undoubtedly a <u>contradiction</u> that embodied opposing forces, symbolized opposing ideas, and unleashed opposing impulses.

On the one hand, the wilderness was a refuge, a flourishing paradise to which Europeans fled in order to escape difficult, even fatal, circumstances. Arriving from lands where poverty existed widely and religious persecution was <u>prevalent</u>, those early Americans imagined the wilderness as a place of beauty, freedom, and opportunity. What was <u>uppermost</u> in their minds was the chance the wilderness provided to create their own lives. To them, the natural wilderness was a new Eden and they were all Adams and Eves.

On the other hand, the wilderness was also a place of danger, an environment of evil itself, and <u>strenuous</u> efforts were necessary simply to ensure survival in it. Americans had to take every <u>precaution</u>, exercise every care, when venturing into the forest, and anyone who was too <u>squeamish</u>, too sensitive about what might be found there, was probably better off staying in town or returning to Europe. The forest was huge and dark, uncivilized and unforgiving.

So the American wilderness grew in the imagination as both divine and diabolical. It was a place of delight and independence and, at the same time, an abode of crime, sin, and death. It was a place that offered freedom, but it also demanded that a man or woman face it <u>steadfastly</u>, with physical hardiness, moral courage, and firm resolve. The wilderness was a place where an American might create his identity, meet his doom—or both.

1. Underline the word that helps explain <u>disclosed</u>. Name a fact *disclosed* recently in the news.

2. Circle the words that help explain <u>contradiction</u>. Identify the prefix in *contradiction* that indicates two things being "against" each other.

3. Underline the words that help explain <u>prevalent</u>. Identify an attitude you think is *prevalent* in your school.

4. Name an antonym for *uppermost*.

5. Explain why the early Americans' efforts had to be <u>strenuous</u>. What is a synonym for *strenuous*?

6. Circle the word that means <u>precaution</u>. Name a common *precaution* that people take in their daily lives.

7. Circle the words that explain <u>squeamish</u>. Name something about which many people are *squeamish*.

8. Underline the words that help explain <u>steadfastly</u>. Describe a situation in which someone acts *steadfastly*.

"The Devil and Tom Walker" by Washington Irving
Literary Analysis: Characterization

Characterization is the way a writer reveals and develops characters. With **direct characterization,** the writer makes explicit statements about a character. With **indirect characterization,** the writer makes statements that allow the reader to make inferences about a character.

Examples: Tom Walker was a miserly fellow. (direct characterization)
Tom Walker fed his horse the bare minimum. (indirect characterization)

DIRECTIONS: *The numbered items are examples of indirect characterization. The lettered items are examples of direct characterization. On the line, write the letter of the item that has the same meaning.*

_____1. Passersby often heard her voice raised in arguments with her husband.

_____2. Tom sat down and had a comfortable conversation with Old Scratch.

_____3. The one thing Tom would not do was to become a slave-trader.

_____4. Tom refused to allow his debtor any more time, foreclosing on the home.

_____5. Seeing Old Scratch outside, Tom turned pale and his knees shook.

_____6. Tom's wife urged him to do whatever he had to do in exchange for wealth.

_____7. Tom began to go to church every Sunday, praying loudly and strenuously.

_____8. Tom had his horse buried with his feet uppermost, so he would be ready for riding on the last day, when the world would be turned upside down.

a. Tom was not afraid of the Devil.

b. Tom was a heartless money-lender.

c. Tom was afraid of the Devil.

d. Tom was outwardly religious.

e. Tom's wife loved money more than she loved her husband.

f. Tom was not completely bad.

g. Tom was superstitious.

h. Tom's wife was a quarrelsome woman.

"The Devil and Tom Walker" by Washington Irving

Reading Strategy: Evaluate Social Influences of the Historical Period

The characters in "The Devil and Tom Walker" are American colonists living in New England in the late 1720s and early 1730s. The dialogue, the narrator's comments about the characters, and the events that the characters experience help the reader to recognize and **evaluate the social influences of the period.** Of course, some of these influences and attitudes are often exaggerated in Irving's satirical story. Nevertheless, readers do get a picture of colonial life in the New England of Tom Walker's day.

DIRECTIONS: *On the basis of each passage that follows, evaluate the social influences of New Englanders, or American colonists in general, in the 1720s and 1730s. Write your evaluation on the lines provided.*

1. Tom Walker . . . had a wife as miserly as himself: they were so miserly that they even conspired to cheat each other . . . many and fierce were the conflicts that took place about what ought to have been common property.

   _____

   _____

   _____

2. "I [the Devil] amuse myself by presiding at the persecutions of Quakers and Anabaptists; I am the great patron and prompter of slave dealers, and the grandmaster of the Salem witches."

   _____

   _____

   _____

3. About the year 1727, just at the time that earthquakes were prevalent in New England, and shook many tall sinners down upon their knees. . . .

   _____

   _____

   _____

4. Such was the end of Tom Walker and his ill-gotten wealth. Let all griping money brokers lay this story to heart.

   _____

   _____

   _____

"The Devil and Tom Walker" by Washington Irving
Vocabulary Builder

Using the Latin Prefix *ex-*

A. DIRECTIONS: *The prefix* ex- *often means "out." To* extort *is "to twist out of, or force to give away." Complete each sentence with a word from the list below.*

exhale   export   extrovert   exoskeleton

1. If you ship a product out of the country, you _____ it.
2. An _____ is an outgoing person.
3. When you breathe out, you _____.
4. An insect's outer shell is called an _____.

Using the Word List

discord   extort   ostentation   parsimony   prevalant   treacherous

B. DIRECTIONS: *The following sentences are missing two words. On the line before each number, write the letter of the pair of terms that best completes each sentence.*

____ 1. He was a(n) _____ who tried to _____ money.
    A. criminal—extort   C. discord—steal
    B. ostentation—acquire   D. parsimony—save

____ 2. The house was _____, a monument to _____.
    A. treacherous—loyalty   C. extorted—love
    B. bright—parsimony   D. lavish—ostentation

____ 3. The _____ was evidence of her _____.
    A. discord—calm   C. small portion—parsimony
    B. extortion—generosity   D. tasteful decor—ostentation

____ 4. Because of the _____ mood of joy, everyone was _____.
    A. ostentatious—crying   C. preferred—parsimonious
    B. prevalent—smiling   D. fleeting—treacherous

____ 5. The man's _____ deed was motivated by his _____.
    A. parsimonious—courage   C. upsetting—discord
    B. treacherous—greed   D. ostentatious—stinginess

____ 6. Their constant _____ reflected the _____ in their marriage.
    A. bickering—discord   C. cheerfulness—parsimony
    B. treachery—excitement   D. ostentation—gloom

"The Devil and Tom Walker" by Washington Irving
Support for Writing

As you prepare to write an updated **retelling** of "The Devil and Tom Walker," enter information in the chart below. Remember that you want to communicate the same message but with different plot elements and details about the characters. Also remember to use modern examples of food, clothing, and current events.

Modern Retelling of "The Devil and Tom Walker"	
New title:	
Characters with new details: Tom Tom's wife The Devil	
New plot elements: Where Tom and Wife live Where they meet Devil What happens with characters How story ends	
Modern day references: Clothing Food Current events	

On a separate page, write a draft of your updated version of the Irving tale. When you revise your draft, be sure you have updated the elements of the nineteenth-century story to reflect today's world.

Name _____ Date _____

Enrichment: Narrative Point of View

Film directors use many techniques to tell their stories. They may shoot a scene using an unusual camera angle, filters, or animation. They may add a voice-over, music, or sound effects to a particular scene. They may even film part of a scene using a "fantasy" sequence, where the audience "sees" objects as if through the character's mind. If you think about films you have seen, you could list other techniques film directors use.

DIRECTIONS: *Choose three scenes from "The Devil and Tom Walker" that you might portray in a film. First, briefly describe each scene. Then, describe the techniques you might use to film each scene, keeping the viewpoint of the omniscient (all-knowing) narrator. Write your answers on the lines provided.*

Scene 1: _____

_____

Techniques for filming: _____

_____

_____

_____

Scene 2: _____

_____

Techniques for filming: _____

_____

_____

_____

Scene 3: _____

_____

Techniques for filming: _____

_____

_____

_____

from **"The Devil and Tom Walker"** by Washington Irving
Open-Book Test

Short Answer *Write your responses to the questions in this section on the lines provided.*

1. In the beginning of "The Devil and Tom Walker," Irving gives the reader some background about the treasure of the pirate Captain Kidd. Reread the first paragraph and determine what meaning the reader is meant to infer from this information. What is the writer setting up for the reader?

   _____

   _____

   _____

2. In paragraph 3 of "The Devil and Tom Walker," does Irving use direct or indirect characterization to describe the character of Tom's wife? Briefly explain your answer.

   _____

   _____

   _____

3. In paragraph 3 of "The Devil and Tom Walker," what information shows you the level of selfishness to which Tom and his wife have sunk? How do they treat each other?

   _____

   _____

   _____

4. In "The Devil and Tom Walker" locate the paragraph beginning, "Oh, I go by various names. . . ." Does Irving use direct or indirect characterization in revealing the character of the Devil? Briefly explain your answer.

   _____

   _____

   _____

5. Read the paragraph toward the middle of "The Devil and Tom Walker," which begins "The most current and probable story. . . ." Then explain how Tom feels about the disappearance of his wife.

   _____

   _____

   _____

   _____

6. In the sixth paragraph of "The Devil and Tom Walker," find context clues to help you figure out the meaning of the vocabulary word *treacherous*.

_____

_____

7. In "The Devil and Tom Walker," the reader does not learn the name of Tom's wife. She is simply referred to as "Tom's wife." What does this suggest about the attitudes toward women during this Puritan period?

_____

_____

_____

8. Read the passages in the Graphic Organizer. What do you learn about Tom Walker's character through each of these examples of either direct or indirect characterization? Fill in the right side of the chart with words that tell you about Tom's character. Then identify the example as direct characterization (**DC**) or indirect characterization (**IC**).

"Your grounds! . . . no more your grounds than mine;" [Tom said to the Devil.]	
In proportion to the distress of the applicant was the hardness of [Tom's] terms.	
"You have made so much money out of me," said the speculator [to Tom].	

9. In "The Devil and Tom Walker," reread the paragraph which follows the passage in which Tom makes his deal with the Devil, beginning, "His reputation for a ready-moneyed man. . . ." What is Irving telling the reader about people's attitudes toward money in the early 1700s?

_____

_____

_____

10. In the third paragraph from the end of "The Devil and Tom Walker," what do you learn about the beliefs of the Boston Puritans during this period? In what kinds of supernatural beings did they believe? Were they frightened by events that seemed to be of a supernatural nature?

_____

_____

_____

Essay

Write an extended response to the question of your choice or to the question or questions your teacher assigns you.

11. Reread the section in "The Devil and Tom Walker" in which the Devil and Tom set out the terms of their working agreement. Identify the one activity the Devil asks of Tom that Tom refuses. Write a brief essay to explain what this refusal by Tom reflects about the social and moral beliefs of Washington Irving and the Puritans of this time period.

12. Toward the end of "The Devil and Tom Walker," Tom begins to wonder what kind of future he faces, given the deal he has made with the Devil. Write a short essay about how Tom tries to assume the role of a devoted religious man. Cite three actions he takes toward this end and give your opinion about whether these actions actually change his life.

13. In "The Devil and Tom Walker," are Tom and his wife evenly matched, do you think? Write a brief essay to state your opinion, and support it with at least two examples from the story.

14. **Thinking About the Essential Question: How does literature shape or reflect society?** Based on "The Devil and Tom Walker," how do you think Washington Irving and the Puritans felt about the amassing of great wealth, or greed? Write a brief essay using examples from the story to support your answer.

Oral Response

15. Go back to question 3, 4, 6, or 9 or to the question your teacher assigns to you. Take a few minutes to expand your answer and prepare an oral response. Find additional details in "The Devil and Tom Walker" that will support your points. If necessary, make notes to guide your response.

"The Devil and Tom Walker" by Washington Irving
Selection Test A

Critical Reading *Identify the letter of the choice that best answers the question.*

____ 1. Which answer choice shows that the third-person omniscient point of view is used in "The Devil and Tom Walker"?

    I. The narrator is not a character in the story.

    II. Tom's and his wife's feelings are both described.

    III. Tom argues with the Devil about the buried money.

    IV. The narrator comments on the death of Captain Kidd.

  A. I, II, III

  B. II, III, IV

  C. I, III, IV

  D. I, II, IV

____ 2. Based on "The Devil and Tom Walker," what was one of the major social influences of this period that Irving criticized?

  A. freedom of religion

  B. striving for wealth

  C. westward expansion

  D. civil rights for Native Americans

____ 3. In "The Devil and Tom Walker," how does the writer show that Tom's wife is meant to represent many women rather than one specific woman?

  A. Her character has no name.

  B. She is a strong woman.

  C. She is a Puritan.

  D. Her character is fearless.

____ 4. In "The Devil and Tom Walker," why does Tom's wife go off into the forest with her best silver?

  A. She hopes to sell it and leave Tom.

  B. She is taking a gift to a relative.

  C. She wants to deal with the Devil.

  D. She plans to trade it for food.

____ 5. Based on "The Devil and Tom Walker," which of the following beliefs did the Puritans of this time hold?

  A. Husbands and wives are considered to be equal.

  B. The Devil can sometimes take a human form.

  C. You can always tell who is a respected businessman.

  D. Those who say loud prayers are the truest worshippers.

_____ 6. Based on Tom's behavior in "The Devil and Tom Walker," which of these groups did Irving likely support?

   A. Salem witches

   B. slave-traders

   C. abolitionists

   D. money-lenders

_____ 7. What most likely happens to Tom at the end of "The Devil and Tom Walker"?

   A. He rides off to escape the anger of people to whom he loaned money.

   B. The Devil kidnaps him to get his money and horses.

   C. The Devil ends his life and takes him to hell.

   D. He takes his riches and retires to another town.

_____ 8. Which of these sentences about "The Devil and Tom Walker" reflects the third-person omniscient point of view?

   A. He saw a dark, coarsely dressed man sitting on a log.

   B. Tom hoped to spite his wife and she hoped to outwit him.

   C. Tom got rich by lending money to the townspeople.

   D. I saw a name written on the bark of the huge tree.

Vocabulary

_____ 9. In which sentence is the meaning of the word *parsimony* expressed?

   A. The Devil carried Tom off forever on his black horse.

   B. Tom and his wife were equally greedy for riches.

   C. The other worshippers suspected Tom's false prayers.

   D. Tom built a mansion but spent little to furnish it.

_____ 10. Tom had "long been picking his way cautiously through this treacherous forest." What is another word for *treacherous*?

   A. sunny

   B. shadowed

   C. widespread

   D. dangerous

Essay

11. In literature, a one-dimensional character is a person who does not change his or her basic nature. Do you think Tom and his wife are one-dimensional characters who always act greedy in "The Devil and Tom Walker"? Why or why not? Write a brief essay to give your opinion. Support it with at least two examples from the story.

12. Do you think Tom Walker deserved his fate in "The Devil and Tom Walker," based on the kind of person he was and the job he held? Why or why not? Write a brief essay to explain your point of view. Use at least two examples from the story to support your opinion.

13. **Thinking About the Essential Question: How does literature shape or reflect society?** Based on "The Devil and Tom Walker," how do you think Washington Irving and the Puritans felt about the amassing of great? wealth, or greed? Write a brief essay using examples from the story to support your answer.

"**The Devil and Tom Walker**" by Washington Irving
Selection Test B

Critical Reading *Identify the letter of the choice that best completes the statement or answers the question.*

____ 1. The opening descriptions of the forest suggest that what Tom will find there will be
   A. treacherous and malignant.
   B. fortunate and useful.
   C. hot-tempered and vengeful.
   D. dull and depressing.

____ 2. Which of these details most clearly suggests that the figure Tom meets is the Devil?
   A. His voice is hoarse and growling, and his hair is black.
   B. His eyes are red, and he is covered with soot.
   C. He is powerfully built and is holding an ax.
   D. He wears rude, half-Indian garb and is sitting on a tree stump.

____ 3. What is the significance of Tom's finding most of the tall trees in the forest each "marked with the name of some great man of the colony"?
   A. The townspeople carved great men's names on trees.
   B. Landowners carved their names on trees on their property.
   C. The men had carved their own names on the trees to ensure their fame.
   D. Carved onto the trees in the Devil's forest are the names of those who made a deal with him.

____ 4. What seems to be Tom's prime motivation in agreeing to the Devil's terms?
   A. the desire to spite his wife
   B. gratitude for the Devil's involvement in his wife's disappearance
   C. the desire to win the respect of the community
   D. greed

____ 5. A main lesson of this story is that
   A. greed and mean-spiritedness lead to misery.
   B. husbands and wives should love each other.
   C. prayer can erase all past sins.
   D. great wealth can never produce happiness.

____ 6. The story implies that God expresses His disapproval of humans' sins by
   A. ignoring their prayers.
   B. making them poor.
   C. causing natural disasters.
   D. giving them nightmares.

____ 7. In what way is Tom Walker a one-dimensional character?
   A. He has no personality traits.
   B. He uses other people for his own gain.
   C. He does not fear the Devil.
   D. He symbolizes human greed and miserliness.

____ 8. It can be inferred from the story that New England Puritans of Tom Walker's day
believed in
A. many gods.
B. witches and spirits.
C. tolerance of all religious faiths.
D. reincarnation.

____ 9. Tom's "violent" religious devotion tells us that among Puritan New Englanders, one of
the major cultural influences was
A. adherence to Quakerism
B. a public, dramatic display of religious fervor
C. religious tolerance
D. acceptance of violence

____ 10. Which of these statements does *not* apply to an omniscient narrator?
A. The narrator stands outside the story.
B. The narrator provides the thoughts or feelings of many characters.
C. The narrator may comment on events in the story.
D. The narrator is a character in the story who refers to himself or herself with the
first-person pronoun *I*.

____ 11. Which of these statements best demonstrates an omniscient narrator?
A. Tom was walking through the forest.
B. Tom's wife was tall and greedy.
C. Mrs. Walker hoped that Tom would make the pact, but Tom would not agree, just to
spite her.
D. As Tom grew older, he began to worry about what would happen after he died.

____ 12. With which special-interest group of Irving's day does the story suggest Irving had the
most sympathy?
A. abolitionists
B. New England shipbuilders
C. Puritans
D. bankers

____ 13. Which of these observations about the story stems from the use of an omniscient
narrator?
A. The narrator focuses on Tom's experiences.
B. The narrator never tells us what happened to Tom's wife.
C. The narrator makes clear the motives and desires of Tom and his wife.
D. The narrator keeps the Devil shrouded in mystery.

Vocabulary

____ 14. When the Devil says "You shall extort bonds," what is the meaning of the word *extort*?
A. to write in legal language
B. to sell by auction
C. to break, unlink, or untie
D. to obtain by threat or violence

____ 15. Why is Tom's "vast house" an act of *ostentation*?
  A. It is too small for him.
  B. It is a boastful display of wealth.
  C. It is very beautiful.
  D. He got the money for it through unscrupulous means.

____ 16. Which relationship best describes the italicized words in this sentence?

He built himself, as usual, a vast house, out of *ostentation*; but left the greater part of it unfinished and unfurnished, out of *parsimony*.

  A. They are identical in meaning.
  B. They are similar in meaning.
  C. They are opposite in meaning.
  D. There is no relationship.

____ 17. In indicating that Tom and his wife live in *discord*, the narrator suggests that
  A. the two are often arguing.
  B. the two are very greedy.
  C. their house is small but comfortable.
  D. their behavior is hypocritical.

Essay

18. Which tree do you think is hit by the thunderbolt falling at the end of the story? In a brief essay, state your theory and then support it with information from the selection.

19. How does the use of an omniscient narrator affect this story? Analyze the effects in an essay that supports your general statements with examples from the selection. Be sure to include examples of scenes or dialogue that might *not* have been included if the story did not have an omniscient narrator.

20. At the end of the story, all of Tom's possessions disappear or are destroyed. Why do you think this happens? Offer your theory in an essay that uses information from the story to support your ideas.

21. **Thinking About the Essential Question: How does literature shape or reflect society?** Based on "The Devil and Tom Walker," how do you think Washington Irving and the Puritans felt about the amassing of great wealth, or greed? Write a brief essay, using examples from the story, to support your answer.

Name _____ Date _____

"Crossing the Great Divide" by Meriwether Lewis
"Commission of Meriwether Lewis" by Thomas Jefferson
Primary Sources Worksheet

The two documents in this selection are concerned with the exploration of the Louisiana Purchase. Thomas Jefferson's memorandum outlines what Meriwether Lewis is expected to do and learn. Meriwether Lewis's journal describes his experiences as he follows Jefferson's suggestions.

DIRECTIONS: *Use the table below to compare Lewis's experiences with what Jefferson expects of him.*

What Lewis Says or Does	How This Fulfills Jefferson's Orders
1.	
2.	
3.	
4.	

"Crossing the Great Divide" by Meriwether Lewis
"Commission of Meriwether Lewis" by Thomas Jefferson
Vocabulary Builder

Using the Root -spec-

A. DIRECTIONS: *The Latin root -spec- means "to look" or "to see." Keep that in mind as you write on the line the letter of the choice that best completes each sentence.*

1. A *spectator* is someone who _____ a game.
   A. participates in
   B. watches
   C. referees
   D. scores

2. A health *inspector* comes to a restaurant in order to _____.
   A. eat dinner
   B. criticize the food
   C. see if food is being properly handled
   D. entertain clients

3. You wear *spectacles* _____.
   A. to see better
   B. to protect against the rain
   C. to change your appearance
   D. to keep warm

Using the Word List

celestial	conciliatory	conspicuous	discretion	dispatched
latitude	longitude	membrane	practicable	prospect

B. DIRECTIONS: *Write the vocabulary word or words that best complete the sentence.*

1. It did not seem _____ to carry heavy equipment over the mountains.

2. The explorers noted their _____ and _____ in their report about their location.

3. The explorers were told to use their own _____ about when to return home.

4. The scouts were _____ down the river to gather information about the surroundings.

5. Not wishing to surprise the natives, the explorers tried to be as _____ as possible.

6. The _____ of a hostile reception was always on the explorers' minds.

7. The explorers made _____ gestures toward the natives, in an attempt to win their trust.

8. The natives used the _____ of certain trees to line their canoes.

9. The explorers sometimes depended on _____ navigation to determine their positions.

Unit 2 Resources: A Growing Nation
26

Primary Sources Thomas Jefferson/Meriwether Lewis
Selection Test

MULTIPLE CHOICE

Critical Reading *Identify the letter of the choice that best answers the question.*

____ 1. Who is the audience for Jefferson's Commission?
   A. the Indian peoples of the west   C. the Congress
   B. Meriwether Lewis   D. U.S. scientists

____ 2. Which body of water does Jefferson instruct Meriwether Lewis to use as his basis for the exploration?
   A. the Mississippi River   C. the Pacific Ocean
   B. the Columbia River   D. the Missouri River

____ 3. What main information does Jefferson hope to learn from Meriwether's explorations?
   A. an all-water route to the Pacific   C. a list of all native animals and plants
   B. a cure for smallpox   D. new ways of growing crops

____ 4. What fact in Jefferson's Commission tells the reader about the period of history in which it was written?
   A. the reference to different diseases   C. the reference to latitude and longitude
   B. the references to birchbark paper   D. the reference to animals and plants

____ 5. Reread this passage from Jefferson's Commission:

   The commerce which may be carried on with the people inhabiting the line you will pursue, renders a knowledge of thoese people important. You will therefore endeavor to make your- self acquainted, . . . with the names of the nations and their numbers.

   What interests of the U.S. does Jefferson focus on in this passage?
   A. scientific   C. commercial
   B. political   D. medical

____ 6. What can you infer about Jefferson from these passage in his Commission to Meriwether Lewis?

   Other objects worthy of notice will be - The soil and face of the country, its growth and vegetable productions, especially those not of the United States:

   Climate, as characterized by the . . . proportion of rainy, cloudy, and clear days; . . . by the access and recess of frost; . . . the dates at which particular plants put forth, or lose their flower or leaf; . . .
   A. He has not been president for long.   C. He has spent time as a farmer.
   B. He thinks the soil in Washington is bad   D. He dislikes cold and rainy weather.

_____ 7. Who is the audience for Meriwether Lewis's "Crossing the Great Divide"?
   A. the people of the Pacific northwest
   B. Sacajawea and her tribal people
   C. Thomas Jefferson and others
   D. doctors and scientists

_____ 8. In the passage from "Crossing the Great Divide," who is reunited at the river's edge?
   A. Lewis and Clark
   B. Sacajawea and Lewis
   C. Clark and the interpreter Charbono
   D. Clark and the Indians

_____ 9. How would you describe the approach of Lewis and Clark to the Indians they met on the Missouri?
   A. hostile and threatening
   B. friendly but controlling
   C. helpful and submissive
   D. commercial and scientific

_____ 10. What conclusion can you draw from both primary sources?
   A. Exploration in this period was tedious and slow.
   B. Knowledge of the unknown region was crucial to the U.S.
   C. The Indians were very willing to help Lewis and Clark.
   D. The Missouri River was a good river along which to camp.

_____ 11. What skill did Meriwether Lewis have that would have been particularly helpful to the readers of his accounts?
   A. He could speak several languages.
   B. He could sketch the things he saw.
   C. He could break camp quickly.
   D. He was friendly to everyone.

Essay

12. **Thinking about the Essential Question: What is the relationship between place and literature?** When the U.S. purchased the Louisiana territory, it gained a huge swath of new land about which European Americans knew nothing. Choose one of the following areas of interest that Jefferson commissioned Meriwether Lewis to investigate-climate, animals and plants, Indian people, minerals, and compass markings. Write a brief essay about why knowing about this element of the region would have been important to the new nation.

"The Song of Hiawatha" and "The Tide Rises,
The Tide Falls" by Henry Wadsworth Longfellow
"Thanatopsis" by William Cullen Bryant and "Old Ironsides" by Oliver Wendell Holmes
Vocabulary Warm-up Word Lists

Study these words from the selections. Then, complete the activities.

Word List A

blight [BLYT] *n.* something that withers growth, hopes, and ambitions
   A job with good pay can help to lift the <u>blight</u> of poverty.

communion [kuh MYOON yuhn] *n.* the act of sharing deep thoughts and feelings with another or others
   The meeting turned into a <u>communion</u> of ideas from around the globe.

eyries [AIR eez] *n.* the nests of eagles built in high places (also *aeries*)
   The bald eagles raised chicks in their <u>eryies</u> in the treetops.

insensible [in SEN suh buhl] *adj.* without sensations or awareness
   The boxer knocked his opponent <u>insensible</u>.

moors [MOORS] *n.* rolling, open grassy lands, often marshy
   Rocks and wet patches were scattered throughout the wide, green <u>moors</u>.

musings [MYOO zingz] *n.* meditations; reflections
   After a long walk to think things over, Jacob shared his <u>musings</u> with us.

palisades [pal uh SAYDZ] *n.* fences made of tall stakes and used for fortifications; also the stakes themselves
   <u>Palisades</u> guarded the perimeter of the old fort.

vales [VAYLZ] *n.* valleys
   The trail to the mountaintop first led us up and down through three <u>vales</u>.

Word List B

efface [uh FAYS] *v.* erase completely
   Workers were able to <u>efface</u> the graffiti that had covered the wall.

pensive [PEN siv] *adj.* deeply thoughtful
   She sat in the corner, <u>pensive</u> and serious, staring out the window.

reverberations [ri VER buh RAY shuhnz] *n.* echoing sounds
   The <u>reverberations</u> of the announcer's voice boomed across the stadium.

summons [SUM uhnz] *n.* an order to attend or appear somewhere
   The witness received a <u>summons</u> to the court to testify at the trial.

sustained [suh STAYND] *v.* supported; strengthened; comforted
   Your friendship <u>sustained</u> me when I most needed help.

threadbare [THRED bair] *adj.* worn thin; shabby
   A <u>threadbare</u> coat cannot keep you warm in the winter.

unfaltering [un FAWL ter ing] *adj.* unswerving; not failing; persistent
   With <u>unfaltering</u> courage, Mason rescued Tim from the burning house.

vanquished [VANG kwishd] *adj.* conquered; defeated
   The champions behaved respectfully toward the <u>vanquished</u> team.

"The Song of Hiawatha" and **"The Tide Rises,**
The Tide Falls" by Henry Wadsworth Longfellow
"Thanatopsis" by William Cullen Bryant and **"Old Ironsides"** by Oliver Wendell Holmes
Vocabulary Warm-up Exercises

Exercise A *Fill in the blanks, using each word from Word List A only once.*

Whenever Madison felt down, as if a [1] _____ were threatening to
destroy her hopes and ambitions, she visited the zoo. Perhaps she imagined her feelings of [2] _____ with the other creatures, because they could not
exactly speak their thoughts and ideas back to her. Well, that was not exactly true:
there was one brown owl which eyed her during every visit as if to say it had important
thoughts and wanted to share its own [3] _____. If no humans were
looking, Madison hooted at it, and it hooted right back at her. Nearby was the bald
eagle exhibit, fenced with tall [4] _____, where the birds nested high up
in their [5] _____. The zoo's trail led up and down through several natural [6] _____ and across open, grassy, wet meadows that resembled
[7] _____. The zoo was such a good place for meditation that even the
inanimate, [8] _____ rocks seemed to offer comfort to her.

Exercise B *Answer the following questions with complete explanations. Be sure to use the
underlined vocabulary word in your answer.*

1. If you <u>efface</u> the name on a monument, can you still read it?
   _____

2. If someone is <u>pensive</u>, does he have something on his mind?
   _____

3. If you hear <u>reverberations</u>, can you expect them to become louder with each
   repetition?
   _____

4. If you receive a <u>summons</u> to court, can you decline because you are not in the
   mood to go?
   _____

5. If you were selling a new coat, would you advertise it as <u>threadbare</u>?
   _____

6. Would you congratulate a <u>vanquished</u> candidate for winning an election?
   _____

7. If your dog shows <u>unfaltering</u> obedience, does he sometimes disobey?
   _____

8. If a snack <u>sustained</u> you, how were you able to survive until dinnertime?
   _____

"The Song of Hiawatha" and **"The Tide Rises,
The Tide Falls"** by Henry Wadsworth Longfellow
"Thanatopsis" by William Cullen Bryant and **"Old Ironsides"** by Oliver Wendell Holmes

Reading Warm-up A

Read the following passage. Then, complete the activities.

Sanjay and his father hiked part of the way up Mt. Lafayette in New Hampshire's White Mountains to spend the night at Greenleaf Hut. The hut could accommodate forty-eight hikers each night. Dinner was served family-style at long tables, which offered an opportunity for communion among all the guests. They shared their impressions, trail information, and their general thoughts and musings about their experiences in the mountains.

One man asked where to see bald eagles in the White Mountains. Sanjay, who knew about eagles, replied that they often nested near bodies of water in high places. He said the man might be more likely to find eagles' eyries in the vales, or valleys, near lakes or rivers, rather than up in the mountains.

After dinner, Sanjay and his father went outside for a stroll. Near the hut, tall palisades made a fence around a storage area, to keep out bears. The pair sat on a large rock and watched shooting stars. Then they went to sleep in the men's bunk room.

At breakfast the next morning, Sanjay had the amusing thought that even an insensible object, like his bowl of oatmeal, seemed to be welcoming him and encouraging him about the day's hike. The weather was cooperative too. He and his father had fine, 360-degree views when they reached the top of Mt. Lafayette. In one direction, they saw a protected wilderness area, some of which appeared to be rolling, open, grassy moors. An inspiring view like this erased any possibility of a blight dampening or withering your spirits, Sanjay reflected, and that was a great reason to keep on hiking.

1. Underline the words that are a clue to the meaning of the word underline communion. Write a sentence describing the opposite of **communion**.

2. Circle the word that has the same meaning as musings. Write a new sentence using the word **musings**.

3. Underline the word in a nearby sentence that is a clue to the meaning of eyries. Why does it make sense for eagles to build their **eyries** in high places?

4. Circle the word that has the same meaning as vales. Write a sentence telling about one or two of the **vales** you have seen.

5. Underline the phrase that explains the purpose for the fence made of palisades. Name another use for a fence made of **palisades**.

6. Circle the words that describe what is insensible. Write your own definition of the word **insensible**.

7. Underline the words that describe moors. Write a new sentence using the word **moors**.

8. Circle the words that help to explain the meaning of the word blight. Write a synonym for the word **blight**.

"The Song of Hiawatha" and **"The Tide Rises,
The Tide Falls"** by Henry Wadsworth Longfellow
"Thanatopsis" by William Cullen Bryant and **"Old Ironsides"** by Oliver Wendell Holmes

Reading Warm-up B

Read the following passage. Then, complete the activities.

When people think of the great nineteenth-century writers, it may be hard to imagine these writers starting out as untried and uncertain teenagers. An anecdote about the young Longfellow can help to <u>efface</u> that impression and wipe away those images.

On November 17, 1820, the *Portland Gazette* published a poem called "The Battle of Lovell's Pond." The author was identified only as "Henry" but, in fact, the poet was the overjoyed thirteen-year-old Longfellow. Although he had told no one that his first poem had been published, he felt optimistic about his future.

As it happened, Longfellow had been invited to the home of a friend for dinner that night. His friend's father, the respected Judge Mellen, mentioned the poem he had read that morning. Not knowing that the author was sitting at his table, he scornfully called the poem "remarkably stiff," a <u>threadbare</u> fabric of words, ragged, full of holes. He even accused the poet of borrowing words from another writer. Longfellow did not dare argue with a well-educated adult, one who was powerful enough to issue a court <u>summons</u> that commanded people to appear before him. The boy tried to ignore the <u>reverberations</u> of the judge's harsh words so they would not keep echoing in his mind. Silent and <u>pensive</u>, he sat and thought, concealing his disappointment until he returned home, where he cried himself to sleep.

If that early criticism left Longfellow with temporarily <u>vanquished</u> hopes, he somehow managed to keep writing, even though he was feeling defeated. After that inauspicious beginning, or because of it, his belief in himself became fierce, unwavering and <u>unfaltering</u>. The sting of that criticism—and more important, his response to it—<u>sustained</u> him throughout the years, supporting his resolve. Eventually, "Henry" became the best-selling poet in the English language.

1. Underline the words that have the same meaning as <u>efface</u>. Name something that you believe time cannot ***efface***.

2. Underline the words that help to explain the meaning of <u>threadbare</u>. Use the word ***threadbare*** in a sentence.

3. Circle the word that is a clue to the meaning of <u>summons</u>. What is the difference between a ***summons*** and an invitation?

4. Underline the phrase that is a clue to the meaning of <u>reverberations</u>. Use the word ***reverberations*** in a sentence.

5. Circle the words that help to explain the meaning of <u>pensive</u>. Describe the behavior of someone who appears ***pensive***.

6. Circle the word that explains the meaning of <u>vanquished</u>. Name two synonyms for the word ***vanquished***.

7. Circle the word that is a synonym for <u>unfaltering</u>. Describe a situation in which someone behaves with ***unfaltering*** devotion.

8. Underline the word that helps to explain the meaning of <u>sustained</u>. Describe a situation in which someone's words or actions ***sustained*** you.

from "The Song of Hiawatha" and **"The Tide Rises, The Tide Falls"**
by Henry Wadsworth Longfellow
"Thanatopsis" by William Cullen Bryant
"Old Ironsides" by Oliver Wendell Holmes

Literary Analysis: Meter

The **meter** of a poem is the rhythmic pattern created by the arrangement of stressed and unstressed syllables. The basic unit of meter is the **foot**, which usually consists of one stressed syllable and one or more unstressed syllables. The most common foot in English-language poetry is the **iamb**, an unstressed syllable followed by a stressed syllable, as in the word *today*.

The type and number of feet per line determine the poem's meter. For example, a pattern of three iambs per line is called **iambic trimeter**; four iambs per line, **iambic tetrameter**; five iambs per line, **iambic pentameter**. The process of analyzing a poem's meter is called **scansion**, or **scanning** the poem. Here are examples of scanned lines.

Iambic tetrameter:	Beneath it rung the battle shout
Iambic pentameter:	To him who in the love of Nature holds

DIRECTIONS: *Scan the following stanza of "Old Ironsides" by marking the stressed and unstressed syllables. Then, describe the metrical pattern of the poem on these lines:*

_____

_____

Oh, better that her shattered hulk

   Should sink beneath the wave;

Her thunders shook the mighty deep,

   And there should be her grave;

Nail to the mast her holy flag.

   Set every threadbare sail,

And give her to the god of storms,

   The lightning and the gale!

from **"The Song of Hiawatha"** and **"The Tide Rises, The Tide Falls"**
by Henry Wadsworth Longfellow
"Thanatopsis" by William Cullen Bryant
"Old Ironsides" by Oliver Wendell Holmes

Reading Strategy: Summarizing to Repair Comprehension

Summarizing is a valuable way to check and **repair your reading comprehension.** When you summarize something, you briefly state its main points and key details in your own words.

DIRECTIONS: *Summarize each stanza below on the lines provided.*

1. "Thanatopsis":

> Yet not to thine eternal resting place
> Shalt thou retire alone, nor couldst thou wish
> Couch more magnificent. Thou shalt lie down
> With patriarchs of the infant world—with kings,
> The powerful of the earth—the wise, the good,
> Fair forms, and hoary seers of ages past,
> All in one mighty sepulcher.

_____

_____

_____

2. "Old Ironsides":

> Oh, better that her shattered hulk
>   Should sink beneath the wave;
> Her thunders shook the mighty deep,
>   And there should be her grave;
> Nail to the mast her holy flag.
>   Set every threadbare sail,
> And give her to the god of storms,
>   The lightning and the gale!

_____

_____

_____

from **"The Song of Hiawatha"** and **"The Tide Rises, The Tide Falls"**
by Henry Wadsworth Longfellow
"Thanatopsis" by William Cullen Bryant
"Old Ironsides" by Oliver Wendell Holmes
Vocabulary Builder

Using the Latin Root *-fac-*

A. DIRECTIONS: *One of the meanings of the word root -fac- is "the face," or, by extension, "outward appearance." Keeping that in mind, write on the line the letter of the choice that best completes each item.*

_____ 1. If you make a *facsimile* of a document, what will it look like?
    A. a different color from the original   C. identical to the original
    B. a reverse image of the original   D. smaller or larger than the original

_____ 2. The *façade* of a building is its
    A. front.   C. back.
    B. courtyard.   D. interior.

_____ 3. A *facet* of a gemstone is one of
    A. the ways it might be set.   C. the imperfections inside it.
    B. its small, polished surfaces.   D. the places where it is found in nature.

Using the Word List

> eloquence   efface   pensive   venerable

B. DIRECTIONS: *On the lines provided, rewrite each sentence, substituting the correct word from the Word List in place of its italicized definition.*

1. The valleys were blanketed in a *thoughtful* quietness.

_____

2. The old man was knowledgeable and *worthy of respect*.

_____

3. The ravages of time will soon *erase* the letters on the monument.

_____

4. The speaker's *skillful use of language* moved the audience to tears.

_____

from **"The Song of Hiawatha"** and **"The Tide Rises, The Tide Falls"**
by Henry Wadsworth Longfellow
"Thanatopsis" by William Cullen Bryant
"Old Ironsides" by Oliver Wendell Holmes
Support for Writing

Use this chart to prepare for writing your **compare-and-contrast** essay. First, choose one five to ten-line passage each from two poems in this grouping (Longfellow's poems, "Thanatopsis," "Old Ironsides"). Then, list the stylistic devices that help create the mood of each passage.

Poem:	Lines: Mood:
Subject	
Meter	
Images	
Word Choice	
Other Details That Affect Mood	

Poem:	Lines: Mood:
Subject	
Meter	
Images	
Word Choice	
Other Details That Affect Mood	

On a separate page, draft your summary of the selection. When you revise your work, be sure you have included only the main ideas and images from each part of the poem.

from **"The Song of Hiawatha"** and **"The Tide Rises, The Tide Falls"**
by Henry Wadsworth Longfellow
"Thanatopsis" by William Cullen Bryant
"Old Ironsides" by Oliver Wendell Holmes
Enrichment: Science

The curlew mentioned in "The Tide Rises, The Tide Falls" is a large, long-legged wading bird whose call is associated with the evening. Knowing information about subjects discussed in a poem or story often helps the reader interpret meaning. In this case, knowing that a curlew's call is associated with the evening helps the reader visualize the setting of the poem and establish mood.

DIRECTIONS: *Research the curlew and four other birds of the Northeast. Use encyclopedias, field guides, or ornithology texts. As you find facts about each bird, fill in the following chart, explaining how the facts can be used to help establish a mood.*

Bird	Facts	How Can Knowing This Information Help Establish a Mood?
Curlew		

Name _____ Date _____

"Song of Hiawatha" and **"The Tide Rises, The Tide Falls"** by Longfellow;
"Thanatopsis" by Bryant; **"Old Ironsides"** by Holmes

Open-Book Test

Short Answer *Write your responses to the questions in this section on the lines provided.*

1. Reread stanzas 1–4 from "The Song of Hiawatha." Below, summarize each stanza by writing a sentence that briefly describes what the speaker says.

Stanza 1	
Stanza 2	
Stanza 3	
Stanza 4	

2. The metric form, or foot, in "The Song of Hiawatha" is the trochee, one stressed syllable followed by an unstressed syllable. Look at the marking of the metric feet in the example below. The stressed syllable is marked (/) and the unstressed syllable is marked (u).

   / u / u / u / u

   With the rushing of great rivers

   Mark the metric feet in these two lines from "Song of Hiawatha" : "Listen to these wild traditions, To this Song of Hiawatha!"

   _____

   _____

3. The meter in lines 5, 10, and 15 of "The Tide Rises, The Tide Falls" is different from the meter in the rest of the poem. How does this difference affect the mood of the poem?

   _____

   _____

   _____

4. In "The Tide Rises, The Tide Falls," you find the following lines: "The little waves, with their soft, white hands,/*Efface* the footprints in the sands." What word or phrase might you use as a synonym for the word *efface*? You may choose more than one.

   _____

   _____

5. What image is conveyed by the "calling" of the sea and the waves with their "soft, white hands" in "The Tide Rises, the Tide Falls?" How does this image relate to the theme of the poem?

_____

_____

_____

6. In "Thanatopsis," the poet rarely mentions death. He does, however, include many symbols that represent death. Cite three of these symbols of death from the poem.

_____

_____

_____

7. Reread lines 70–72 in "Thanatopsis." What is the poet's meaning in these lines?

_____

_____

8. Summarize the final stanza of "Thanatopsis" to clarify the poet's message about death.

_____

_____

_____

9. What is the mood of "Old Ironsides?" Why do you think this is the case? How does the meter contribute to the mood of the poem?

_____

_____

_____

10. In the last stanza of "Old Ironsides," why does the poet suggest that the ship be dealt with by giving "her to the storms?"

_____

_____

_____

Essay

Write an extended response to the question of your choice or to the question or questions your teacher assigns you.

11. Choose either "The Tide Rises, The Tide Falls" or "Old Ironsides" and write a brief essay about the meaning of the following images: the curlew and the horses in "The Tide Rises, The Tide Falls"; the harpies of the shore and the eagle of the sea in "Old Ironsides." What does each image represent in the context of the poem?

Name _____ Date _____

12. Choose either "The Song of Hiawatha" or "Thanatopsis" and write a brief essay about the poet's view of nature in the poem. In "The Song of Hiawatha" concentrate on Stanza 3. In "Thanatopsis" concentrate on lines 31–45.

13. Choose either "The Tide Rises, The Tide Falls" or "Thanatopsis" and write a brief esssay on the view of death the poet communicates. Cite examples from the poem to support your opinion.

14. **Thinking About the Essential Question: What makes American literature American?** Choose "The Song of Hiawatha" or "Old Ironsides" and write a brief essay about what makes the work particularly American. Consider the following themes: view of nature, death, change, and the history of the nation and its peoples.

Oral Response

15. Go back to question 1, 5, 6, or 8 or to the question your teacher assigns to you. Take a few minutes to expand your answers and prepare an oral response. Find additional details in "The Song of Hiawatha," "The Tide Rises, The Tide Falls," "Thanatopsis," or "Old Ironsides" that will support your points. If necessary, make notes to guide your response.

from "**The Song of Hiawatha**" and "**The Tide Rises,
The Tide Falls**" by Henry Wadsworth Longfellow
"**Thanatopsis**" by William Cullen Bryant
"**Old Ironsides**" by Oliver Wendell Holmes
Selection Test A

Critical Reading *Identify the letter of the choice that best answers the question.*

____ 1. The stories to be told in "The Song of Hiawatha" are taken from what sources?
   A. Native American legends
   B. European traditions
   C. North Dakota
   D. early North American trappers and settlers

____ 2. Which sentence best summarizes the prologue to "The Song of Hiawatha"?
   A. Longfellow loves meadows, forests, and rushing streams.
   B. The prologue introduces traditional stories from Native American culture.
   C. The prologue describes trade agreements between Native American peoples.
   D. The prologue contains the lyrics to a song written by a Native American composer.

____ 3. How does the prologue's repetitive, insistent meter set the mood for "The Song of Hiawatha"?
   A. It creates the lively feeling of a barn dance or hoedown.
   B. It sounds like the waters of a rushing stream.
   C. It imitates animal sounds, such as an owl's hoot.
   D. It echoes the rhythm of tom-toms, as at a powwow.

____ 4. According to the poet in "Thanatopsis," what will happen to his listeners after they die?
   A. They will be buried in kings' tombs.
   B. They will be buried far out at sea.
   C. They will become less bitter.
   D. They will become part of the earth.

____ 5. In the following lines from "Old Ironsides," which syllables are accented?
   Her deck, once red with heroes' blood, / Where knelt the vanquished foe,

   A. every first syllable
   B. every second syllable
   C. every third syllable
   D. every syllable

____ 6. What kind of ship is "Old Ironsides"?

    A. a motorboat

    B. a sailboat

    C. a battleship

    D. a cruise ship

____ 7. Which statement below is the best summary of these lines from "Old Ironsides"?

    Her deck, once red with heroes' blood, / Where knelt the vanquished foe, / When winds were hurrying o'er the flood, / And waves were white below, / No more shall feel the victor's tread, / Or know the conquered knee;—

    A. The blood of past battles will be washed off the ship by water.

    B. The ship will no longer see people battling on her deck.

    C. The ship was best in battle when the waves were high.

    D. The winners no longer stay on deck but are honored on shore.

____ 8. Which line is in iambic pentameter?

    A. "And the tide rises, the tide falls."

    B. "The day returns, but never more . . ."

    C. "Of ages glide away, the sons of men . . ."

    D. "From his footprints flowed a river . . ."

____ 9. Which line is in iambic tetrameter?

    A. "To mix forever with the elements"

    B. "Communion with the visible forms, she speaks . . ."

    C. "Her deck, once red with heroes blood . . ."

    D. "Darkness settles on roofs and walls . . ."

Vocabulary

____ 10. In which of the following is the meaning of *venerable* expressed?

    A. The traveler will never return to the shore.

    B. The poet urges people to approach death with trust.

    C. "Old Ironsides" had fought and won many a battle.

    D. If you ask me, I will tell you the story.

____ 11. In "The Tide Rises, the Tide Falls," the ocean's waves "efface the footprints in the sands." What does the word *efface* mean?

    A. wipe away, erase

    B. deepen, make more prominent

    C. form new footprints

    D. follow the trail of human footprints

Essay

12. In "Thanatopsis," Bryant says to people who will eventually die, "Thou shalt lie down / With patriarchs of the infant world—with kings, / The powerful of the earth—the wise, the good, / Fair forms, and hoary seers of ages past . . ." What do you think he is saying to readers about what will happen to them after death? What does he seem to suggest about how humans might be valued in death, compared to how they are valued in life? Write a brief essay to express your opinion of this passage.

13. What attitude toward death do you think Bryant has, based on "Thanatopsis"? Is he afraid of death? How does he want his readers to view death? Write a brief essay giving your ideas about the poet's view of death. Use evidence from the poem to support your ideas.

14. **Thinking About the Essential Question: What makes American literature American?** Choose "The Song of Hiawatha" or "Old Ironsides" and write a brief essay about what makes the work particularly American. Consider the following themes: view of nature, death, change, and the history of the nation and its peoples.

from **"The Song of Hiawatha"** and **"The Tide Rises,
The Tide Falls"** by Henry Wadsworth Longfellow
"Thanatopsis" by William Cullen Bryant
"Old Ironsides" by Oliver Wendell Holmes

Selection Test B

Critical Reading *Identify the letter of the choice that best completes the statement or answers the question.*

_____ 1. In line 1 of the prologue to "The Song of Hiawatha," what is the meaning of the question "whence these stories"?
  A. "When will you tell us these stories?"
  B. "Why should I tell you these stories?"
  C. "Where did these stories come from?"
  D. "Are these stories fact or fiction?"

_____ 2. Longfellow believes that Native American tales derive their power from what source?
  A. the skill of the storytellers, who are clever at plot and characterization
  B. nature itself, whose spirit is expressed in native peoples and their cultures
  C. great deeds of warfare, conquest, and nobility
  D. Europe, where Longfellow learned about myths and folk tales

_____ 3. The title "Thanatopsis" means
  A. a vision of death.
  B. the process of decaying.
  C. a metamorphosis or transformation.
  D. a feeling of euphoria or well-being.

_____ 4. According to the speaker in "Thanatopsis," what will happen to him after death?
  A. His soul will go to heaven.
  B. His spirit will cease to exist.
  C. His body will be preserved in the earth.
  D. His body will become part of nature.

_____ 5. Bryant's line "Shall send his roots abroad, and pierce thy mold" is an example of iambic _____.
  A. trimeter
  B. tetrameter
  C. pentameter
  D. hexameter

_____ 6. "Old Ironsides" was the nickname of
  A. the *U.S.S. Constitution,* a War of 1812 battleship.
  B. the *Clermont,* an early steamship.
  C. the *Titanic,* a famous luxury liner.
  D. Oliver Wendell Holmes.

_____ 7. Which of these qualities does Holmes's poem attribute to "Old Ironsides"?
  A. ruthlessness
  B. heroism
  C. holiness
  D. modesty

_____ 8. Which of these statements best expresses the author's view in "Old Ironsides"?
  A. A remarkable national relic should be saved.
  B. Old ships are architectural treasures.
  C. Ships are the foundation of a country's defense.
  D. Older things are built better than newer things.

_____ 9. In "The Tide Rises, The Tide Falls," to what do these lines refer?
  The little waves, with their soft, white hands,
  Efface the footprints in the sands . . .
  A. the footprints of the curlew
  B. the hostler's footprints
  C. the traveler's footprints
  D. the footprints of the steeds

_____ 10. What is the best summary of these lines from "The Tide Rises, The Tide Falls"?
  Darkness settles on roofs and walls,
  But the sea, the sea in the darkness calls
  A. Because it is nighttime, the sea is calling.
  B. Dark clouds cause the noises of the sea.
  C. The village is agitated because of the calling of the sea.
  D. Even though the night is quiet, the sea is not.

_____ 11. Which of the following lines is *not* written in iambic tetrameter?
  A. Her deck, once red with heroes' blood
  B. Where knelt the vanquished foe
  C. The harpies of the shore shall pluck
  D. And give her to the god of storms

_____ 12. Which of these lines most varies the regular iambic meter?
  A. Yet not to thine eternal resting place
  B. Should sink beneath the wave
  C. In the full strength of years, matron and maid
  D. We reached the barn with merry din

Vocabulary

_____ 13. Which word below could replace the italicized word in the phrase "*thoughtful* quietness"?
  A. pensive   C. efface
  B. venerable   D. eloquence

_____ 14. Which word best describes a respected father figure?
   A. efface
   B. eloquence
   C. venerable
   D. pensive

_____ 15. In writing about "the vales/Stretching in pensive quietness," what human quality does Bryant attribute to this natural setting?
   A. longing for a golden past
   B. thoughtful reflectiveness
   C. nervous anticipation
   D. joyful exuberance

Essay

16. Oliver Wendell Holmes helped convince the public to rally to save the ship called *Old Ironsides* from destruction. If Holmes had written an editorial instead of a poem, do you think it would have had the same effect on the public? Why or why not? Answer these questions in a brief essay. To support your opinion, cite specific examples from the poem, and consider the emotional responses that the examples produce.

17. Poets often use images from nature to provoke an emotional response. Describe how nature images in at least two of the poems provoke different emotions. Consider the emotions the speaker or narrator attempts to convey and the emotional response in the reader.

18. **Thinking About the Essential Question: What makes American literature American?**
   Choose "The Song of Hiawatha" or "Old Ironsides" and write a brief essay about what makes the work particularly American. Consider the following themes: view of nature, death, change, and the history of the nation and its peoples.

Vocabulary Warm-up Word Lists

Study these words from the selection. Then, complete the activities.

Word List A

amiss [uh MIS] *adv.* in error; wrongly
    Please don't take my comment <u>amiss</u>, but I think your tie is crooked.

apprehensive [ap ree HEN siv] *adj.* worried; fearful about the future
    Because the teacher said the exam would be difficult, Sandra was <u>apprehensive</u>.

averse [uh VERS] *adj.* opposed to
    Most cats are <u>averse</u> to getting wet.

iniquity [in IK wuh tee] *n.* sin; corruption
    In the Bible, the Old Testament has many passages denouncing sin and <u>iniquity</u>.

instinctive [in STINK tiv] *adj.* prompted by an inborn or natural feeling
    It is <u>instinctive</u> that birds find their way south in the fall.

intellect [IN tuh lekt] *n.* mental capacity
    Terry's <u>intellect</u> allowed her to read at an 8th-grade level in the 3rd grade.

ostentatious [ahs ten TAY shuhs] *adj.* showy; flamboyant
    Although she is extremely wealthy, Irene is not flashy or <u>ostentatious</u>.

refrain [ree FRAYN] *n.* repeated phrase
    At the end of each stanza of that poem, there was a stirring <u>refrain</u>.

Word List B

amiable [AY mee uh buhl] *adj.* friendly; congenial
    At Donna's party, we enjoyed <u>amiable</u> conversations with lots of friends.

attribute [AT ri byoot] *n.* characteristic; quality or trait
    Concern for students is a valuable <u>attribute</u> in a teacher.

censure [SEN shuhr] *n.* criticism
    The congressman's conduct was so shocking that it provoked official <u>censure</u>.

energetic [en er JET ik] *adj.* active; vigorous
    The senator mounted an <u>energetic</u> campaign to ban smoking in public places.

multitude [MUL ti tood] *n.* large crowd
    There was a <u>multitude</u> of spectators for the Fourth of July parade on Main Street.

placid [PLAS id] *adj.* peaceful; calm
    The sailboat traveled on <u>placid</u> waters all day.

retained [ree TAYND] *v.* held or kept in possession
    In the contract, the company <u>retained</u> the right to alter the terms of the pension fund.

venerable [VEN uh ruh buhl] *adj.* worthy of respect because of age and experience
    In his old age, his colleagues regarded Alvin as a <u>venerable</u> and wise advisor.

"The Minister's Black Veil" by Nathaniel Hawthorne
Vocabulary Warm-up Exercises

Exercise A *Fill in the blanks, using each word from Word List A only once.*

As Kent thought about the math exam coming up the next day, he grew more worried and
[1] _____. He was not [2] _____ to math, but it was not his
best subject. He felt that his [3] _____ was more suited to English and history. He had a(n) [4] _____ feel for language, for characters, and
eventful situations. Numbers, he felt, were comparatively abstract, and he found it
hard to relate to them. Kent had also frittered away some of his precious study time
by staying out at the movies. He did not feel guilty, as if he had been indulging in
[5] _____, but he did consider that he had acted [6] _____.
He could try to fake illness with a(n) [7] _____ display of coughing and
wheezing. He'd be ashamed to do that, though. Bleak as it seemed, he would have to
make "CRAM!" his repeated [8] _____ for the rest of the night.

Exercise B *Revise each sentence so that the underlined vocabulary word is logical. Be sure to
keep the vocabulary word in your revision.*

Example: Because the work was so <u>tedious</u>, we greatly enjoyed it.
Because the work was so <u>tedious</u>, we soon grew bored.

1. Meg was strongly repelled by Ben's <u>amiable</u> behavior.

   _____

2. Mike's greatest <u>attribute</u> was loyalty, which was foreign to his personality.

   _____

3. Before bestowing the prize, the principal made remarks in <u>censure</u> of Jay's conduct.

   _____

4. Inez did an <u>energetic</u> workout, performing her routines slowly and without enthusiasm.

   _____

5. Through the telescope on a cloudy night, we could see a <u>multitude</u> of twinkling stars.

   _____

6. The dog had a <u>placid</u> disposition, barking loudly and threatening to bite.

   _____

7. Mr. Lindgren <u>retained</u> a large part of his fortune, giving most of his money to charity.

   _____

8. A <u>venerable</u> advisor has provided reliable counsel for only a short time.

   _____

"The Minister's Black Veil" by Nathaniel Hawthorne
Reading Warm-up A

Read the following passage. Pay special attention to the underlined words. Then, read it again, and complete the activities. Use a separate sheet of paper for your written answers.

Nathaniel Hawthorne often makes use of the super-natural in his stories. A good example is "Dr. Heidegger's Experiment." In this story, four elderly friends gather at the house of Dr. Heidegger, an old eccentric, who likes to perform scientific experiments. Old age has made the friends <u>apprehensive</u> and fearful. They have all led unhappy lives, wasting their energy and talents. One of them, for example, has indulged in sin and <u>iniquity</u> so much that he is tormented with pains in both body and soul. Another visitor has been a prosperous merchant, but he has behaved <u>amiss</u> and has lost all his money. A third character is a ruined politician, <u>ostentatious</u> for his corruption. Finally, there is the Widow Wycherly, whom scandalous stories have forced into a life of seclusion.

Dr. Heidegger announces to his guests that he has received a package from an acquaintance containing water from the legendary Fountain of Youth, which is located in Florida. He demonstrates the water's powers by placing a crumbling, withered rose in it. When the flower revives to recover its original freshness, the visitors are convinced. Hardly <u>averse</u> to recovering their lost youth, they eagerly accept Dr. Heidegger's invitation to taste the liquid.

In a remarkable transformation, the visitors become young and vigorous. "Give us more!" is their <u>refrain</u>, uttered again and again. By the third drink, though, their <u>instinctive</u> rivalries get the better of them. The men scuffle over the Widow Wycherly. The vase is overturned and shatters, with all the water trickling away. Suddenly, the characters grow old again.

The reader's <u>intellect</u> may find this story hard to accept, because the Fountain of Youth is a product of myth, not science. On a symbolic level, however, Hawthorne's story is an effective morality tale, underlining the dangers of greed.

1. Underline the word in this sentence that gives a clue to the meaning of <u>apprehensive</u>. Use a word meaning the opposite of *apprehensive* in an original sentence.

2. Circle the words in this sentence that give a clue to the meaning of <u>iniquity</u>. What is an antonym for *iniquity*?

3. Underline the words in this sentence that hint at the meaning of <u>amiss</u>. What is an antonym for *amiss*?

4. What are two synonyms for <u>ostentatious</u>? Use the word *ostentatious* in an original sentence.

5. Circle the words in this sentence that hint at the meaning of <u>averse</u>. What is a synonym for *averse*?

6. Underline the words in this sentence that give a clue to the meaning of <u>refrain</u>. Is a *refrain* uttered only once, or is it repeated?

7. Circle the words in this sentence that offer a clue to the meaning of the word <u>instinctive</u>. What is a noun related to this adjective?

8. Underline the words that give a clue to the meaning of <u>intellect</u>. What is a synonym for *intellect*?

"The Minister's Black Veil" by Nathaniel Hawthorne
Reading Warm-up B

Read the following passage. Pay special attention to the underlined words. Then, read it again, and complete the activities. Use a separate sheet of paper for your written answers.

Like everybody else, Marcy had grown up hearing the old saying that you can't judge a book by its cover. The saying had a <u>venerable</u> status, one of those ancient bits of wisdom that everyone accepted. Ever since her earliest childhood, though, Marcy had <u>retained</u> a strong doubt about the saying's actual truth. Walk into any high school, she would argue, and you would find just the opposite: people judging each other by their appearance, particularly by their clothes. Like a face, clothes often became an <u>attribute</u> of a person's identity.

In her English class one afternoon, Marcy made a mental survey of how people's clothes revealed their personalities. Tina, the head cheerleader, a peppy, <u>energetic</u> girl, wore a pink mini-dress and big hoop earrings, while a boy named Max, on the other hand, wore black clothes to proclaim his seriousness. In a way, Max's black clothes issued a challenge to Tina's bright attire, inviting disapproval, even <u>censure</u>, as if clothes could pose a threat to other people. But as Marcy looked around, she found that most people chose to wear ordinary clothes—jeans, baseball caps, T-shirts. She guessed that most people wanted to blend in with the <u>multitude</u> of the crowd, appearing not too much like Tina, not too much like Max.

Marcy found it particularly intriguing to look at her English teacher, Mr. Bryant, to see if he too made an effort to express himself through his clothes. She realized that Mr. Bryant arrived at school each day in a tweed jacket and tie, the uniform of a <u>placid</u> man who valued quiet thoughtfulness. She noticed that his encouraging smile became all the more <u>amiable</u> through his wardrobe. The more Marcy thought about it, the more she considered the old saying: The clothes make the man.

1. Underline the words in this sentence that hint at the meaning of the word <u>venerable</u>. What is a synonym for **venerable**?

2. Circle the words in this sentence that hint at the meaning of <u>retained</u>. Use the word **retained** in an original sentence.

3. Underline the words in this sentence that hint at the meaning of <u>attribute</u>. What are two synonyms for the word **attribute**?

4. Underline the words in this sentence that hint at the meaning of <u>energetic</u>. What are two antonyms for **energetic**?

5. Circle the word in this sentence that hints at the meaning of <u>censure</u>. What is an antonym for **censure**?

6. Circle the words in this sentence that give a good clue to the meaning of <u>multitude</u>. Use this word in an original sentence.

7. Underline the words in this sentence that hint at the meaning of <u>placid</u>. What are two synonyms for **placid**?

8. Underline the words in this sentence that hint at the meaning of <u>amiable</u>. Use a word meaning the opposite of **amiable** in a sentence of your own.

"The Minister's Black Veil" by Nathaniel Hawthorne
Literary Analysis: Parable and Symbol

A **parable** teaches a moral lesson through a simple story about humans. Often a parable leaves out specific details about characters or about the location of the story. Parables also often use **symbols** to suggest universal truths. These techniques make the story more applicable to all readers. For example, in "The Minister's Black Veil," Hawthorne does not reveal the reason Parson Hooper is wearing the veil because the people's reaction to the veil and what it may symbolize is the critical part of the parable.

Hawthorne calls "The Minister's Black Veil" a parable because he feels strongly about the moral lesson of the story.

DIRECTIONS: *Look at each of the following excerpts. Then, in the space provided, write how you think the language reinforces the message of the parable for all readers.*

Excerpt	How the Language Conveys the Parable
1. Children, with bright faces, tripped merrily beside their parents, or mimicked a graver gait, in the conscious dignity of their Sunday clothes. Spruce bachelors looked sidelong at the pretty maidens, and fancied that the Sabbath sunshine made them prettier than on weekdays.	
2. At its conclusion, the bell tolled for the funeral of a young lady. The relatives and friends were assembled in the house, and the more distant acquaintances stood about the door, speaking of the good qualities of the deceased . . .	
3. When Mr. Hooper came, the first thing that their eyes rested on was the same horrible black veil, which had added deeper gloom to the funeral, and could portend nothing but evil to the wedding.	

Name _____ Date _____

Reading Strategy: Draw Inferences to Determine Essential Meaning

When you **draw an inference** in reading a story, you use the surrounding details to make a reasonable guess about the essential meaning of the story. To draw thoughtful inferences, look carefully at the writer's description of events and characters and use of literary devices. For example, note Hawthorne's detail as he describes Mr. Hooper's black veil on the Sunday he appears in church.

> Swathed about his forehead, and hanging down over his face, so low as to be shaken by his breath, Mr. Hooper had on a black veil. On a nearer view it seemed to consist of two folds of crape . . . With this gloomy shade before him, good Mr. Hooper walked onward, at a slow and quiet pace, stooping somewhat, and looking on the ground . . .

Based on Hawthorne's description, you might infer that something bad has happened to someone close to Hooper.

DIRECTIONS: *Read the details from "The Minister's Black Veil" in the following chart. Write down what you know from the story and from your own life. Write what you think the author means.*

Details	What I Know	Inference
1. That mysterious emblem was never once withdrawn. It shook with his measured breath . . . it threw its obscurity between him and the holy page . . . and while he prayed, the veil lay heavily upon his uplifted countenance.		
2. It was remarkable that of all the busybodies and impertinent people in the parish, not one ventured to put the plain question to Mr. Hooper . . . Hitherto whenever there appeared the slightest call for such interference, he had never lacked advisers . . .		

"The Minister's Black Veil" by Nathaniel Hawthorne
Vocabulary Builder

Using the Root -*path*-

A. DIRECTIONS: *The word root -path- means "feeling, suffering, or disease." Keep that in mind as you answer the following questions on the lines provided.*

1. *Pathology* is a branch of medicine. With what issues in medicine do you think it is concerned?

   _____

2. The prefix *anti-* means "against." If you felt extreme *antipathy* toward another person, would you want that person to be your friend? Explain.

   _____

3. The prefix *sym-* means "with." If your friend suffered a terrible disappointment, how would you show that you were *sympathetic*?

   _____

Using the Word List

imperceptible   impertinent   inanimate   obstinacy   pathos   venerable

B. DIRECTIONS: *Revise each sentence so that the underlined vocabulary word is used in a logical way. Be sure to keep the vocabulary word in your revision.*

Example: The <u>starving</u> animal just picked at the food that was offered.

Revision: The <u>starving</u> animal gobbled up the food that was offered.

1. Because of Megan's <u>obstinacy</u>, she was always willing to change her mind for good reasons.

   _____

2. No one had any respect for the <u>venerable</u> old man.

   _____

3. The <u>inanimate</u> object jumped all over the room.

   _____

4. The audience laughed uproariously at the <u>pathos</u> in the play.

   _____

5. The <u>impertinent</u> child showed great respect to his elders.

   _____

6. The sound of the lion's roar was <u>imperceptible</u> from twenty feet away.

   _____

"The Minister's Black Veil" by Nathaniel Hawthorne
Grammar and Style: Using Adjective and Adverb Clauses

An **adjective clause** is a subordinate clause that modifies a noun or pronoun by telling *what kind* or *which one*. An **adverb clause** is a subordinate clause that modifies a verb, adjective, adverb, or verbal by telling *where, when, in what way, to what extent, under what condition,* or *why*.

Example: The veil <u>that Mr. Hooper wore</u> was disturbing to the congregation. (adjective clause modifying the noun *veil*)

<u>When Mr. Hooper started wearing the veil</u>, everyone wondered why. (adverb clause modifying the verb *wondered*)

A. PRACTICE: *Underline the adjective or adverb clause in each sentence. On the line, identify it as an adjective clause or adverb clause, and indicate which word it modifies.*

1. As the people approached the meetinghouse, the sexton tolled the bell.

   _____

2. Mr. Hooper, who walked slowly toward the meetinghouse, was wearing a veil.

   _____

3. Mr. Hooper gave a powerful sermon while the parishioners wondered about the veil.

   _____

4. The veil, which was made of black crape, covered most of Mr. Hooper's face.

   _____

5. After he performed the wedding ceremony, Mr. Hooper raised a glass to his lips.

   _____

B. Writing Application: *Use each subordinate clause in a sentence. Tell whether it is an adjective clause or an adverb clause, and tell which word it modifies.*

1. when the visitors were seated in Mr. Hooper's home

   _____

2. who had been engaged to him for some time

   _____

3. as she hinted at the rumors surrounding the veil

   _____

4. that Mr. Hooper suffered

   _____

5. which he refused to remove

   _____

"The Minister's Black Veil" by Nathaniel Hawthorne
Support for Writing

As you gather information for your **interpretive essay about ambiguity,** use this organizer to record details related to the veil. List descriptions of the veil, dialogue about the veil, and characters' actions relating to the veil.

Details in "The Minister's Black Veil"	
Descriptions of the veil	
Dialogue about the veil	
Characters' actions	

On a separate page, write a draft of your interpretive essay. When you go back to revise your work, be sure that you have supported your interpretation with evidence from the story.

"The Minister's Black Veil" by Nathaniel Hawthorne
Enrichment: Art

The painting *Winter Sunday in Norway, Maine* illustrates a New England town much like that in "The Minister's Black Veil."

DIRECTIONS: *Study the painting and then answer the following questions.*

1. Describe the colors in this painting. In general, how do the colors reflect the mood of the story?

    _____

    _____

    _____

2. How is a wintry scene appropriate to the text?

    _____

    _____

    _____

3. What is the effect of the contrast between light and dark in the painting?

    _____

    _____

    _____

4. How are the visual themes of the painting related to the story?

    _____

    _____

    _____

5. How is the painting an appropriate accompaniment to the story?

    _____

    _____

    _____

"The Minister's Black Veil" by Nathaniel Hawthorne
Open-Book Test

Short Answer *Write your responses to the questions in this section on the lines provided.*

1. Early in "The Minister's Black Veil," Hawthorne shows the reader the reactions of the townspeople to the minister's veil. What moral is Hawthorne trying to communicate to the reader by describing these responses?

   _____

   _____

   _____

   _____

2. As the parishioners listen to Mr. Hooper's sermon in "The Minister's Black Veil," they feel a stronger power from his words than from previous sermons. How do the parishioners react? What difference does the veil make in how they react?

   _____

   _____

   _____

3. After the funeral in "The Minister's Black Veil," two of the townspeople have a "fancy"—a feeling or vision—that the minister and the spirit of the dead woman are "walking hand in hand." What inference about the beliefs of these two women can you draw from this imagined moment?

   _____

   _____

   _____

4. Near the beginning of "The Minister's Black Veil," find the paragraph that contains the word *inanimate*. Which word in the same sentence gives you a clue to the meaning of *inanimate* by providing a contrasting, or opposite, meaning?

   _____

   _____

5. In "The Minister's Black Veil," Hawthorne uses the townspeople to symbolize the faults he sees in many people. Cite three faults symbolized by the townspeople that Hawthorne highlights in the story.

   _____

   _____

   _____

   _____

6. In "The Minister's Black Veil," Hawthorne gives Elizabeth a different character from that of the townspeople. From her conversation with Mr. Hooper about his veil, what primary value can you infer is part of Elizabeth's character?

_____

_____

7. In the exchange between Mr. Hooper and Elizabeth in "The Minister's Black Veil," find and read the sentence that contains the word *obstinacy*. Which phrase in the sentence gives you a clue to the meaning of the word *obstinacy*? Which word would you suggest as a synonym?

_____

_____

_____

8. Read each quotation from "The Minister's Black Veil" on the left side of the chart below. Each quote suggests a possibility for the symbolic meaning of the black veil. Use the right side of the chart to write what the possible meaning of the veil is for each of the quotes. Each quote provides a different possibility.

"[the veil] threw its obscurity between it and the holy page as he read the Scriptures;"	
"Were the veil but cast aside, [the townspeople] might speak freely of it, but not till then."	
"This dismal shade must separate me from the world; even you, Elizabeth, can never come behind it!"	

9. Toward the end of "The Minister's Black Veil," read the paragraph beginning "Among all its bad influences. . . ." Explain the one beneficial result of the veil and the message that Hawthorne may be trying to communicate.

_____

_____

_____

10. At the end of "The Minister's Black Veil," the reader learns that Elizabeth has acted as Mr. Hooper's nurse all the years after she refused to marry him. What can you infer from this description of Elizabeth's behavior?

_____

_____

_____

Essay

Write an extended response to the question of your choice or to the question or questions your teacher assigns you.

11. In "The Minister's Black Veil," there are references to the "veil of eternity," a different veil from the material worn by Mr. Hooper. Reread the conversation between Reverend Clark and Mr. Hooper. Write a brief essay to describe the symbolic meaning of the "veil of eternity," and to tell why Mr. Hooper is at the point in his life to have it lifted.

12. What kind of character do you think Mr. Hooper is in "The Minister's Black Veil"? Write a brief essay to state your opinion about whether Mr. Hooper is basically a good person, a bad person, or some combination of both. Use details from the story to support your essay.

13. Toward the very end of "The Minister's Black Veil," reread the paragraph that begins, "Why do you tremble at me alone?" What broad message does Hawthorne mean to communicate in this paragraph? Write a brief essay to answer this question, citing support from the selection.

14. **Thinking About the Essential Question: What is the relationship between place and literature?** Hawthorne sets "The Minister's Black Veil" in a Puritan New England village in colonial times. How does this setting help determine and explain the characters' behavior and attitudes? Write a brief essay explaining the relationship of the setting to the story's events and characters.

Oral Response

15. Go back to question 1, 4, 8, or 9 or to the question your teacher assigns to you. Take a few minutes to expand your answer and prepare an oral response. Find additional details in "The Minister's Black Veil" that will support your points. If necessary, make notes to guide your response.

"The Minister's Black Veil" by Nathaniel Hawthorne
Selection Test A

Critical Reading *Identify the letter of the choice that best answers the question.*

____ 1. In "The Minister's Black Veil: A Parable," what does the word *parable* tell you about the story?
  A. It has animal characters.
  B. It is a science-fiction tale.
  C. It teaches a message.
  D. It is frightening.

____ 2. In "The Minister's Black Veil: A Parable," why do the parishioners have such an intense response to seeing the minister's veil?
  A. They feel it is not religious.
  B. They are frightened by it.
  C. They think it is not appropriate.
  D. They feel he must be dying.

____ 3. From this passage in "The Minister's Black Veil: A Parable," what can you infer about the beliefs of the minister's congregation?

  . . . and while he prayed, the veil lay heavily on his uplifted countenance. Did he seek to hide it from the dread Being whom he was addressing?

  A. They trust God.
  B. They ignore God.
  C. They love God.
  D. They fear God.

____ 4. One meaning of Mr. Hooper's veil is that relationships between people are never completely clear. What can you infer about Elizabeth when she asks him to remove the veil?
  A. She does not understand this essential truth.
  B. She does not love him anymore.
  C. She supports his decision to wear the veil.
  D. She is angry with him for wearing the veil.

____ 5. How does "The Minister's Black Veil: A Parable" convey the Puritan attitude toward human nature?
  A. It is full of optimism.
  B. It is full of enthusiasm.
  C. It is full of pessimism.
  D. It is full of forgiveness.

____ 6. Who takes care of Mr. Hooper during his final illness in "The Minister's Black Veil"?

    A. the couple he married

    B. the town doctor

    C. Elizabeth

    D. a converted sinner

____ 7. A moral lesson of this story might be that

    A. sinners always receive divine justice.

    B. if we wear a veil we should feel guilty.

    C. people are all basically innocent.

    D. guilty secrets separate us from one another.

____ 8. A social lesson of this story might be that

    A. most people have nothing to hide from one another.

    B. people protect their personal privacy by wearing a public mask.

    C. no one needs to worry about other people's opinions.

    D. the best policy is not to wear veils in public.

Vocabulary and Grammar

____ 9. For members of his church, when they first saw Mr. Hooper's veil, "an unsought pathos came hand in hand with awe." How did these people feel about him?

    A. They thought the veil was simply awful.

    B. They felt sorry for him.

    C. They thought he was crazy.

    D. They thought the veil was a joke.

____ 10. "As he stooped, the veil hung straight down from his forehead. . . ." The first three words in this sentence are an

    A. adjective clause.

    B. adverb phrase.

    C. adjective phrase.

    D. adverb clause.

Essay

11. Suppose that the message of "The Minister's Black Veil" is that people are sinful. Suppose that the minister wishes to show that sin is a barrier between people and God, people and their loved ones, as well as people and their happiness. Do you think he communicates this message to his parishioners? Are their lives made more religious or spiritual by his wearing the veil, even after his death? Does he inspire them to be less sinful? Write a brief essay to give your opinions about what value Mr. Hooper's actions have on the people of his congregation.

12. In "The Minister's Black Veil," the minister's last words include these passages: "Why do you tremble at me alone? . . . I look around me, and, lo! on every visage a Black Veil!" What do you think he means? Write a brief essay to state the inference you can draw from the minister's words.

13. Much of Hawthorne's message is that good and evil are not easily separated, and that all people have both qualities within themselves. These ideas are most clearly seen in the contrast between Mr. Hooper and the people who interact with him. In a brief essay, discuss ways in which the following people and events illustrate Hawthorne's themes. Include at least two examples.

    • the morally strict, black-and-white standards of Puritan New England

    • the people's sense of their own righteousness

    • the moral cowardice of the deputies who fail to ask him about the veil

    • parishioners' "speechless, confused" and guiltily uneasy reaction to his presumed judgment on them

    • the "fable" going around that the stares of dead people motivated the veil

    • rumors that Hooper had committed a "great crime"

    • Hooper's whole life becoming "shrouded in dismal suspicions"

14. **Thinking About the Essential Question: What is the relationship between place and literature?** "The Minister's Black Veil" takes place in a small village in Puritan New England during colonial times. Write a brief essay about the relationship of the setting to the events and characters in the story. Your essay should answer this question: How does the setting of the story help determine and explain the characters' behavior and attitudes?

"The Minister's Black Veil" by Nathaniel Hawthorne
Selection Test B

Critical Reading *Identify the letter of the choice that best completes the statement or answers the question.*

_____ 1. Before donning the black veil, what sort of minister was Mr. Hooper?
A. outstanding
B. good
C. frightening
D. despised

_____ 2. Over what group does the veiled minister seem to have the most power?
A. the children of the village
B. other clergymen in the area
C. his congregation
D. souls in agony for sinning

_____ 3. Which statement expresses a central theme of the story?
A. People are attracted by unsolved mysteries.
B. People with faith can overcome any hardship.
C. People are often unwilling to face the truth about themselves.
D. People who sin should not be forgiven.

_____ 4. "The Minister's Black Veil" is a parable, which means that characters, events, and details of setting
A. are described in realistic detail.
B. are gloomy and sometimes terrifying.
C. are usually historical in nature.
D. are simplified to teach a moral lesson.

_____ 5. What does the village physician most likely represent in the story?
A. wealth
B. religious superstition
C. logic and reason
D. human emotion

_____ 6. What message about human nature is most strongly conveyed by Elizabeth's nursing of Mr. Hooper on his deathbed?
A. Love for someone endures despite what that person does.
B. Curiosity leads people to do odd things.
C. Loyalty always leads to learning the truth.
D. Hard work is seldom rewarded in this life.

_____ 7. What message might be conveyed by the veiled minister at the wedding?
A. Weddings are joyful, hopeful occasions.
B. Brides and grooms need to be reminded that they will eventually die.
C. Secrets between people can destroy trust and love.
D. The marriage relationship is very difficult.

_____ 8. What does the black veil most likely represent in the parable?
    A. secret love
    B. secret sin
    C. modesty
    D. violence

_____ 9. Based on this story, how would you describe Hawthorne's view of human nature?
    A. naive
    B. pessimistic
    C. idealistic
    D. uncaring

_____ 10. What can you infer about Hawthorne's message from the following passage?

> The next day, the whole village of Milford talked of little else than Parson Hooper's black veil. That, and the mystery concealed behind it, supplied a topic of discussion between acquaintances meeting in the street, and good women gossiping at their open windows. It was the first item of news that the tavernkeeper told his guests. The children babbled of it on their way to school.

    A. Hawthorne thinks that most human beings are respectful of people's differences.
    B. Hawthorne thinks it's important for people to talk about what is happening in their community.
    C. Hawthorne thinks most human beings gossip too much.
    D. Hawthorne thinks children are the worst gossipers.

_____ 11. Based on the rest of the story, what can you infer about the meaning of the following passage?

> "When the friend shows his inmost heart to his friend; the lover to his best beloved; when man does not vainly shrink from the eye of his Creator, loathsomely treasuring up the secret of his sin; then deem me a monster, for the symbol beneath which I have lived and die! I look around me, and lo! on every visage a Black Veil."

    A. It is sometimes good to hide secrets from other people.
    B. Love is not something to be valued.
    C. It is human nature to follow our hearts.
    D. Each person hides his or her darkest secrets from others for fear of what others will think.

Vocabulary

_____ 12. "It was strange to observe how slowly this venerable man became conscious of something singular in the appearance of his pastor." A synonym for *venerable* is
    A. respected.
    B. fragile, easily wounded.
    C. greedy, selfish.
    D. hypocritical.

_____ 13. Why is the narrator surprised that the *impertinent* people in the congregation fail to ask
Mr. Hooper the reason for the veil?
A. They command a great deal of respect.
B. They would be likely to ask questions that might be considered disrespectful.
C. They are afraid of speaking for fear of appearing disrespectful.
D. They are interested in appearing intelligent.

_____ 14. Which of these events is most likely to arouse *pathos*?
A. a wedding
B. a funeral
C. a graduation
D. a victory celebration

_____ 15. Which of these sentences contains an adverb clause?
A. At the close of the services, the people hurried out.
B. After a brief interval, forth came good Mr. Hooper also.
C. A sad smile gleamed from beneath black veil, and flickered about his mouth.
D. As he stooped, the veil hung straight down from his forehead.

_____ 16. What does the following sentence contain?
At the instance when the clergyman's features were disclosed, the corpse had slightly shud-
dered, rustling the shroud and muslin cap, though the countenance retained the composure
of death.
A. one adverb clause and one adjective clause
B. one adverb clause and no adjective clauses
C. two adverb clauses and one adjective clause
D. three adverb clauses and no adjective clauses

Essay

17. Do you think Mr. Hooper's veil is a form of confession? Is he making a statement? Might it
be both? Write an essay describing the conclusion you reach about the significance of the
veil. Support your solution with examples from the story.

18. What are the characteristics of the Puritans and their religion as portrayed by Hawthorne in
this story? Do you think he has a negative or positive opinion of them? What do you think is
his opinion of Mr. Hooper? Write an essay answering these questions.

19. In the story, a lady of the village says, "How strange. . . that a simple black veil, such as any
woman might wear on her bonnet, should become such a terrible thing on Mr. Hooper's
face!" Write an essay exploring what this statement means in relation to objects and their
symbolic power.

20. **Thinking About the Essential Question: What is the relationship between place and
literature?** Why is the Purtain New England setting important to Hawthorne's story? In a
brief essay, state Hawthorne's attitue toward virtue and vice, good and evil; then, discuss at
least two ways in which the people, their customs, and their religion serve to reveal the
story's possible meanings.

"The Fall of the House of Usher" and "The Raven" by Edgar Allan Poe
Vocabulary Warm-up Word Lists

Study these words from the selections. Then, complete the activities.

Word List A

alternately [AWL tuhr nuht lee] *adv.* in succession; taking turns
   Tom was <u>alternately</u> hopeful and pessimistic, and could not make up his mind.

boon [BOON] *n.* welcome benefit; favor
   The high grade on his math exam was a <u>boon</u> to James, giving him encouragement.

enchantment [en CHANT muhnt] *n.* state of being charmed; magical spell
   During the concert, the flute solo was a delightful source of <u>enchantment</u>.

ghastly [GAST lee] *adj.* horrible; frightful
   The television pictures of the war casualties were <u>ghastly</u>.

maturity [muh CHOOR uh tee] *n.* state or quality of being full-grown
   In <u>maturity</u>, a full-grown male Bengal tiger weighs about 450 pounds.

similarly [SIM uh luhr lee] *adv.* likewise
   Homer's *Iliad* is an epic poem; <u>similarly</u>, *Beowulf* is also an epic focusing on a hero.

sinister [SIN is tuhr] *adj.* threatening harm or evil
   We could tell that the villain in that TV show had <u>sinister</u> intentions.

somber [SOM buhr] *adj.* dark and gloomy; depressed
   The solemn music at the funeral put everyone in a <u>somber</u> mood.

Word List B

acuteness [uh KYOOT nis] *n.* sharpness; keenness
   The <u>acuteness</u> of most dogs' hearing surpasses human abilities.

apathy [AP uh thee] *n.* lack of interest or feeling; indifference
   The class listened with <u>apathy</u> to the speaker.

demeanor [duh MEEN uhr] *n.* outward behavior or conduct
   Sarah was known for her shy <u>demeanor</u>.

gradual [GRAD yoo uhl] *adj.* taking place by slow steps or degrees
   Progress on that issue will have to be <u>gradual</u> and can't be achieved overnight.

inaccessible [in ak SES uh buhl] *adj.* impossible to reach or enter
   Their house is <u>inaccessible</u> except by helicopter.

sensibility [sen si BIL uh tee] *n.* capacity for being affected emotionally
   Pete was respected for his <u>sensibility</u> to other people's problems.

solace [SAHL uhs] *n.* comfort; consolation
   The old man found <u>solace</u> in the visit of his grandchildren.

succumbed [suh KUMD] *v.* yielded to; gave way; submitted to
   Debbie <u>succumbed</u> to temptation and ordered a chocolate ice cream soda.

"The Fall of the House of Usher" and **"The Raven"** by Edgar Allan Poe
Vocabulary Warm-up Exercises

Exercise A *Fill in the blanks, using each word from Word List A only once.*

Tim's new hobby was recording the musical scores of action thrillers. Movies fascinated him, and he felt that when he reached [1] _____ as an adult, his career would somehow be connected with film. Tim [2] _____ considered acting, directing, and composing; he was [3] _____ talented at all three. It was the combination of music and visual images, though, that held the most [4] _____ for him. He appreciated the ways a gifted composer could use music to express a(n) [5] _____ mood of disappointment, or foreshadow an ominous or [6] _____ plot development. Music could create optimism, Tim thought, when the hero or heroine was overjoyed by a(n) [7] _____; music could also drive home the [8] _____ aspects of a horrible catastrophe. Tim thought that before the end of the year, he would try to write his own musical score for a full-length feature film.

Exercise B *Decide whether each statement below is true or false. Circle T or F, and explain your answer.*

1. When someone answers a question with *acuteness*, you can trust the answer as reliable.
   T / F _____

2. *Apathy* usually indicates a person's kindness and concern.
   T / F _____

3. A person's *demeanor* refers to his or her inner emotional state.
   T / F _____

4. A *gradual* series of events often unfolds over a considerable span of time.
   T / F _____

5. An office that is *inaccessible* is easy to find and is open to everyone.
   T / F _____

6. A person whose *sensibility* is fine-tuned does not usually consider others' feelings.
   T / F _____

7. If you find *solace* in a time of grief, your sorrows are increased.
   T / F _____

8. People who have *succumbed* to invaders have mounted a successful challenge to them.
   T / F _____

Name _____ Date _____

"The Fall of the House of Usher" and **"The Raven"** by Edgar Allan Poe
Reading Warm-up A

Read the following passage. Pay special attention to the underlined words. Then, read it again, and complete the activities. Use a separate sheet of paper for your written answers.

In Edgar Allan Poe's poem, the raven is a gloomy, <u>somber</u> bird whose appearance first surprises but then deeply unsettles the speaker. At the start, the raven seems like a <u>boon</u>: a special sign of favor. As the poem progresses, however, the speaker loses all sense of fascination or <u>enchantment</u>. Instead, the raven becomes a <u>ghastly</u>, terrifying reminder of personal tragedy.

In real life, ravens are fascinating, highly intelligent birds that have inspired much study and admiration by humans. The Common Raven (*Corvus corax*) is the largest perching bird in the world. At <u>maturity</u>, adult birds have a length of over two feet and a wingspan of four feet. Ravens are sometimes mistaken for crows. The two species are <u>similarly</u> sooty-colored, but ravens have a much heavier beak and shaggier plumage than crows do.

Although they have often been held to symbolize death and disease, ravens are extremely intelligent and courageous birds. They have inspired many tales, especially among the native peoples of the Northwest Pacific Coast. For Native American storytellers, Raven was a bird-human character who was <u>alternately</u> clever and stupid by turns. He could be a grim and <u>sinister</u> figure, spreading confusion with his irresponsible tricks and greedy appetite. On the other hand, he was also a culture hero, who discovered light to transform the dark earth into a fruitful physical environment. Native American mythology and symbolism of Raven reflect the fascinating contrasts and opposites of this species of bird in real life.

1. Underline the word in this sentence that gives a clue to the meaning of <u>somber</u>. Use the word *somber* in an original sentence.

2. Circle the words in this sentence that give a clue to the meaning of <u>boon</u>. Would a *boon* normally be an advantage or a drawback?

3. Underline the word that hints at the meaning of <u>enchantment</u> here. Does this word have positive or negative associations?

4. Underline the word in this sentence that gives a clue to the meaning of <u>ghastly</u>. What are two synonyms for *ghastly*?

5. Circle the word in this sentence that hints at the meaning of <u>maturity</u>. What is an antonym for *maturity*?

6. Circle the words in this sentence that offer a clue to the meaning of the word <u>similarly</u>. What is a synonym for *similarly*?

7. What is a synonym for <u>alternately</u>? Use the word *alternately* in a sentence of your own.

8. Underline the words that give a clue to the meaning of <u>sinister</u>. What are two synonyms for *sinister*?

"The Fall of the House of Usher" and **"The Raven"** by Edgar Allan Poe
Reading Warm-up B

Read the following passage. Pay special attention to the underlined words. Then, read it again, and complete the activities. Use a separate sheet of paper for your written answers.

In May 1842, Edgar Allan Poe published a magazine review of Nathaniel Hawthorne's first short-story collection, *Twice-Told Tales*. The review continues to be read because it concisely presents Poe's theory of the short story, a form that he called the "prose tale."

Poe believed that stories were superior to novels. In a story, which can be read at one sitting, a writer can present a single total effect. The <u>acuteness</u> with which a reader keenly experiences this effect cannot be duplicated in a novel. The reading of a novel, Poe pointed out, is <u>gradual</u>, with many interruptions from start to finish. The reader's <u>sensibility</u> for the characters and situation is often distracted. Poe thought that the end result might be <u>apathy</u>, or actual indifference to the characters and the storyline. In any event, the length of novels ruled out the impact of a single effect, making such an effect <u>inaccessible</u> to the reader. By contrast, in beginning to read a short story, the reader has <u>succumbed</u> to the writer's control, yielding all of his or her attention from the beginning to the end.

To reinforce his main idea, Poe argued that every detail in a short story should contribute to the writer's single effect. Poe even specified that a story's single effect should be clear in the tale's very first sentence. To test Poe's theory, read the first sentence of "The Fall of the House of Usher" several times. In this long first sentence, you will find at least ten words and phrases with melancholy, even ominous connotations or associations. The narrator's outward <u>demeanor</u> is heavy-hearted and depressed, and he sees no comfort or <u>solace</u> in his horseback ride on a gloomy autumn afternoon. In his first sentence, Poe brilliantly establishes the prevailing mood, or atmosphere, of the tale to come.

1. Underline the words in this sentence that give a clue to the meaning of <u>acuteness</u>. Use the word **acuteness** in an original sentence.

2. Circle the words in this sentence that give a clue to the meaning of <u>gradual</u>. Use a word meaning the opposite of **gradual** in a sentence of your own.

3. Underline the words in this sentence hinting at the meaning of <u>sensibility</u>.

4. Underline the words in this sentence that give a clue to the meaning of <u>apathy</u>. What are two antonyms for **apathy**?

5. Circle the words in this sentence that give a clue to the meaning of the word <u>inaccessible</u>. Use a word meaning the opposite of **inaccessible** in a sentence of your own.

6. Underline the words in this sentence that hint at the meaning of <u>succumbed</u>. What is an antonym of **succumbed**?

7. Underline the word in this sentence that gives a clue to the meaning of <u>demeanor</u>.

8. Circle the word in this sentence that hints at the meaning of the word <u>solace</u>. What is a synonym for **solace**?

"The Fall of the House of Usher" and **"The Raven"** by Edgar Allan Poe
Edgar Allan Poe: Biography

The sad, colorful life of Edgar Allan Poe made him America's first tormented genius. A writer of haunting poetry, brilliant detective fiction and thrilling horror stories, and insightful literary criticism, Poe unfortunately knew only limited success in his lifetime. Yet he eventually became one of the most popular American writers, largely due to his ability to call up the dark, unknown side of human experience.

A. DIRECTIONS: *Edgar Allan Poe has been the subject of many plays, films, and other works. Imagine that you are helping to create a documentary about Poe's life and career. Write a brief summary of each part of Poe's life. Then, suggest a visual or two to use to illustrate each part.*

Part I (childhood): "Orphan Raised Overseas"—**Summary:** _____

_____

Suggested visual(s): _____

Part II (military): "The Poet in the Army"—**Summary:** _____

_____

Suggested visual(s): _____

Part III (literary career): "Turning to Fiction and Criticism"—**Summary:** _____

_____

Suggested visual(s): _____

Part IV (last years): "A Sad End"—**Summary:** _____

_____

Suggested visual(s): _____

B. DIRECTIONS: *Imagine that you are Edgar Allan Poe being interviewed. Give his responses to the following questions.*

Interviewer: You were raised in England and spent time in the army when you started your writing career. What experiences in your life influenced your work?

Poe: _____

_____

Interviewer: Mr. Poe, what sort of reader do you think will be drawn to your stories and poems?

Poe: _____

_____

Interviewer: Finally, Mr. Poe, what qualities do *you* think are distinctly American? How do you show these qualities in your writings?

Poe: _____

_____

"The Fall of the House of Usher" and **"The Raven"** by Edgar Allan Poe
Literary Analysis: Single Effect

Edgar Allan Poe said that a short story should be written to create a **single effect.** Every character, detail, and incident, from the first sentence on, should contribute to this effect. This same principle can be applied to **narrative poems**, poems that tell a story.

DIRECTIONS: *Following are settings and characters described in "The Fall of the House of Usher." On the lines below each setting or character, list three specific details about that setting or character that you feel contribute to the single effect of Roderick's terror and mounting dread.*

1. *Setting:* The room in which Usher spends his days

   A. _____

   B. _____

   C. _____

2. *Setting:* Madeline's tomb

   A. _____

   B. _____

   C. _____

3. *Setting:* The house at the end of the story

   A. _____

   B. _____

   C. _____

4. *Character:* Roderick Usher

   A. _____

   B. _____

   C. _____

5. *Character:* Madeline Usher

   A. _____

   B. _____

   C. _____

Name _____ Date _____

"The Fall of the House of Usher" and **"The Raven"** by Edgar Allan Poe
Literary Analysis: Gothic Style

The gothic style has several well-known characteristics that have made it popular for centuries among writers and other artists. To concoct a gothic style, a writer would use several distinct ingredients and techniques:

Recipe for Gothic Style

- Take one bleak and remote setting.

- Fold in a character who suffers physical and/or psychological torment.

- Mix with events of a macabre or violent nature.

- Add supernatural or otherworldly elements (optional).

- Stir using vivid language with dark and dangerous meanings.

DIRECTIONS: *Now supply your own examples of gothic ingredients in this recipe card:*

My Own Gothic Mix

- Take this setting: _____

- Fold in this character: _____

- Mix with these events: _____

  _____

- Add this otherworldly element: _____

  _____

- Stir with phrases like this: _____

  _____

DIRECTIONS: *For each gothic element listed below, add another example from "The Fall of the House of Usher" or "The Raven," as indicated.*

1. Bleak setting in "The Fall of the House of Usher": <u>Fungus covers the House of Usher.</u>

   Another example: _____

2. Bleak, remote setting in "The Raven": <u>"midnight dreary"</u>

   Another example: _____

3. Characters' torments in "The Fall of the House of Usher": <u>Roderick's acute illness</u>

   Another example: _____

4. Narrator's torments in "The Raven": <u>The narrator is "weak and weary."</u>

   Another example: _____

"The Fall of the House of Usher" and **"The Raven"** by Edgar Allan Poe
Reading Strategy: Break Down Long Sentences

When an author writes a long, complicated sentence, you can clarify the meaning by breaking it down into its logical parts. Look especially for the subject and predicate at its core. After you have identified them, state the core in your own words.

Poe's sentence: A cadaverousness of complexion; an eye large, liquid, and luminous beyond comparison; lips somewhat thin and very pallid, but of a surpassingly beautiful curve; a nose of a delicate Hebrew model, but with a breath of nostril unusual in similar formations; a finely molded chin, speaking, in its want of prominence, of a want of moral energy; hair of a more than weblike softness and tenuity— these features, with an inordinate expansion above the region of the temple, made up altogether a countenance not easily to be forgotten.

Core sentence: These features made up a countenance not easily forgotten.

Own words: He had a memorable face.

DIRECTIONS: *Underline the core of the following sentences from "The Fall of the House of Usher."* *Then restate the core in your own words.*

1. During the whole of a dull, dark, and soundless day in the autumn of that year, when the clouds hung oppressively low in the heavens, I had been passing alone, on horseback, through a singularly dreary tract of country, and at length found myself, as the shades of evening drew on, within view of the melancholy House of Usher.

   _____

2. I reined my horse to the precipitous brink of a black and lurid tarn that lay in unruffled luster by the dwelling, and gazed down—but with a shudder even more thrilling than before—upon the remodeled and inverted images of the gray sedge, and the ghastly tree stems, and the vacant and eyelike windows.

   _____

3. He admitted, however, although with hesitation, that much of the peculiar gloom which thus afflicted him could be traced to a more natural and far more palpable origin—to the severe and long-continued illness—indeed to the evidently approaching dissolution of a tenderly beloved sister, his sole companion for long years, his last and only relative on earth.

   _____

4. Our books—the books which, for years, had formed no small portion of the mental existence of the invalid—were, as might be supposed, in strict keeping with this character of phantasm.

   _____

"The Fall of the House of Usher" and **"The Raven"** by Edgar Allan Poe

Vocabulary Builder

Using the Latin Root -voc-

A. DIRECTIONS: *The root -voc- comes from the Latin* vox, *meaning "voice." On the lines provided, explain how the root -voc- influences the meaning of each of the italicized words.*

1. The environmental board in our town *advocates* passage of a strong law against dumping waste in Lake Jasper.

   _____

2. Studying the works of Poe will probably improve your *vocabulary*.

   _____

3. The cottage was *evocative* of happy childhood memories.

   _____

Using the Word List

anomalous	equivocal	importunate
munificent	sentience	specious

B. DIRECTIONS: *For each item, write on the line the letter of the pair of words that expresses a relationship most like the pair in capital letters.*

___ 1. FALSE : SPECIOUS ::
    A. beautiful : ugly   B. violent : wicked   C. plentiful : abundant

___ 2. NORMAL : ANOMALOUS ::
    A. valuable : worthless   B. blue : color   C. sleepy : tired

___ 3. EQUIVOCAL : SURE ::
    A. physician : disease   B. vocal : talkative   C. vague : clear

___ 4. SENTIENCE : FEELING ::
    A. capable : skill   B. visible : darkness   C. worth : value

___ 5. BENEFACTOR : MUNIFICENT ::
    A. donor : charity   B. giver : taker   C. philanthropist : generous

___ 6. IMPORTUNATE : INSIST ::
    A. unlucky : luck   B. talkative : chat   C. create : thought

"The Fall of the House of Usher" and **"The Raven"** by Edgar Allan Poe
Grammar and Style: Comparative and Superlative Adjectives and Adverbs

Adjectives and adverbs have **comparative** and **superlative** forms.

- When two things are being compared, we use the comparative form. Most comparatives are formed by adding the suffix -er: *smaller, lower, younger.* Some comparatives are formed by using the word *more* or *less: more unusual, more quickly, less expensive.*

- When three or more things are being compared, we use the superlative form. Most superlatives are formed by adding the suffix -est: *smallest, lowest, youngest.* Some superlatives are formed by using the word *most* or *least: most unusual, most quickly, least expensive.*

A. PRACTICE: *Identify the italicized adjective or adverb as a comparative or superlative form. Write* comparative *or* superlative *on the line.*

1. Sandra wore her *most ostentatious* hat in the parade. _____

2. Jan's *prettiest* skirt has ruffles along the hem. _____

3. Jason learned the game *more easily* than he had expected. _____

4. Milo was two inches *taller* than his brother. _____

B. Writing Application: *Write the correct form of the adjective or adverb on the line.*

1. (difficult) Of the two poems, this one is _____ to understand.

2. (surprising) The _____ scene in the whole story was when Madeline Usher got out of the coffin.

3. (dreary) The narrator thought the area was the _____ place he had ever seen.

4. (cheerful) Roderick Usher thought he would become _____ if his friend came for a visit.

5. (peculiar) The _____ thing about Roderick Usher was his tendency to be very reserved.

6. (bleak) The raven tapped at the door on the _____ night in December.

7. (loudly) As the night went on, the raven tapped _____ than before.

8. (ominously) The raven said "Nevermore" _____ the sixth time.

9. (frightening) Which do you think is the _____ stanza in this poem?

10. (effective) Of the two works of literature, which do you think is _____ as an exercise in terror?

"The Fall of the House of Usher" and **"The Raven"** by Edgar Allan Poe
Support for Writing

As you prepare to write a **critical essay** supporting one of the two critics' views of "The Fall of the House of Usher," first reread the story and decide which of the following views you share. Enter details supporting that view on the chart below.

- The narrator and the other two characters are all insane. (Davidson)
- Each character represents part of a single person; for example the conscious mind, the unconscious mind, and the soul. (Lovecraft)
- The house itself is eerily connected to the inhabitants and cannot continue standing after they are dead (Lovecraft)

Critical Appraisal of "The Fall of the House of Usher"	
Main idea about what is going on in story	Expansion of main idea
Support from first part of story	
Support from middle of story	
Support from end of story	

Draft your essay on a separate page. Indicate the cirtic with whom you agree as you state the main idea you share. Then incorporate details supporting that idea. When you revise, be sure that the main idea is clear and that you give enough details from the story to support it.

Name _____ Date _____

"The Fall of the House of Usher" and **"The Raven"** by Edgar Allan Poe

Enrichment: Film Versions of Edgar Allan Poe Stories

Because of their vividly imagined and terrifying worlds, Poe's short stories have often been adapted for film. Film versions of stories such as "The Fall of the House of Usher" (1982), "The Pit and the Pendulum" (1961), "The Tell-Tale Heart" (1963), "The Premature Burial" (1962), and "The Murders in the Rue Morgue" (1971) exist in video form today. Others appear from time to time on television.

DIRECTIONS: *Choose a scene from "The Fall of the House of Usher" or "The Raven" that you think would be especially suitable for a film or video interpretation. Recalling horror stories you have seen on television or at the movies, consider how you might film your scene. Focus on creating the right mood and effect. You may want to begin by looking at some suspense and horror videos of Poe's work. Note the techniques used to create mood and effect. Think about how you will handle the narration in Poe's stories. What will the setting be like? How will the characters look, dress, and move? Write a script for your scene that includes not only lines, but also descriptions of the setting, the characters and their actions, camera shots, and special visual and sound effects.*

Plan your scene in the following space.

Chosen scene:

_____

_____

Notes on the setting:

_____

_____

Notes on the characters:

_____

_____

Ideas for special camera shots:

_____

_____

Ideas for visual and sound effects:

_____

_____

"The Fall of the House of Usher" and **"The Raven"** by Edgar Allen Poe
Open-Book Test

Short Answer *Write your responses to the questions in this section on the lines provided.*

1. In the first four paragraphs of "The Fall of the House of Usher," Poe is striving to create a single effect for the reader. What do you think it is? Give at least two examples from this section to support your answer.

   _____

   _____

   _____

2. In paragraph 6 of "The Fall of the House of Usher," reread the sentence that begins, "While the objects around me . . . ." Break down this long sentence into smaller, simpler ideas. Rewrite the sentence as three or four sentences. You may put them in different order for clarity, if you wish.

   _____

   _____

   _____

   _____

3. In paragraphs 8–10 of "The Fall of the House of Usher," Poe describes Roderick Usher. What picture does the reader get of the character of Roderick Usher from these paragraphs? What is he like physically and mentally?

   _____

   _____

4. In "The Fall of the House of Usher," find the highlighted vocabulary word *munificent*. What context clues in the same sentence help you figure out the meaning of the word *munificent*?

   _____

   _____

5. In paragraph 11 of "The Fall of the House of Usher," what do you learn that Roderick Usher fears? Does this surprise you?

   _____

   _____

   _____

6. In "The Fall of the House of Usher," how does the narrator react to the situation? Is he frightened like his friend? Support your answer with details from the story.

   _____

   _____

7. By breaking down the long sentence in Stanza 1 of "The Raven," describe what is occurring in this stanza in two or three simple sentences.

_____

_____

_____

8. What is the single effect Poe achieves in "The Raven" through the repeated use of the Raven's "Neveremore?"

_____

_____

_____

9. Reread lines 67–72 of "The Raven." Break down this one long sentence into three or four smaller sentences that have a clearer meaning.

_____

_____

_____

_____

10. Read each passage from "The Raven" in the numbered boxes below. Then determine what single effect is created by the words, and write this in the box underneath. Consider sound, repeated words, rhyme, and ideas when you make your choice of each single effect.

Deep into that darkness peering, long I stood there wondering, fearing,
Doubting, dreaming dreams no mortal every dared to dream before;

_____
_____

And the only word there spoken was the whispered word, "Lenore?"
This I whispered, and an echo murmured back the word, "Lenore!"
Merely this and nothing more.

_____
_____

Leave my loneliness unbroken! quit the bust above my door!
Take thy beak from out my heart, and take they form from off my door!"
Quoth the Raven, "Nevermore."

_____
_____
_____

Essay

Write an extended response to the question of your choice or to the question or questions your teacher assigns you.

11. Both Roderick Usher in "The Fall of the House of Usher" and the speaker in "The Raven" are solitary men. How does this affect them? How does it affect the outcome of the selections in which they appear as characters? Choose one of the selections and write a brief essay to answer these questions.

12. Choose one:

    What do you think the effect of the events in "The Fall of the House of Usher" is on the narrator? Write a brief essay to give your opinion on how the narrator might remember the events after months, or even years have passed. Remember why he has come to Roderick's home and what he has hoped to do there.

    In "The Raven," Poe uses rhyming and rhythmic techniques to create a sense of impending doom. Write a brief essay to show how these techniques are used, citing at least two examples from the poem.

13. In both "The Fall of the House of Usher" and "The Raven" the poet uses symbols. Choose one of the following and write a brief essay to explain your opinions: What does the house symbolize in "The Fall of the House of Usher?" What does the Raven symbolize in "The Raven?" Cite details from the works to support your opinion.

14. **Thinking About the Essential Question: What is the relationship between place and literature?** Choose either Poe's "The Fall of the House of Usher" or "The Raven." Write a brief essay on the effect of the setting, the place in which the action happens. How does it affect the main characters?

Oral Response

15. Go back to question 1, 3, 8, or 9 or to the question your teacher assigns to you. Take a few minutes to expand your answers and prepare an oral response. Find additional details in the "The Fall of the House of Usher" or "The Raven" that will support your points. If necessary, make notes to guide your response.

Name _____ Date _____

Selection Test A

Critical Reading *Identify the letter of the choice that best answers the question.*

____ 1. In "The Fall of the House of Usher," which word best describes the single effect created by the opening description of the house?

    A. interest

    B. gloom

    C. enthusiasm

    D. sorrow

____ 2. Which choice below best restates this long sentence from "The Fall of the House of Usher"?

> Feeble beams of encrimsoned light made their way through the trellised panes, and served to render sufficiently distinct the more prominent objects around; the eye, however, struggled in vain to reach the remoter angles of the chamber or the recesses of the vaulted and fretted ceiling.

    A. Not enough light came through the windowpanes, and I had trouble seeing even the larger objects in the room.

    B. The light that came through the windows was so dim that it made everything in the room seem shadowy.

    C. The dim light coming through the windows lit up the larger objects, but my eye could not see anything in the corners of the room.

    D. The reddish light coming through the windows helped my eyes focus on everything in the room.

____ 3. In "The Fall of the House of Usher," what does the narrator find to be the explanation for his host's sad situation?

    A. the condition of the old house

    B. the unending gloomy weather

    C. his sister's mortal illness

    D. his own failing health

____ 4. What gothic element may be seen in details such as the black tarn, decayed trees, and vacant, eyelike windows of Usher's house?

    A. macabre or violent incidents

    B. bleak or remote settings

    C. characters in psychological and/or physical torment

    D. strong language full of dangerous meanings

_____ 5. Which choice below best restates this long sentence from "The Fall of the House of Usher"?

> Oppressed, as I certainly was, upon the extraordinary coincidence, by a thousand conflicting sensations, in which wonder and extreme terror were predominant, I still retained sufficient presence of mind to avoid exciting, by an observation, the sensitive nervousness of my companion.

    A. Though I was oppressed by many feelings, the feelings of terror and nervousness were the two strongest.

    B. I was overcome by many difficult emotions and was unable to avoid upsetting my friend.

    C. I felt many different responses, but realized that my friend had not observed it at all.

    D. Though the coincidence overcame me with many feelings, including terror, I was careful to avoid upsetting my friend.

_____ 6. What macabre or violent incident contributes to the gothic element of the story?

    A. the narrator's decision to visit his childhood friend

    B. Roderick's guitar playing

    C. the long hours spent alone by the narrator

    D. Roderick's having buried his sister alive

_____ 7. When the poet in "The Raven" thinks that Lenore may be at his door, what are his feelings?

    A. fear and anguish

    B. hope and doubt

    C. anger and disgust

    D. curiosity and relief

_____ 8. Which of these identifies a main cause-and-effect relationship in "The Raven"?

    A. poetry and happiness

    B. loss and heartbreak

    C. sleeplessness and illness

    D. strange visitors and dreams

Vocabulary and Grammar

___ 9. "To an anomalous species of terror I found him a bounden slave." What is the meaning of *anomalous*?
   A. something clearly understood by all
   B. something catching, like the flu
   C. something wonderful and amazing
   D. something mysterious, having no name

___ 10. In the phrase ". . . closer and still closer intimacy . . . ," the word *closer* is a
   A. superlative adverb
   B. comparative adverb
   C. superlative adjective
   D. comparative adjective

Essay

11. In what ways are Roderick and Madeline Usher, and the house in which they live, alike? Are they healthy and lively, or dying and decaying? Why have they fallen into the state of health they are in? Write a brief essay to compare the siblings and the house from "The Fall of the House of Usher."

12. Many writers often use birds as symbols of hope, freedom, and light. In what different way does Poe use the image of the raven in his poem, "The Raven"? Write a brief essay to give your opinion about what the raven symbolizes in Poe's poem. Use at least two examples from the poem to support your opinion.

13. How does the setting of "The Fall of the House of Usher" create a mood of gloomy, gothic fantasy? In a short essay, describe and discuss the landscape, the grounds, the house, and the weather. Include at least three specific details.

14. **Thinking About the Essential Question: What is the relationship between place and literature?** Choose either Poe's "The Fall of the House of Usher" or "The Raven." Write a brief essay on the effect of the setting, the place in which the action happens. How does it affect the main characters?

Name _____ Date _____

"The Fall of the House of Usher" and **"The Raven"** by Edgar Allan Poe
Selection Test B

Critical Reading *Identify the letter of the choice that best completes the statement or answers the question.*

____ 1. Which of these words best describes the single effect created by the opening description of the house in "The Fall of the House of Usher"?
   A. sadness
   B. terror
   C. wariness
   D. curiosity

____ 2. The letter that the narrator receives hints that Roderick Usher will be
   A. dull and depressed.
   B. suspicious and cruel.
   C. cautious and glum.
   D. nervous and passionate.

____ 3. In contrast to Roderick Usher, the narrator presents himself as someone who values
   A. reason.
   B. money.
   C. nature.
   D. a juicy horror tale.

____ 4. Which passage most underscores the single effect of "The Fall of the House of Usher"?
   A. "There was an iciness, a sinking, a sickening of the heart—an unredeemed dreariness of thought which no goading of the imagination could torture into aught of the sublime."
   B. "Although, as boys, we had been even intimate associates, yet I really knew little of my friend."
   C. "Beyond this indication of extensive decay, however, the fabric gave little token of instability."
   D. "It had been used, apparently, in remote feudal times, for the worst purposes of a donjon-keep, and, in later days, as a place of deposit for powder."

____ 5. Which choice below presents the core meaning of the following sentence?
   One of the phantasmagoric conceptions of my friend, partaking not so rigidly of the spirit of abstraction, may be shadowed forth, although feebly, in words.

   A. The phantasmagoric conceptions partake not so rigidly.
   B. One of the phantasmagoric conceptions of my friend may be shadowed.
   C. The spirit of abstraction may be shadowed forth in words.
   D. One of the phantasmagoric conceptions of my friend may be shadowed forth in words.

____ 6. Which statement expresses a central theme of "The Fall of the House of Usher"?
   A. Too much contact with the world leads to a distortion of reality.
   B. Isolation of the mind leads to death of the body.
   C. A person cut off from the world can fall prey to irrational fears and mental illness.
   D. The mind cannot affect the body in any way.

____ 7. Which detail early in "The Fall of the House of Usher" most clearly foreshadows, or hints at, the story's ending?

A. the narrator's memories of Roderick as a boy

B. the narrator's fear of the tarn

C. the narrator's concern for Roderick and his sister

D. the lofty, high-windowed room

____ 8. Why does the narrator "start" when Roderick Usher mentions "the gradual yet certain condensation of an atmosphere . . . about the waters and the walls" of the House of Usher?

A. The narrator himself felt such an atmosphere when he approached the estate.

B. Usher's idea is so incredible that it frightens the narrator.

C. It gives the narrator his first inkling of his friend's instability.

D. Usher is predicting the destruction of the house in a terrifying way.

____ 9. What does the speaker in "The Raven" feel when he first thinks that Lenore may be at his door?

A. joy and passion   C. relief and pleasure

B. terror and hope   D. confusion and melancholy

____ 10. When the speaker describes Lenore as "nameless *here* for evermore," what does he mean?

A. He cannot remember Lenore's name.

B. No one will speak Lenore's name because the angels took her.

C. Lenore is never mentioned in the speaker's chamber because she deserted him.

D. Lenore is so special that she is nameless in the speaker's heart.

____ 11. What is the core meaning of the following sentence from "The Fall of the House of Usher"?

"A letter, however, had lately reached me in a distant part of the country—a letter from him—which, in its wildly importunate nature, had admitted of no other than a personal reply."

A. I had received a letter so insistent that I had to reply personally.

B. He wrote me a letter to which I immediately replied.

C. His letter, which was distant in tone, deserved no reply.

D. The letter I received in a distant place was full of wild ideas.

____ 12. Which of these statements expresses a central theme of "The Raven"?

A. Loss of love causes a person to become bitter.

B. Belief in superstition can be dangerous.

C. Grief can cause hallucinations.

D. Isolation can lead to madness.

____ 13. Which choice below presents the core meaning of the following sentence?

But the Raven, sitting lonely on the placid bust, spoke only / That one word, as if his soul in that one word he did outpour.

A. But the Raven sitting lonely that one word did outpour.

B. The raven on the placid bust his soul in that one word he did outpour.

C. The raven spoke only that one word.

D. His soul in that one word he did outpour.

Vocabulary and Grammar

___ 14. Poe writes of ". . . the *specious* totality of old woodwork which has rotted for years."
Specious means that such woodwork is
A. stronger than stonework.
B. unsurpassed in quality.
C. rarely found in houses anymore.
D. unsound, not to be trusted.

___ 15. Which of the phrases below contains a superlative adjective?
A. ". . . at an exceeding depth below the surface of the earth."
B. ". . . a ghastly and inappropriate splendor."
C. "I was, perhaps, more forcibly impressed with it. . . ."
D. ". . . moments of the highest artificial excitement."

___ 16. The phrase "*equivocal* appellation of the 'House of Usher'" refers to the fact that
A. the final destiny of the House of Usher is doubtful.
B. good and evil are equally mixed within the House of Usher.
C. Roderick and Madeline often speak their family name in a booming tone.
D. the title "House of Usher" seems to include both the estate and the family.

___ 17. How many comparative adjectives does this line from "The Raven" contain?
Nothing farther then he uttered—not a feather then he fluttered.
A. none
B. one
C. two
D. three

Essay

18. Suppose that you had an encounter with Poe's raven. How would you feel? How would you react? How would your response to the raven compare and contrast to that of the speaker in "The Raven"? Write an essay that answers these questions.

19. Some critics believe that the point Poe is making in "The Fall of the House of Usher" is that when creative artists like Roderick Usher completely turn away from the external world and are drawn into the internal world of their imagination, they destroy their ability to create and may eventually destroy themselves. Do you agree or disagree with this interpretation? Write an essay that states your position and supports it with examples from the story.

20. How does Poe use the poem "The Haunted Palace" to imbue Roderick Usher's mansion, pre-sumably a real place, with elements of the fantastic and supernatural? In a brief essay, and with specific textual references, describe at least three instances of this.

21. **Thinking About the Essential Question: What is the relationship between place and literature?** Choose either Poe's "The Fall of the House of Usher" or "The Raven." Write a brief essay on the effect of the setting, the place in which the action happens. How does it affect the main characters?

"The Fall of the House of Usher" by Edgar Allan Poe
"Where *Is* Here?" by Joyce Carol Oates
Literary Analysis: Comparing Gothic Literature

Gothic literature, whether traditional or modern, has as its chief characteristic an air of mystery, magic, and the supernatural. Elements of horror are rampant; the reader can expect the sense of impending doom to culminate in some horrific or violent incident. The setting in a work of gothic literature is often a bleak or remote setting that contributes to the gloomy atmosphere.

DIRECTIONS: *Read these passages from the selections. Then, on the lines below, comment on the similarities and differences between them.*

. . . I scanned more narrowly the real aspect of the building. Its principal feature seemed to be that of an excessive antiquity. The discoloration of ages had been great. Minute fungi overspread the whole exterior, hanging in a fine tangled web-work from the eaves. Yet all this was apart from any extraordinary dilapidation. No portion of the masonry had fallen; and their appeared to be a wild inconsistency between its still perfect adaptation of parts, and the crumbling condition of the individual stones. (from "The Fall of the House of Usher")

The father had moved to another window and stood quietly watching, his cheek pressed against the glass. "He's gone down to the old swings. I hope he won't sit in one of them, for memory's sake, and try to swing—the posts are rotted almost through." The mother drew breath to speak but sighed instead, as if a powerful current of feeling had surged through her. The father was saying, "Is it possible he remembers those swings from his childhood? I can't believe they're actually that old." The mother said vaguely, "They were old when we bought the house." (from "Where *Is* Here?")

_____

_____

_____

_____

_____

_____

_____

_____

_____

_____

_____

_____

_____

_____

"The Fall of the House of Usher" by Edgar Allan Poe
"Where *Is* Here?" by Joyce Carol Oates
Vocabulary Builder

Using the Latin Root *-pul-*

A. DIRECTIONS: *The root -pul- means "to push into motion." Using that information, write on the line the letter of the choice that best completes each sentence.*

_____1. If Linda has the *compulsion* to keep her room tidy,
A. she never tidies her room.
B. she keeps her room tidy all the time.
C. she does not care at all about her room.

_____2. A company that specializes in jet *propulsion* is concerned with
A. building jets.
B. recycling jet parts.
C. making jets go.

_____3. *Expulsion* is a penalty principals use when
A. they want to get a student out of the school.
B. they want to include a student in the school.
C. they want to make class sizes equal.

_____4. If attendance at a school event is *compulsory*,
A. students can choose to go or not.
B. everyone must attend.
C. the event will take place after school.

Using the Word List

cavernous   exasperation   fastidious   impulsively   stealthily

B. DIRECTIONS: *On the line, write the letter of the pair of words that expresses a relationship most like the pair in capital letters.*

_____1. STEALTHILY : SNEAKY : :
A. spy : patriot
B. slyly : secretive
C. happily : gladly
D. sad : unhappy

_____2. FASTIDIOUS : SLOPPY : :
A. neat : clean
B. careful : meticulous
C. tidy : messy
D. dust : vacuum

_____3. EXASPERATION : ANNOYANCE : :
A. temper : shouting
B. ant : picnic
C. anger : calm
D. vexation : irritant

_____4. IMPULSIVELY : HESITATE : :
A. reflectively : think
B. painstakingly : plod
C. quickly : fast
D. generously : hoard

_____5. CAVERNOUS : VAST : :
A. miniature : tiny
B. beauteous : ugly
C. enormous : elephant
D. cave : rock

"The Fall of the House of Usher" by Edgar Allan Poe
"Where *Is* Here?" by Joyce Carol Oates
Support for Writing

As you gather information about the settings for your **compare-and-contrast essay,** keep track of details on this Venn diagram.

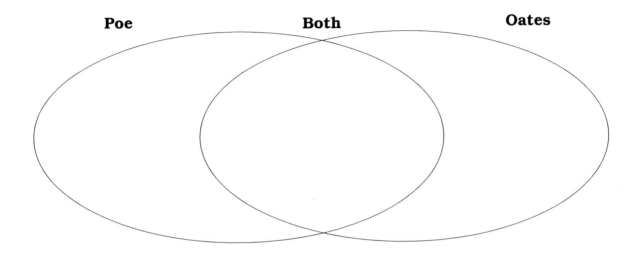

Poe   Both   Oates

Below or on a separate page, write a draft of your comparison-and-contrast essay. When you revise your work, be sure that you support your points with evidence from the stories.

Name _____ Date _____

"Where _Is_ Here?" by Joyce Carol Oates
Selection Test

Critical Reading *Identify the letter of the choice that best completes the statement or answers the question.*

_____ 1. The setting of "Where _Is_ Here?" by Joyce Carol Oates is
  A. a chill, damp November evening at dusk.
  B. early morning, just before sunrise.
  C. a breezy afternoon in summer.
  D. a snowy day at a cottage in the mountains.

_____ 2. At the beginning of Oates's story, the stranger says that he would like to
  A. meet the children in the house
  B. make an offer to buy the house
  C. take photographs of the house
  D. poke around

_____ 3. Which of the following passages most clearly signals Oates's gothic style in the story?
  A. "My father was a unique man. Everyone who knew him admired him."
  B. "Mother too had plants on this windowsill but I don't recall their ever blooming."
  C. "I hate riddles—they're moronic some of the time and obscure the rest of the time."
  D. "I'm sorry," the mother said. "Please don't be," the stranger said. "We've all been dead—*they've* all been dead—a long time."

_____ 4. Which event triggers the father's abrupt intervention when he announces, "The visit is over"?
  A. the stranger's insistence on going upstairs
  B. the stranger's bursting into tears
  C. the stranger's demonstration of a mathematical riddle
  D. the stranger's request to sit on the basement steps in the dark

_____ 5. As Oates portrays him in the story, the stranger is a person of
  A. zany humor
  B. fierce loyalty
  C. mysterious power
  D. absolute integrity

____ 6. Read the following excerpt from the last part of "Where *Is* Here?":

> In the living room he saw that the lights were flickering as if on the brink of going out; the patterned wallpaper seemed drained of color; a shadow lay upon it shaped like a bulbous cloud or growth.

Which of the following best characterizes this passage?
A. a flashback to the stranger's childhood
B. an ironic reversal of the father's opinions about the stranger
C. an ominous, otherworldly element
D. a humorous reference to one of the stranger's remarks

____ 7. Which of the following identifies an important similarity between Roderick Usher in Poe's "The Fall of the House of Usher" and the stranger in Oates's "Where *Is* Here?"
A. Both characters have a sister.
B. Both characters are intensely sensitive.
C. Roderick Usher and the stranger predict their own deaths.
D. Both characters claim they can communicate with the spirit world.

____ 8. Which of the following is an accurate statement about the setting in the works by Poe and the story by Oates?
A. The setting is not closely linked to the plot.
B. In all three works, the setting is closely linked to the overall atmosphere, or mood.
C. The cheerful setting contrasts with the characters' inner turmoil.
D. The setting is only vaguely described.

____ 9. The works by Poe and Oates are similar in that they focus on which of the following?
A. the precise, mathematical design of the universe
B. the strange power of the irrational in human behavior
C. tension between family members
D. the beauty of nature

Essay

10. Modern gothic fiction uses many of the same elements as traditional gothic fiction, but usually presents these elements in more modern circumstances. In an essay, discuss the ways in which Joyce Carol Oates uses the following elements or patterns to weave a modern gothic tale in "Where *Is* Here?": setting, atmosphere or mood, characterization, and hints of violence and otherworldliness. Be sure to illustrate your main ideas with specific details and examples from the story.

Study these words from the selection. Then, complete the activities.

Word List A

accumulated [uh KYOOM yuh lay tuhd] *v.* collected; gathered together
   By 6:00 o'clock this morning, six inches of snow had <u>accumulated</u> overnight.

acquiescence [ak wee ES uhns] *n.* agreement
   Paul said his <u>acquiescence</u> to our plan did not necessarily imply his approval.

cringing [KRINJ ing] *v.* fearfully shrinking back or away from
   The dog shrank back, <u>cringing</u> before its owner, who was shouting commands.

dislodged [dis LOJD] *v.* removed; forced from a position or place
   The heavy rain <u>dislodged</u> some of the tiles from our roof.

downcast [DOUN kast] *adj.* sad; depressed
   Olga looked <u>downcast</u>, as if she had just suffered a major disappointment.

foreboding [for BOHD ing] *n.* prediction or portent, especially of something bad
   Halfway through the movie, a dark musical theme created a mood of <u>foreboding</u>.

imperial [im PEER ee uhl] *adj.* having supreme authority; like an emperor
   In ancient Rome, many of the more important provinces were under <u>imperial</u> control.

outrageous [out RAYJ uhs] *adj.* very offensive or shocking
   We thought their statement was <u>outrageous</u>, worthy of a strong reprimand.

Word List B

admonitions [ad muh NISH uhnz] *n.* warnings
   The Surgeon General gave <u>admonitions</u> concerning the need for exercise.

haughty [HAW tee] *adj.* extremely proud; arrogant
   Richard's sneering remark was good evidence of his <u>haughty</u> attitude.

heroic [hi ROH ik] *adj.* very courageous
   The main character in an epic poem often performs <u>heroic</u> deeds.

inscrutable [in SKROOT uh buhl] *adj.* obscure and mysterious; not easily understood
   With that <u>inscrutable</u> look on his face, we couldn't tell what Max was thinking.

intercept [in ter SEPT] *v.* to stop or interrupt the course of
   You should try to <u>intercept</u> Ken before he leaves on that dangerous journey.

pagan [PAY guhn] *adj.* not religious; heathen
   During the Age of Discovery, most Europeans considered native peoples as <u>pagan</u>.

specific [spuh SIF ik] *adj.* particular; distinct; definite
   Jack's <u>specific</u> problems got him in trouble.

vengeance [VEN juhns] *n.* revenge
   The urge to take <u>vengeance</u> for an injury is natural.

from **Moby-Dick** by Herman Melville
Vocabulary Warm-up Exercises

Exercise A *Fill in the blanks, using each word from Word List A only once.*

Professional dog training is an amazing field. Trainers who have [1] _____

years of knowledge and experience seem to work wonders with dogs. Animals under their

control are not [2] _____ with fear or guilty of [3] _____

behavior. Instead, a trainer has [4] _____ the anxiety and

[5] _____ of a poorly adjusted dog and turned the animal into a well-

behaved, affectionate pet. How does a trainer secure a dog's [6] _____ and

cooperation? Experts agree that there is no substitute for firmness, repetition, and a

sensible structure of commands. Trainers cannot afford to seem unhappy or

[7] _____ to a dog. Instead, they must always have an optimistic, benign

look and a hearty voice. At the opposite end of the spectrum, they must avoid appearing

or sounding [8] _____. A dog must know who is boss, but this knowledge

must come with benevolent authority, not with tyranny.

Exercise B *Decide whether each statement below is true or false. Circle T or F, and explain your answer.*

1. *Admonitions* are speeches of praise.
   T / F _____

2. Someone with a *haughty* attitude behaves arrogantly.
   T / F _____

3. *Heroic* behavior typically involves fraud or deceit.
   T / F _____

4. It is hard to figure out the motives of someone who appears *inscrutable*.
   T / F _____

5. If you *intercept* a message, the message eludes or gets away from you.
   T / F _____

6. In the Middle Ages, many Christians were likely to call non-Christian rituals *pagan*.
   T / F _____

7. A *specific* argument is usually general and vague.
   T / F _____

8. If you take *vengeance* on a person, you want to get satisfaction for an injury or wrong.
   T / F _____

Name _____ Date _____

from **Moby-Dick** by Herman Melville
Reading Warm-up A

Read the following passage. Pay special attention to the underlined words. Then, read it again, and complete the activities. Use a separate sheet of paper for your written answers.

Ever since arriving on Cape Cod, Jason had been hounding his mother to go on a whale-watching trip. She worried about getting seasick, having spent a miserable day on a boat twenty years ago in a thunderstorm. Jason persisted, though, doing everything his mother asked. Eventually, he had <u>accumulated</u> such a record of good conduct that his mother couldn't refuse. When he finally got her <u>acquiescence</u>, they made reservations on the *Bayman* and set off the next morning to look for whales.

The sky, gray and ominous, filled the morning with <u>foreboding</u>, as if a violent storm might erupt and send the boat tossing over enormous waves. His mother watched her feet carefully as she climbed aboard, her <u>downcast</u> face showing her nervousness. She seemed terrified as the boat <u>dislodged</u> itself from the dock and set out for the open sea. After that, she sat gripping the edge of her seat, <u>cringing</u> with anxiety each time the boat went over even the smallest wave.

They cruised the waters outside Provincetown for almost two hours without seeing even the slightest trace of a whale. Jason abandoned his mother and stood at the front of the boat, growing ever more impatient for a sighting. It would be <u>outrageous</u> to go to all this trouble and not see even a tail or a fin in the distance. Then, just as he was about to give up hope, the captain shouted. A sperm whale jumped out of the water once, then twice, then a third time. The huge whale dominated the entire ocean, an <u>imperial</u> shape of enormous power. Even Jason's mother stood up to watch him as he appeared once more above the surface.

1. Underline the words in this sentence that give a clue to the meaning of <u>accumulated</u>. Use the word *accumulated* in an original sentence.

2. Circle the words in the previous sentence that give a clue to the meaning of the word <u>acquiescence</u>. What is a synonym for *acquiescence*?

3. Underline the words that give a clue to the meaning of <u>foreboding</u>. Use the word *foreboding* in a sentence of your own.

4. Circle the words that offer a clue to the meaning of <u>downcast</u> here. What are two antonyms for the word *downcast*?

5. Circle the words in this sentence that offer clues to the meaning of <u>dislodged</u>. Use a word meaning the opposite of *dislodged* in a sentence.

6. Underline the words in this sentence that give a clue to the meaning of <u>cringing</u>. What is a synonym for *cringing*?

7. Circle the words that give a clue to the meaning of <u>outrageous</u>. Use the word *outrageous* in an original sentence.

8. Underline the words that hint at the meaning of <u>imperial</u>. Is this word used literally or figuratively here?

Name _____ Date _____

from **Moby-Dick** by Herman Melville
Reading Warm-up B

Read the following passage. Pay special attention to the underlined words. Then, read it again, and complete the activities. Use a separate sheet of paper for your written answers.

In the mid-nineteenth century, the city of New Bedford in southeastern Massachusetts was the whaling center of America. In New Bedford, there were countless <u>heroic</u> tales of captains, sailors, and ships that had won fame in rough and challenging quests to hunt whales. It is hardly surprising, then, that Melville makes this town the home port of the *Pequod,* the whaling ship of the mysterious, <u>inscrutable</u> Captain Ahab in *Moby-Dick.*

New Bedford was founded in 1652 by settlers from Plymouth Colony. A century later, it had become a fishing community. The deepwater harbor was used by American privateers during the Revolutionary War. These ships would <u>intercept</u> and damage British vessels whenever they could. When the Americans ignored British <u>admonitions</u> to stop these raids, the British sought <u>vengeance</u>. In a <u>haughty</u> display of arrogance, they burned New Bedford in 1778.

The town recovered swiftly, however, and by 1820 it was one of the world's most important whaling ports. In *Moby-Dick,* Melville describes the magnificence of the town's private houses, gardens, and public parks. He also gives a detailed, <u>specific</u> account of the Whaleman's Chapel, where sailors, as well as their wives and widows, would gather for religious consolation. The vast ocean must have seemed to them like a <u>pagan</u> universe, ruled by no caring divinity but rather by the hostile forces of nature. In the Whaleman's Chapel, by contrast, they could recover their faith and cherish the hope that their dangerous journeys at sea would be successful and they would enjoy a safe return. The Whaleman's Chapel, which is now known as the Seamen's Bethel, may still be visited today in New Bedford.

1. Underline the words in this sentence that give a clue to the meaning of <u>heroic</u>. Use the word **heroic** in an original sentence.

2. Circle the word in this sentence that gives a clue to the meaning of <u>inscrutable</u>. What is a synonym for **inscrutable**?

3. Underline the words in this and the previous sentence hinting at the meaning of <u>intercept</u>. What is a synonym for the word **intercept**?

4. Underline the words in this sentence that give a clue to the meaning of <u>admonitions</u>. Use **admonitions** in a sentence of your own.

5. Circle the words in this and the next sentence that give a clue to the meaning of <u>vengeance</u>. What are two synonyms for **vengeance**?

6. Underline the words in this sentence that hint at the meaning of <u>haughty</u>. Use a word meaning the opposite of **haughty** in a sentence of your own.

7. Underline the word in this sentence that gives a clue to the meaning of <u>specific</u>. What are two antonyms of **specific**?

8. Circle the words in this sentence that hint at the meaning of the word <u>pagan</u>.

Name _____ Date _____

from **Moby-Dick** by Herman Melville
Literary Analysis: Symbol

In *Moby-Dick*, many elements take on symbolic meanings as the novel progresses. A **symbol** is a person, place, action, or thing that also represents an abstract meaning beyond itself. In the following passage, for example, the sharks may be symbols of Ahab's destructive behavior or the destructive response of nature to Ahab's mad pursuit of the whale.

> And still as Ahab glided over the waves the unpitying sharks accompanied him; and so pertinaciously stuck to the boat; and so continually bit at the plying oars, that the blades became jagged and crunched, and left small splinters in the sea, at almost every dip.

DIRECTIONS: *Read the following passages from* Moby-Dick. *On the lines provided after each passage, identify one symbol that the passage contains and explain what the symbol might represent.*

1. "I came here to hunt whales, not my commander's vengeance. How many barrels will thy vengeance yield thee even if thou gettest it, Captain Ahab? It will not fetch thee much in our Nantucket market."

   "Nantucket market! hoot! But come closer, Starbuck. . . ."

   "Vengeance on a dumb brute!" cried Starbuck, "that simply smote thee from blindest instinct! Madness! To be enraged with a dumb thing, Captain Ahab, seems blasphemous."

   _____

   _____

   _____

2. "The ship? Great God, where is the ship?". . . Concentric circles seized the lone boat itself, and all its crew, and each floating oar, and every lance pole, and spinning, animate and inanimate, all round and round in one vortex, carried the smallest chip of the *Pequod* out of sight.

   _____

   _____

   _____

3. A sky hawk that tauntingly had followed the main-truck downwards from its natural home among the stars, . . . this bird now chanced to intercept its broad fluttering wing between the hammer and the wood: and simultaneously feeling that ethereal thrill, the submerged savage beneath, in his deathgrasp, kept his hammer frozen there: and so the bird of heaven, with archangelic shrieks, and his imperial beak thrust upwards, and his whole captive form folded in the flag of Ahab, went down with his ship, which like Satan, would not sink to hell till she had dragged a living part of heaven along with her.

   _____

   _____

   _____

from **Moby-Dick** by Herman Melville
Reading Strategy: Identify Relevant Details

To recognize and understand the symbols and theme of a work of literature, **identify the relevant details** that the author uses. Such details can lead you to the essential message or main idea of the work. Consider, for example, the following passage:

> "Give way!" cried Ahab to the oarsmen, and the boats darted forward to the attack; but maddened by yesterday's fresh irons that corroded in him, Moby-Dick seemed combinedly possessed by all the angels that fell from heaven.

Here Melville connects Moby-Dick to a larger idea by comparing him to "all the angels that fell from heaven," or devils. This detail suggests that Moby-Dick might be a symbol of evil or of the darker side of human nature.

DIRECTIONS: *Read the following passage, which opens your textbook selection from* Moby-Dick. *Then, on the lines provided, answer the questions about the passage.*

> One morning shortly after breakfast, Ahab, as was his wont, ascended the cabin gangway to the deck. There most sea captains usually walk at that hour, as country gentlemen, after the same meal, take a few turns in the garden.
>
> Soon his steady, ivory stride was heard, as to and fro he paced his old rounds, upon planks so familiar to his tread, that they were all over dented, like geological stones, with the peculiar mark of his walk. Did you fixedly gaze, too, upon that ribbed and dented brow; there also, you would see still stranger footprints—the footprints of his one unsleeping, ever-pacing thought.
>
> But on the occasion in question, those dents looked deeper, even as his nervous step that morning left a deeper mark. And, so full of his thought was Ahab, that at every uniform turn that he made, now at the mainmast and now at the binnacle, you could almost see that thought turn in him as he turned, and pace in him as he paced; so completely possessing him, indeed, that it all but seemed the inward mold of every outer movement.

1. Which details suggest that Ahab is a symbol?

   _____

   _____

2. With what abstract idea or ideas does Melville seem to connect him here?

   _____

   _____

3. Identify one more detail in the passage that might have symbolic significance.

   _____

   _____

4. Which details suggest that it is a symbol?

   _____

5. What abstract idea or ideas does it seem to symbolize?

   _____

   _____

from **Moby-Dick** by Herman Melville
Vocabulary Builder

Using the Prefix *mal-*

A. DIRECTIONS: *The prefix* mal- *means "bad." The word* maledictions *combines the prefix* mal- *with the root* -dict-, *which means "speak." Keep that in mind as you write on the line the letter of the choice that best completes each of these sentences.*

1. _____ is often described as malodorous.
   A. Cinnamon
   B. A rose
   C. A squirrel
   D. A skunk

2. A *malnourished* child most likely eats _____ meals.
   A. well-balanced
   B. skimpy
   C. hearty
   D. tasty

3. A *malcontent* probably _____ his or her job.
   A. loves
   B. hates
   C. is puzzled by
   D. never complains about

4. A man with a *malady* has _____.
   A. a disease
   B. great wealth
   C. happiness
   D. an aristocratic wife

5. A woman might be called a *malefactor* if she _____.
   A. gives to charity
   B. teaches math
   C. commits a crime
   D. loves her husband

Using the Word List

impulsive   inarticulate   inscrutable   maledictions   pedestrian   prescient

B. DIRECTIONS: *On the line before each word in the left column, write the letter of its definition in the right column.*

___ 1. inscrutable
___ 2. maledictions
___ 3. prescient
___ 4. inarticulate
___ 5. impulsive
___ 6. pedestrian

A. having foreknowledge
B. not able to speak
C. curses
D. not able to be easily understood
E. ordinary; commonplace
F. acting suddenly and without careful thought

Name _____ Date _____

from **Moby-Dick** by Herman Melville
Grammar and Style: Using Participles, Gerunds, and Infinitives

A **participle** is a verb form, typically ending in -ed or -ing, used as a modifier, either alone or in a phrase.

Examples: The *astonished* sailors listened as Ahab raged about the whale.
Starbuck, *worried* about the captain, remained silent.

A **gerund** is a verb form, typically ending in -ing or -ed, used as a noun, either alone or in a phrase.

Examples: *Pacing* the deck was Ahab's morning activity.
Ahab was obsessed with *avenging* himself on the whale.

An **infinitive** is the form of the verb with *to*. It can function as a noun, an adjective, or an adverb, either alone or in a phrase.

Examples: Ahab was determined to *destroy* the white whale.
The crew had many tasks *to accomplish*.

A. PRACTICE: *In each of the following sentences, identify the underlined phrase as a gerund, infinitive, or participial phrase.*

1. <u>To encourage the crew,</u> Ahab offered a reward. _____

2. The dolphins, <u>breaking the surface of the ocean</u>, were beautiful. _____

3. The team of harpooners <u>selected by the captain</u> did excellent work. _____

4. After <u>assembling on the deck</u>, the crew listened to the captain. _____

5. <u>To keep the ship running smoothly</u>, the crew performs various duties. _____

6. The vortex seized the *Pequod*, <u>carrying the ship out of sight</u>. _____

B. Writing Application: *Write three sentences, using a gerund, infinitive, or participial phrase. Use each type of phrase at least once, and label each one.*

1. _____

_____

2. _____

_____

3. _____

_____

from **Moby-Dick** by Herman Melville
Support for Writing

As you think about writing a **character study**, think about why Captain Ahab seems to you either mad or great. Also, think about the main events of the selection and what they reveal about Ahab. Enter the information into the chart below.

Ahab's Character	
Main Events First Part of Selection	
Main Events Middle Part of Selection	
Main Events End of Selection	
My Opinion of Ahab/ Reasons for My Opinion	

On a separate page, write a draft that gives your opinion about whether Ahab is mad or great. Explain why you drew these conclusions or made these judgements about Ahab. When you revise your work, be sure you have justified your opinion with examples from the selection.

from **Moby-Dick** by Herman Melville
Enrichment: Art

You probably know the saying "A picture is worth a thousand words." Whether or not you think this is true, you would probably agree that visual art can be a powerful narrative tool. Study Rockwell Kent's pen-and-ink drawings that illustrate the selection from *Moby-Dick*. Then answer the following questions.

1. What does the picture of Captain Ahab reveal about him? How does the use of shadow add to the impression?

    _____

    _____

    _____

2. What feelings do you get from the drawing of Moby-Dick leaping from the surface of the ocean? Explain how details such as the stars and the indication of water convey movement.

    _____

    _____

    _____

3. What theme of the selection does the picture of the whale and the boat express? How does it do this?

    _____

    _____

    _____

4. How do you feel about the use of color to illustrate this selection? Would black-and-white illustrations have been more effective? Why or why not?

    _____

    _____

    _____

    _____

from **Moby Dick** by Herman Melville
Open-Book Test

Short Answer *Write your responses to the questions in this section on the lines provided.*

1. Reread the first three paragraphs of the first section in *Moby-Dick*. What is Captain Ahab doing in these paragraphs? What do these actions symbolize in terms of Ahab's character?

_____

_____

_____

_____

2. In the first section from *Moby-Dick*, why does Captain Ahab decide to offer his men a gold piece for finding the great whale? What does he do with the piece as he shows it to them?

_____

_____

_____

_____

3. In the paragraph in the first section from *Moby-Dick* that begins "Hark ye yet again, . . ." to what does Ahab compare *Moby-Dick*? What does this symbolism tell you about Ahab's obsession?

_____

_____

_____

_____

4. In the first section, how do the men in Ahab's crew view Moby-Dick? How is this different from Ahab's view of the whale?

_____

_____

_____

_____

5. In the "Quarter-Deck" section of *Moby-Dick*, Ahab has his crew drink from their weapons as they swear to hunt Moby Dick. What theme does this action symbolize?

_____

_____

_____

_____

6. In the last part of the third paragraph of "The Chase—Third Day" section of *Moby-Dick*, Ahab discusses the wind. How does he feel about this element of nature? Cite at least one description of the wind to support your opinion.

_____

_____

_____

7. In "The Chase—Third Day" section of *Moby-Dick*, find the paragraph that begins "Yet the voice spake true . . . ." Read the sentence that uses the word *prescient*. If a dog was *prescient*, would it be surprised by an earthquake? Explain your answer based on the way the word prescient is used in the story.

_____

_____

_____

8. Toward the end of *Moby-Dick*, reread the paragraph that begins, "I turn my body from the sun." What message is Ahab communicating in this paragraph?

_____

_____

_____

9. What symbolic meaning do the sharks have when they appear in this selection from *Moby-Dick*? What do they represent, and what message is Melville trying to convey? Cite one description from the selection to support your answer.

_____

_____

_____

_____

10. Toward the end of the selection from *Moby-Dick*, the ship's line breaks and Ahab makes a connection between this action and his own body. What inference can the reader make about the connection between Ahab and his ship?

_____

_____

_____

Essay

Write an extended response to the question of your choice or to the question or questions your teacher assigns you.

11. What do you interpret the final paragraph of this selection from *Moby-Dick* to mean? Write a brief essay to explain what images are used in the final paragraph and what symbol each image represents. What message does Melville suggest through these symbols?

12. Toward the end of the selection from *Moby-Dick*, Melville uses a descriptive passage about "a red arm and a hammer hovered backwardly uplifted in the open air, in the act of nailing the flag . . ." to communicate a specific action and a larger meaning. Write a brief essay to explain what action is taking place and how Melville uses it to symbolize a larger meaning. Look back at the paragraph a page or two before this quote, which begins, "Meantime, for that one beholding instant . . ." for clues.

13. In this selection from *Moby-Dick*, the fate of the sky hawk at the end becomes a part of the fate of Ahab and the men on the ship. Write a brief essay to discuss the symbolism of this action and the way in which it is related to Melville's theme of humankind versus nature.

14. **Thinking About the Essential Question: Essential Question: What makes American literature American?** Melville's novel *Moby-Dick* is mainly the story of one obsessed man's quest for conquest and revenge. Although the *Pequod's* mission is superficially a commercial one, what really motivates it is Captain Ahab's unrelenting quest to vanquish the white whale that took his leg on a previous voyage. Is Ahab's stubborn persistence, his determination to succeed at all costs, an especially American trait or a universal human one? Develop your thoughts in an essay supported by details from the selection.

Oral Response

15. Go back to question 3, 5, 6, or 8 or to the question your teacher assigns to you. Take a few minutes to expand your answer and prepare an oral response. Find additional details in the selection from *Moby-Dick* that will support your points. If necessary, make notes to guide your response.

from **Moby-Dick** by Herman Melville
Selection Test A

Critical Reading *Identify the letter of the choice that best answers the question.*

____ 1. In *Moby-Dick,* why does Captain Ahab seek vengeance against the white whale?
   A. The whale keeps escaping his harpoon.
   B. The whale has taken his leg in a struggle.
   C. The whale chases other whales away.
   D. The whale keeps attacking the *Pequod.*

____ 2. How does Ahab persuade the crew to help him find the whale in *Moby-Dick?*
   A. He appeals to their pride.
   B. He appeals to their loyalty.
   C. He appeals to their skills.
   D. He appeals to their greed.

____ 3. In *Moby-Dick,* what does the gold coin symbolize for the crew?
   A. Ahab's fortune from his business
   B. their reward for finding the whale
   C. the *Pequod's* profits from whaling
   D. Ahab's wish to seem better than them

____ 4. In *Moby-Dick,* who continually tries to make Ahab call off his mission of revenge?
   A. Stubb
   B. Queequeg
   C. Daggoo
   D. Starbuck

____ 5. Ahab tells Starbuck, "Talk not to me of blasphemy, man; I'd strike the sun if it insulted me," Of what larger theme is this a detail?
   A. Ahab sins by putting himself in place of God.
   B. The sun shines very intensely on the *Pequod.*
   C. Ahab does not like to be lectured to by his officers.
   D. Starbuck is jealous of Ahab's power.

_____ 6. In *Moby-Dick*, what is the symbolic meaning of Ahab having his crew drink from their weapons?
   A. They are promising not to hunt while drunk.
   B. They are toasting Ahab's great leadership.
   C. They are promising to find the white whale.
   D. They are cleaning their weapons for later use.

_____ 7. In *Moby-Dick*, why is it symbolic for Ahab to compare himself with his ship's mast?
   A. Both are part of the whaling ship.
   B. The mast is stronger than Ahab.
   C. Ahab has a leg made of wood.
   D. The whale is seen from the mast.

_____ 8. In *Moby-Dick*, what does the whale symbolize to Ahab in this passage?
   Retribution, swift vengeance, eternal malice were in his whole aspect . . . his forehead smote the ship's starboard bow, till men and timbers reeled.
   A. a force of nature
   B. an important helper
   C. a strong god
   D. a powerful enemy

Vocabulary and Grammar

_____ 9. In which sentence is the meaning of the word *maledictions* expressed?
   A. Ahab vowed to hunt Moby-Dick to the end of his life.
   B. The captain shouted curses at the whale who escaped him.
   C. The *Pequod's* crew grew afraid of Ahab's obsession.
   D. Ahab died without fulfilling his vow to kill the whale.

_____ 10. In the sentence "Men, ye seem the years; so brimming life is gulped and gone," *brimming* is a
   A. gerund.
   B. infinitive.
   C. participle.
   D. noun.

Essay

11. As you read *Moby-Dick,* you encountered many uses of symbols: Moby-Dick, the wind, the ship's mast, the gold coin, the sea, and so on. What do you think the character of Ahab symbolizes? Write a brief essay about how Ahab is used as a symbol, perhaps of a struggle of some kind. Provide at least two examples from the text. Remember that a symbol can have more than one meaning.

12. Do you think Captain Ahab in *Moby-Dick* is a character who is free? Does he act as a free person and think as a free person because he can sail when he wishes? Or does his obsession keep him in a kind of prison? Write a brief essay to give your response to these questions. Use at least two examples from *Moby-Dick* to support your response.

13. At the end *Moby-Dick,* the sky hawk shares the same fate as Ahab and his crew. Write a brief essay to tell what the hawk might symbolize and how it illustrates Melville's theme of humankind versus nature.

14. **Thinking About the Essential Question: Essential Question: What makes American literature American?** Melville's novel *Moby-Dick* is mainly the story of one obsessed man's quest for conquest and revenge. Although the *Pequod's* mission is superficially a commercial one, what really motivates it is Captain Ahab's unrelenting quest to vanquish the white whale that took his leg on a previous voyage. Is Ahab's stubborn persistence, his determination to succeed at all costs, an especially American trait or a universal human one? Develop your thoughts in an essay supported by details from the selection.

from Moby-Dick by Herman Melville
Selection Test B

Critical Reading *Identify the letter of the choice that best completes the statement or answers the question.*

_____ 1. The name of the whaling ship that Ahab captains is the _____.
A. *Pequod*
B. *Quarter-Deck*
C. *Tashtego*
D. *Nantucket*

_____ 2. The white whale against whom Ahab seeks vengeance
A. never appears.
B. treats the ship's crew indifferently when he finally appears.
C. caused Ahab to lose his leg in a previous encounter.
D. is never seen by anyone but Ahab.

_____ 3. Ahab persuades his crew members to chase the white whale by appealing mainly to their _____.
A. patriotism
B. hunger
C. greed
D. loyalty

_____ 4. Ahab's rambling monologues show that he is _____.
A. practical
B. uneducated
C. vulnerable
D. single-minded

_____ 5. What is the chief significance of Ahab's being drowned by his own harpoon line?
A. It stresses his inexperience as a sailor.
B. It stresses the idea that obsession and vengefulness are self-destructive.
C. It stresses the idea that manmade objects are more powerful than nature.
D. It stresses Ahab's defiance.

_____ 6. One of the central themes conveyed in this selection is that
A. only the strongest survive.
B. revenge is justifiable.
C. whaling is indefensible.
D. human understanding is limited.

_____ 7. The selection portrays nature as
A. sympathetic and soothing.
B. violent but tamable.
C. majestic and elusive.
D. foolish and vengeful.

____ 8. As the ship is sinking, we see a crew member frantically nailing Ahab's flag to the mast. This detail exemplifies the larger theme of
A. the futility of human efforts to dominate nature.
B. the supremacy of American culture.
C. America's loss of innocence.
D. nature's essential evil.

____ 9. In the following passage, what larger issue is related to Ahab's footprints?

> Soon his steady, ivory stride was heard, as to and fro he paced his old rounds, upon planks so familiar to his tread, that they were all over dented, like geological stones, with the peculiar mark of his walk. Did you fixedly gaze, too, upon that ribbed and dented brow; there also, you would see still stranger footprints—the footprints of his one unsleeping, ever-pacing thought.

A. the decline in morale among the ship's crew
B. footprints in the sands of time
C. the idea that we always kill the thing we love
D. Ahab's obsession with Moby-Dick

____ 10. Which of these aspects of nature does the white whale *not* symbolize?
A. destructiveness
B. immortality
C. spiritual comfort
D. beauty

____ 11. To Ahab's mind, Moby-Dick symbolizes a wall that
A. keeps the ship from its business of whaling.
B. protects Ahab from his own inner thoughts and desires.
C. must be broken through to reach the truth behind it.
D. has grown up between Ahab and his crew.

____ 12. What behavior of Ahab most clearly symbolizes the restlessness and obsessive nature of his thoughts?
A. his pacing up and down on deck
B. his offering mugs of grog to the crew
C. his nailing a coin to the mast
D. his being hoisted up the mast in a basket

____ 13. What does the sea probably symbolize in this final sentence from the selection?

> Then all collapsed, and the great shroud of the sea rolled on as it had rolled five thousand years ago.

A. humanity's power over nature
B. nature's power over humanity
C. the goodness of nature
D. the changeability of nature

Vocabulary and Grammar

_____ 14. Which of these characters would most likely be described as *prescient*?
    A. a politician
    B. a dog catcher
    C. a whaler
    D. a prophet

_____ 15. Which word has a meaning most nearly opposite that of *maledictions*?
    A. blessings
    B. lies
    C. curses
    D. pleas

_____ 16. In the sentence "The three mates quailed before his strong, sustained, and mystic aspect," which word is a participle?
    A. mystic
    B. quailed
    C. strong
    D. sustained

_____ 17. Identify an infinitive phrase in the sentence "Yon ratifying sun now waits to sit upon it."
    A. ratifying sun
    B. now waits
    C. to sit
    D. upon it

Essay

18. Examine Ahab in his role as captain of the whaling ship. In what ways does he seem to be a good captain? In what ways is he a bad one? Answer these questions in an essay in which you support your opinions with details from the selection.

19. At one point Ishmael, the narrator, states, "For with little external to constrain us, the innermost necessities in our being, these still drive us on." Write an essay that shows how this statement applies to one or more characters in this selection.

20. At one point in the selection, the members of the crew gather to hear Ahab describe his goal and persuade everyone else to join him. Why do you think Melville felt that such a scene was necessary? What are some things that the scene accomplishes? Address these questions in an essay.

21. In this selection from *Moby-Dick*, the fate of the sky hawk at the end becomes a part of the fate of Ahab and the men on the ship. Write a brief essay to discuss the symbolism of this action and the way in which it is related to Melville's theme of humankind versus nature.

22. **Thinking About the Essential Question: What makes American literature American?** Is Ahab's stubborn persistence, his determination to succeed at all costs, an especially American trait or a universal human one? Develop your thoughts in an essay supported by details from the selection.

Name _____ Date _____

from **Nature**, *from* **Self-Reliance**, and **"Concord Hymn"** by Ralph Waldo Emerson
Vocabulary Warm-up Word Lists

Study these words from the selections. Then, complete the activities.

Word List A

brink [BRINK] *n.* the edge of a steep place; verge, often used figuratively
   Sam was on the <u>brink</u> of ordering dinner when the chef yelled, "Fire!"

embattled [em BAT uhld] *adj.* in the midst of fighting
   The <u>embattled</u> troops stood their ground and kept fighting.

exhilaration [eg ZIL uh RAY shuhn] *n.* great joy; high spirits
   After learning about his high score on the exam, Ray felt <u>exhilaration</u>.

harmony [HAHR muh nee] *n.* peaceful agreement
   We live in <u>harmony</u> with our respectful, considerate neighbors.

melancholy [MEL uhn KAHL ee] *n.* sadness; gloom
   The barren winter landscape filled her with <u>melancholy</u>.

misunderstood [mis un der STOOD] *adj.* wrongly understood; misinterpreted
   Theo felt <u>misunderstood</u>, so he explained his opinion more clearly.

resides [ri ZYDZ] *v.* lives in; dwells
   My grandmother hugs me and says that a lot of love <u>resides</u> in my heart.

testify [TES tuh fy] *v.* to bear witness or give evidence
   Several eyewitnesses agreed to <u>testify</u> at the trial.

Word List B

blithe [BLYTH] *adj.* cheerful and lighthearted
   Even under pressure, Rajiv remains <u>blithe</u> and carefree.

contradict [kahn truh DIKT] *v.* to assert the opposite of what is stated
   It is not considered polite for children to <u>contradict</u> their elders.

immortal [i MAWRT uhl] *adj.* never dying; everlasting
   Some teenagers, considering themselves <u>immortal</u>, take dangerous risks.

imparted [im PAHRT id] *v.* communicated; told; revealed
   Natalia <u>imparted</u> the news only to her closest friends.

integrity [in TEG ruh tee] *n.* honesty; moral uprightness
   The mayor was re-elected because she was known for her <u>integrity</u>.

occurrence [uh KUR uhns] *n.* event; happening
   A total solar eclipse is a relatively rare <u>occurence</u>.

perennial [puh REN ee uhl] *adj.* lasting; reappearing regularly or every year
   The <u>perennial</u> flowers in Juan's garden bloom every spring.

tranquil [TRANG kwuhl] *adj.* calm; peaceful
   After the thunderstorm, a <u>tranquil</u> blue sky returned.

from Nature, from Self-Reliance, and "Concord Hymn" by Ralph Waldo Emerson
Vocabulary Warm-up Exercises

Exercise A *Fill in the blanks, using each word from Word List A only once.*

The strength of a great nation often [1] _____ in its ability to respond to enormous challenges. The year 1776 was a critical turning point for the [2] _____ Continental Army under General George Washington. Many thought the Revolution was on the [3] _____ of failure. A mood of [4] _____ prevailed as Washington was forced to retreat from New York through New Jersey. Washington, though, never gave up. He was [5] _____ by the British, who nicknamed him the "fox" for his ability to slip away. The Battle of Trenton in late December would [6] _____ to Washington's gift for bold-ness and surprise. When news of the American victory spread, the colonists' mood changed from disappointment to [7] _____, and the revolutionary cause was embraced with a new, cooperative [8] _____.

Exercise B *Revise each sentence so that the underlined vocabulary word is used in a logical way. Be sure to keep the vocabulary word in your revision.*

Example: Because rainfall was <u>abundant</u>, the newly planted shrubs withered.
Because rainfall was <u>abundant</u>, the newly planted shrubs flourished.

1. Their habitual frowns showed us that our cousins had a <u>blithe</u> outlook on life.
   _____

2. Otis was not afraid to <u>contradict</u> the boss by saying that he completely agreed with her.
   _____

3. Morris invited us to his <u>perennial</u> holiday party, which he was holding for the first time.
   _____

4. Hercules was thought to be <u>immortal</u> since he died when he was young.
   _____

5. Sam gladly <u>imparted</u> the news by revealing very little of the story.
   _____

6. Mayor Zeiss, known for her <u>integrity</u>, is facing a corruption inquiry.
   _____

7. If an event is described as an <u>occurrence</u>, it has never happened.
   _____

8. The sea seemed <u>tranquil</u>, with high, brutal waves lashing the shoreline.
   _____

from **Nature,** *from* **Self-Reliance,** and **"Concord Hymn"** by Ralph Waldo Emerson
Reading Warm-up A

Read the following passage. Then, complete the activities.

Serena sat in the cramped office of her high school newspaper, *The Tattler*. She felt sad and <u>melancholy</u>. It all had to with an essay and a cartoon she did for the paper. They were about the cross-country team, which had never won a single meet in the 40-year history of the school. The team's coach had gone to Mr. Street, the principal, and demanded that every copy of the newspaper be confiscated.

The next day, Mr. Street told *The Tattler* staff he was sorry, but the ultimate responsibility for such matters in a school always <u>resides</u> with its principal. Therefore, he would store all 2,000 copies of the paper in his office until a teacher advisory committee could meet and reach a peaceful agreement, and some <u>harmony</u>, about what to do.

The Tattler's faculty advisor, Ms. Thistle, insisted the coach had <u>misunderstood</u> Serena's work, misinterpreting her intent. She brought Serena to <u>testify</u> before the faculty committee to explain that her writing and art were intended to poke fun at the school's tradition of losing and not meant to criticize the coach or any particular team member.

For a week, the <u>embattled</u> *Tattler* staff printed fliers protesting that their rights to freedom of speech were being denied. Meanwhile, Serena's gloom deepened. She felt she might go over the edge; she was on the <u>brink</u> of despair.

As Serena sat in *The Tattler* office before school, word came from Mr. Street of the advisory committee's final decision. They had sided with the newspaper. Suddenly, despair was replaced by <u>exhilaration</u>. Cheers went up in the office. At lunch that day, it was a great joy to see people reading copies of *The Tattler* in the cafeteria.

1. Circle the word that has a meaning similar to <u>melancholy</u>. Write an antonym for **melancholy**.

2. Underline the phrase that tells what <u>resides</u> with the principal. Describe a responsibility that **resides** with you.

3. Underline the word that has a meaning similar to <u>harmony</u>. Use the word **harmony** in a sentence.

4. Circle the words that explain what was <u>misunderstood</u>. Use the word **misunderstood** in a sentence.

5. Underline the phrase that describes what Serena did when she went to <u>testify</u>. Write a sentence describing another situation in which a person might have to **testify**.

6. Circle the words that tell what was <u>embattled</u>. Use the word **embattled** in a sentence.

7. Underline the words that explain the meaning of <u>brink</u>. Describe another situation in which a person is on the **brink**.

8. Circle the words in a nearby sentence that have the same meaning as <u>exhilaration</u>. Write an antonym for **exhilaration**.

from Nature, from Self-Reliance, and **"Concord Hymn"** by Ralph Waldo Emerson
Reading Warm-up B

Read the following passage. Then, complete the activities.

Henry David Thoreau, who greatly admired Emerson, became famous for his decision to search out a peaceful, tranquil life of solitude in a simple cabin at Walden Pond. Thoreau spent two years and two months living alone at the Pond, which is located near the site of Emerson's home in Concord, Massachusetts. It is easy to admire Thoreau for his integrity, for he had an utterly honest goal: to find out what really matters in life.

Thoreau's uncomplicated lifestyle seemed to contradict what the majority of his fellow men pursued at the time—a life of increasing prosperity and ease. During his stay at Walden, Thoreau did not let any occurrence or natural event in the woods go unnoticed. He shared his experiences and imparted what he had learned in his book *Walden*. It has become a perennial classic that appears on college reading lists year after year. In fact, *Walden* remains one of the best-known works of nonfiction ever published in the United States.

At about the same time as Thoreau, a group of people known as Transcendentalists carried out a very different lifestyle experiment in another part of Massachusetts. They started Brook Farm, a communal farm on 175 acres in West Roxbury, now part of Boston. Residents shared property, farm chores, and meals. They aimed to create a place where people could work and live in blithe and peaceful harmony.

Brook Farm generated an enormous amount of interest among intellectuals and writers. It existed only six years, so it was hardly immortal, but its name lives on because so many distinguished figures were associated with it, including educational theorist Bronson Alcott, feminist author Margaret Fuller, and Emerson. Writer Nathaniel Hawthorne, an original member, created a fictionalized portrait of Brook Farm in his novel *The Blithedale Romance.*

1. Circle the word that has the same meaning as tranquil. Write an antonym for the word *tranquil*.

2. Underline the words that give a clue to the meaning of integrity. Write a sentence using an antonym for the word *integrity*.

3. Underline the words that tell what Thoreau's life at Walden Pond seemed to contradict. Write a synonym for the word *contradict*.

4. Circle the words that give a clue to the meaning of occurrence. Use the word *occurrence* in a sentence of your own.

5. Underline the phrase that gives a clue to the meaning of imparted. Write a synonym for *imparted*.

6. Underline the words that give a clue to the meaning of perennial. Write a sentence using the word *perennial*.

7. Who hoped to live in blithe and peaceful harmony? Write two antonyms for the word *blithe*.

8. Underline the words that hint at the meaning of immortal. Write a synonym for the word *immortal*.

from **Nature,** *from* **Self-Reliance,** and **"Concord Hymn"**
by Ralph Waldo Emerson

Literary Analysis: Figurative Language

Emerson uses various types of **figurative language** to express his meaning and make his abstract ideas seem more concrete. Figurative language is language that is used imaginatively rather than literally. Here are some types of figurative language:

- **imagery**, or word pictures that appeal to the senses
- **metaphor**, or a comparison between two or more unlike things without the use of the word *like* or *as*
- **description**, or a detailed portrayal of something in words
- **synecdoche**, or the use of one part of something to stand for the whole

When Emerson uses these tools in his writing, he clarifies his ideas and makes them easier for the reader to understand.

DIRECTIONS: *Read these passages from Emerson's work. Then, on the lines provided, identify the underlined sections as imagery, metaphor, description, or synecdoche.*

1. In good health, <u>the air is a cordial of incredible virtue.</u> _____
   _____

2. I become <u>a transparent eyeball</u>. _____
   _____

3. For nature is not always tricked in holiday attire, but the same scene which yesterday <u>breathed perfume and glittered</u> as for the frolic of the nymphs is overspread with melancholy today. _____
   _____

4. <u>Society is a joint-stock company</u> in which the members agree for the better securing of his bread to each shareholder. _____
   _____

5. He who would gather <u>immortal palms</u> must not be hindered by the name of goodness.
   _____

6. He may as well concern himself with <u>his shadow on the wall</u>. _____
   _____

7. Here once the embattled farmers stood / And fired <u>the shot heard round the world</u>.
   _____

8. Down <u>the dark stream which seaward creeps</u>. _____
   _____

from **Nature,** *from* **Self-Reliance,** and **"Concord Hymn"**
by Ralph Waldo Emerson

Reading Strategy: Challenging, or Questioning, the Text

One way to gain more understanding of a work is to **challenge the text**, or **question** the author's assertions. Here are some guidelines:

- Identify the author's opinions and restate them in your own words.
- Evaluate the examples, reasons, or other evidence the author provides to support his or her opinions.
- Consider other evidence that supports or refutes the author's opinions.
- On the basis of the evidence, decide if you agree or disagree with the author.

DIRECTIONS: *Read the following passage from* Self-Reliance. *Then challenge the text by performing the numbered activities below. Write your responses on the lines provided.*

Society everywhere is in conspiracy against the manhood of every one of its members. Society is a joint-stock company in which the members agree for the better securing of his bread to each shareholder, to surrender the liberty and culture of the eater. The virtue in most request is conformity. Self-reliance is its aversion. It loves not realities and creators, but names and customs.

1. Restate Emerson's basic opinion about society.

   _____

   _____

2. Identify and evaluate the evidence Emerson uses to support that opinion.

   _____

   _____

   _____

3. Provide examples from everyday life to support and refute Emerson's opinion of society.

   Support: _____

   _____

   _____

   Refute: _____

   _____

   _____

from **Nature,** *from* **Self-Reliance,** and **"Concord Hymn"**
by Ralph Waldo Emerson
Vocabulary Builder

Using the Latin Prefix *ab-*

A. DIRECTIONS: *The Latin prefix ab- means "away" or "from." Absolve means "to free from guilt or blame, or from having to fulfill a duty or a promise." On the line after each sentence below, explain how the italicized word reflects the meaning of the prefix- ab-.*

1. That idea is *absurd*—please come up with a less ridiculous suggestion.

   _____

2. It is usually pleasant this time of year, but today was *abnormally* hot.

   _____

3. Poerty uses images to make *abstract* ideas or emotions more concrete.

   _____

4. Unwilling to decide about the issue, Senator Díaz *abstained* from voting.

   _____

5. Most of the class came to school today, but two students were *absent*.

   _____

Using the Word List

> absolve   aversion   chaos   conviction   decorum   perpetual   tranquil

B. DIRECTIONS: *On the line, write the letter of the word that is most nearly the same in meaning as the word in capitals.*

____ 1. CHAOS: A. joy   B. pain   C. confusion   D. silence
____ 2. AVERSION: A. attraction   B. distaste   C. discrepancy   D. revision
____ 3. PERPETUAL: A. passive   B. weak   C. constant   D. fussy
____ 4. DECORUM: A. decoration   B. rudeness   C. quota   D. rightness
____ 5. CONVICTION: A. wish   B. dream   C. belief   D. promise
____ 6. ABSOLVE: A. pardon   B. worry   C. insult   D. harm
____ 7. TRANQUIL: A. peaceful   B. excited   C. full   D. wistful

Name _____ Date _____

from Nature, *from* Self-Reliance, and "Concord Hymn"
by Ralph Waldo Emerson
Support for Writing

To gather material for your critical evaluation of the selection from *Self-Reliance*, enter key points into the chart below.

My Critique of *Self-Reliance*	
Main Ideas of Essay/Beginning	
Main Ideas of Essay/Middle	
Main Ideas of Essay/End	
Emerson's Argument/Summary Statement	
My Opinion/Support from Text	

On a separate page, write a first draft of your critical evaluation. When you revise your work, be sure you have made your critical opinion of the essay clear and have supported it with examples from the selection.

Name _____ Date _____

from **Nature,** *from* **Self-Reliance,** and **"Concord Hymn"**
by Ralph Waldo Emerson
Enrichment: Local Landmarks

Like the statue of the Minute Men commemorated in "Concord Hymn," monuments honoring historic figures and events can be found in just about every town and city in the United States. Locate one such memorial in your own area. Then, on the lines provided, answer the following questions about the monument. To answer, you may need to visit the monument and do additional research at a local library or historical society. If an answer is unavailable, write "unknown" or "does not apply."

1. Where is the monument located?

   _____

2. What form does the monument take—statue, plaque, or other?

   _____

3. What occasion, person, or group does the monument celebrate?

   _____

4. When was the monument erected?

   _____

5. Who erected the monument?

   _____

6. What inscription, if any, accompanies the monument?

   _____

7. What visual symbols, if any, does the monument include?

   _____

8. How is the monument like and unlike the monument honored in "Concord Hymn"?

   _____

   _____

9. In the space below or on a separate piece of paper, write your own poem or brief speech that could have accompanied the dedication of the monument. If possible, provide a photograph, drawing, or model of the monument to share with the class as you read your tribute aloud.

   _____

   _____

   _____

   _____

from **Nature,** *from* **Self-Reliance,** and **"Concord Hymn"** by Ralph Waldo Emerson
Open-Book Test

Short Answer *Write your responses to the questions in this section on the lines provided.*

1. What figurative language does Emerson use near the beginning of *Nature* to show that a person becomes younger in the presence of the natural world?

_____

_____

_____

2. Read the sentence in the first paragraph of *Nature* that begins "There I feel that nothing can befall me in life-no disgrace . . . ." From this sentence, which of his senses is most important to Emerson in his experience of the natural world? Why do you think so?

_____

_____

_____

_____

3. When Emerson says in *Nature* that he becomes "a transparent eyeball," what is he communicating through this descriptive image?

_____

_____

_____

4. Do you agree with Emerson's statement in *Nature* that "Nature is a setting that fits equally well a comic or mourning piece?" Explain what he means and state whether you agree or disagree.

_____

_____

_____

5. In the sentence from *Nature*, "In good health, the air is a cordial of incredible virtue," what literary form does Emerson use? What two things does he compare?

_____

_____

_____

_____

6. Emerson states in *Self-Reliance* that society values conformity above all else. Do you agree or disagree with this statement? Give one or two examples from the essay to support your opinion.

_____

_____

_____

7. What does Emerson mean in *Self-Reliance* when he says that "God will not have his work made manifest by cowards?" Supply a detail or quotation from the essay that helps the reader interpret Emerson's idea.

_____

_____

_____

8. Reread the paragraph in *Self-Reliance* that begins, "Society is everywhere in conspiracy against . . . ." Toward the end of the paragraph note the word *aversion.* Think about what Emerson is saying about the demand society makes for conformity from its members. Since Emerson counsels self-reliance instead of conformity, what do you think is the meaning of the sentence "Self-reliance is its [conformity's] *aversion?*"

_____

_____

_____

9. Reread lines 5 and 6 of "Concord Hymn." What message is Emerson communicating in these lines?

_____

_____

_____

10. What is the meaning of Stanza 3 of "Concord Hymn?"

_____

_____

_____

Essay

Write an extended response to the question of your choice or to the question or questions your teacher assigns you.

11. One of the key concepts in Emerson's writing is how the individual sees himself or herself in relation to nature and society. Choose either *Nature* or *Self-Reliance* and write a brief essay to discuss how Emerson views the individual. Use two examples to support your opinion from whichever selection you choose.

12. Choose one of the following:

A synecdoche is a form of figurative language in which a part is used to stand for the whole, as in "All hands went on strike at the factory." The word *hands* stands for the word *workers* or *employees*. In the first stanza of "Concord Hymn," Emerson uses a synecdoche. Identify this figure of speech and determine what the "part" is and for what "whole" it stands. Write a brief essay to explain the synecdoche and what it represents in the context of the poem.

In the final paragraph of the selection from *Nature*, Emerson describes nature in a way that suggests that it is perceived through the emotional state of the person observing it. In what way does the poet describe nature to show that nature can appear either beautiful or sad? Write a brief essay to explain your ideas.

13. Choose one:

Reread the paragraph in *Self-Reliance* that begins "Society everywhere is in conspiracy against the manhood of every one of its members." Find the metaphor in the paragraph and write a brief essay about what it means. What two unlike things does Emerson compare in the metaphor? What is the effect of the comparison in Emerson's mind?

Reread the paragraph in *Nature* that begins "The greatest delight which the fields and woods minister is the suggestion . . . ." Write a brief essay about what Emerson is saying in this paragraph.

14. **Thinking about the Essential Question: Essential Question: How does literature shape or reflect society?** Although Ralph Waldo Emerson began his career as a minister, he found his true vocation as an independent thinker and philosopher who prized above all a spirit of independence and nonconformity in seeking out an authentic life. In what respect do Emerson's views—as expressed in "Nature," Self-Reliance," and "Concord Hymn"—seek to inspire his readers to reshape and rethink the kind of society they live in? Develop your ideas in an essay supported by details from the selections.

Oral Response

15. Go back to question 2, 3, 4, or 6 or to the question your teacher assigns to you. Take a few minutes to expand your answer and prepare an oral response. Find additional details in the selections from *Nature*, *Self-Reliance*, and "Concord Hymn" that will support your points. If necessary, make notes to guide your response.

Name _____   Date _____

from Nature, *from* Self-Reliance, and "Concord Hymn"
by Ralph Waldo Emerson
Selection Test A

Critical Reading *Identify the letter of the choice that best answers the question.*

____ 1. How does a reader question any text?
A. by questioning the writer's opinions
B. by proofreading the material for errors
C. by agreeing with the writer's opinions
D. by rereading the text for clarity

____ 2. Which of the following sentences or phrases from *Nature* is an example of figurative language?
A. "I have enjoyed a perfect exhilaration."
B. "the waving of the boughs in the storm"
C. "There I feel nothing can befall me . . ."
D. "To a man laboring under calamity . . ."

____ 3. Which of these suggests a meaning for Emerson's words from *Nature:* "In the woods is perpetual youth"?
A. Only young people like to walk in the woods.
B. People feel refreshed and young in the woods.
C. The woods attracts those who don't like to grow up.
D. The natural world is found only in the woods.

____ 4. Which of the following expresses a key idea of the selection from *Self-Reliance?*
A. Be guided by the will of the majority.
B. It is wise to try to be like others.
C. The individual mind is the only guide.
D. Social customs are necessary for peace.

____ 5. The following sentence from *Self-Reliance* is which type of figurative language?
Society is a joint-stock company

A. description
B. synecdoche
C. metaphor
D. imagery

_____ 6. In "Concord Hymn," what does Emerson mean by the synecdoche "the shot heard round the world"?

    A. a battle fought with very large and noisy weapons

    B. a battle written about in many foreign newspapers

    C. the opening battle of the Revolutionary War

    D. a battle farmers wrote about to their European relatives

_____ 7. Which best describes the image Emerson evokes in the following lines from "Concord Hymn"?

> By the rude bridge that arched the flood,/Their flag to April's breeze unfurled,/Here once the embattled farmers stood . . .

    A. farmers carrying weapons and a flag marching over a bridge in April

    B. armed farmers standing by a bridge that has been flooded by April rains

    C. a flag waving in the April breeze over a flooded bridge

    D. armed farmers standing by a bridge, carrying a flag waving in the April breeze

_____ 8. In *Nature,* what might Emerson mean by the metaphor, "Nature always wears the colors of the spirit"?

    A. Nature is always colorful.

    B. A person's mood affects his or her view of nature.

    C. The spirit of nature colors the feelings of human beings.

    D. The colors in nature reveal its spirit.

Vocabulary

_____ 9. In which of the following sentences is the meaning of the word *aversion* expressed?

    A. To be self-reliant is to trust one's own heart and experiences.

    B. Many great men have also been misunderstood.

    C. The conformist is hostile to the person who respects individuality.

    D. The world will support a person who acts with integrity.

_____ 10. Which of the following words is a synonym of the italicized word in this sentence?

> The Revolutionary War was not a *tranquil* time in America.

    A. calm

    B. violent

    C. exciting

    D. memorable

Essay

11. In *Self-Reliance*, does Emerson express respect for the expectations of society, or does he criticize society's expectations? Write a brief essay to give your description of Emerson's position. Use at least two examples from the selection.

12. Reread the paragraph in *Nature* that begins "The greatest delight which the fields and woods minister. . . ." Write a brief essay about what Emerson is saying in this paragraph and how that is central to the whole selection. State what you feel is the main idea of the paragraph. Then, support that idea by citing details from the paragraph and elsewhere in the selection.

13. **Thinking About the Essential Question: How does literature shape or reflect society?** Although Ralph Waldo Emerson began his career as a minister, he found his true vocation as an independent thinker and philosopher who prized above all a spirit of independence and nonconformity in seeking out an authentic life. In what respect do Emerson's views—as expressed in *Nature, Self-Reliance,* and "Concord Hymn"—seek to inspire his readers to reshape and rethink the kind of society they live in? Develop your ideas in an essay supported by details from the selections.

from Nature, *from* Self-Reliance, and "Concord Hymn"
by Ralph Waldo Emerson
Selection Test B

Critical Reading *Identify the letter of the choice that best completes the statement or answers the question.*

____ 1. In *Nature*, what does Emerson mean by the metaphor in the following statement?
  In good health, the air is a cordial of incredible virtue.

  A. Virtuous and friendly humans enjoy good health.
  B. The air is friendly to people who are in good health.
  C. When one is in good health, the air itself is a delicious and healthy drink.
  D. Pure and healthy air is incredibly friendly to human beings.

____ 2. "Concord Hymn" was written to celebrate
  A. music and poetry.
  B. a monument to the Revolution.
  C. Massachusetts.
  D. the end of the Civil War.

____ 3. Readers question a writer's text when they
  A. refuse to read.
  B. lend the text to others.
  C. question the writer's opinions.
  D. proofread articles to make them more accurate.

____ 4. As "a joint-stock company" in Emerson's metaphor from *Self-Reliance*, what does society require from people?
  A. to make bread for its members who have conformed
  B. to conform to become members of the company
  C. surrender of liberty to become part of the larger culture
  D. conformity and surrender of liberty in order to gain resources

____ 5. How might a reader question the following text from *Self-Reliance*?
  Trust thyself: every heart vibrates to that iron string.

  A. The reader might reflect on personal experience to judge the statement.
  B. The reader might show that the word *thyself* is archaic, or outdated.
  C. The reader might defend the statement because it is written by a famous American philosopher.
  D. The reader might research the facts on how the heart functions.

____ 6. Which view of nature does Emerson take?
  A. Nature is indifferent to human suffering.
  B. Nature must be studied and dissected.
  C. Urban dwellers have little conception of the cruelty of nature.
  D. Nature can inspire the human spirit.

_____ 7. What is the implication of the following image from *Nature*?

> To a man laboring under calamity, the heat of his own fire hath sadness in it.

  A. The heat of one's fire should give warmth and pleasure.
  B. Fire can be a sad thing to watch.
  C. Sometimes a fireplace can be too warm.
  D. Feeling the heat of one's fire is often a sad experience.

_____ 8. Which of these statements best characterizes the central idea of *Self-Reliance*?
  A. Meekness is the virtue that fosters self-awareness.
  B. Rely on your own instincts.
  C. Social customs serve a valuable purpose.
  D. Cruelty may be necessary to achieve philosophical goals.

_____ 9. Emerson's romanticism is most clearly displayed in his
  A. careful descriptions of nature.
  B. exaggerated sense of loneliness.
  C. logically constructed arguments.
  D. reliance on emotional truth.

_____ 10. In "Concord Hymn," what does Emerson mean by "the shot heard round the world"?
  A. the brave farmer-soldiers
  B. the Battle of Lexington and Concord
  C. the Declaration of Independence
  D. the battle monument

_____ 11. In *Self-Reliance*, Emerson writes that society "loves not realities and creators, but names and customs." Which of these adjectives best reflects Emerson's attitude in that statement?
  A. disapproving
  B. accepting
  C. encouraging
  D. forgiving

_____ 12. Why does Emerson allude to individuals such as Socrates, Jesus, and Galileo in *Self-Reliance*?
  A. to suggest that they agreed with his philosophy
  B. to encourage readers to learn about historical figures
  C. to inspire readers through the example of their struggles
  D. to question their contribution to society

_____ 13. Which of these statements could be used to question the text of a written work?
  A. The author presents a thorough analysis of the subject.
  B. The author constructs a rational defense of the position.
  C. The author cites excellent research.
  D. The author expresses opinions as if they were facts.

Vocabulary

_____ 14. Which pair of words expresses a relationship that is most similar to the relationship of these words in capital letters?

INFINITY : PERPETUAL ::

A. warm : hot   C. star : small
B. glowing : moon   D. perfume : fragrant

_____ 15. Which of the following words best completes the following sentence?

A bow to the queen shows proper _____.

A. conviction
B. decorum
C. absolve
D. tranquil

_____ 16. Which word below is most nearly *opposite* in meaning to the italicized word in this statement?

He has an *aversion* to joining the team.

A. plan   C. distaste
B. liking   D. hope

_____ 17. Which word below can be substituted for the italicized word in this statement?

Modern philosophers theorize that there may be order in *chaos*.

A. disorder   C. pain
B. nature   D. self-reliance

Essay

18. Write an essay in which you describe two examples from Emerson's essay *Nature* that suggest a relationship between the human spirit and nature.

19. In "Concord Hymn," the imagery in the first stanza evokes feelings and attitudes about the Minutemen of Concord. In a brief essay, explain these feelings and attitudes and how the images evoke them. Use examples from the poem to support your point.

20. Reread the paragraph in Nature that begins "The greatest delight which the fields and woods minister. . . ." Write an essay about what Emerson is saying in this paragraph and its relationship to the selection as a whole. State what you feel is his main idea in the paragraph, and support your statement with details from the paragraph and elsewhere in the selection.

21. **Thinking About the Essential Question: How does literature shape or reflect society?** Although Ralph Waldo Emerson began his career as a minister, he found his true vocation as an independent thinker and philosopher who prized above all a spirit of independence and nonconformity in seeking out an authentic life. In what respect do Emerson's views—as expressed in Nature, Self-Reliance, and "Concord Hymn"—seek to inspire his readers to reshape and rethink the kind of society they live in? Develop your ideas in an essay supported by details from the selections.

Contemporary Commentary
Gretel Ehrlich Introduces *Walden* by Henry David Thoreau

DIRECTIONS: *Use the space provided to answer the questions.*

1. At first, why was Thoreau's landscape at Walden Pond unfamiliar to Ehrlich?

    _____

    _____

2. What examples from *Walden* does Ehrlich use to support her assertion that the heart of an essay is "an attempt to understand the nature of things"?

    _____

    _____

    _____

3. A. In her commentary, Ehrlich stresses Thoreau's philosophical idea that "life is change." What details does Ehrlich cite to support this idea?

    _____

    _____

    B. Do you agree with the claim that "life is change"? Briefly explain why or why not.

    _____

    _____

4. According to Ehrlich, how would Thoreau advise us to cope with the speed and complexity of modern life?

    _____

    _____

5. Explain what Thoreau means by the "auroral character."

    _____

    _____

6. Do you believe that Thoreau was right in encouraging us to "march to a different drummer" if that's where our destiny takes us? Briefly explain your opinion.

    _____

    _____

    _____

7. What questions about Thoreau's *Walden* does Ehrlich's commentary raise in your mind at this point?

    _____

    _____

    _____

Gretel Ehrlich
Listening and Viewing

Segment 1: Meet Gretel Ehrlich
- Why does Gretel Ehrlich recommend traveling to other countries?
- What have you learned from either moving to or visiting a place different from your hometown?

_____

_____

_____

_____

Segment 2: Gretel Ehrlich Introduces *Walden* by Henry David Thoreau
- How has Gretel Ehrlich's writing been influenced by Thoreau?

_____

_____

_____

_____

Segment 3: The Writing Process
- Why does Gretel Ehrlich believe it is important to constantly record one's observations and thoughts by taking notes?
- What method of collecting information do you rely on when writing?

_____

_____

_____

_____

Segment 4: The Rewards of Writing
- What does Gretel Ehrlich believe is the obligation of a writer?
- What insights about humanity do you think you could gain by reading books about other cultures?

_____

_____

_____

_____

Vocabulary Warm-up Word Lists

Study these words from the selections. Then, complete the activities.

Word List A

anticipated [an TIS uh payt uhd] *v.* expected
   The storm was worse than the weather forecasters had <u>anticipated</u>.

calculation [kal kyoo LAY shuhn] *n.* precise reckoning
   Mario realized that a simple <u>calculation</u> would give him the answer.

cluttered [KLUT uhrd] *adj.* crowded; congested
   Jimmy <u>cluttered</u> his room with books and newspapers.

enterprises [ENT uhr pryz uhz] *n.* undertakings; business ventures
   Restaurants are difficult <u>enterprises</u> to run, requiring long hours of hard work.

essentially [uh SEN shuhl ee] *adv.* basically
   The corner lot was <u>essentially</u> bare, with just one tree on the property.

external [ek STERN uhl] *adj.* outer
   That medicine is for <u>external</u> use only.

premises [PREM is uhs] *n.* grounds; piece of real estate
   Lana lived in gorgeous <u>premises</u>—a lavish mansion overlooking the bay.

superfluous [soo PER floo uhs] *adj.* more than is needed; excessive
   You can say all you need to in a brief speech; anything more is <u>superfluous</u>.

Word List B

conformity [kuhn FORM uh tee] *n.* action according to customs or rules
   The mayor brought the municipal ordinance into <u>conformity</u> with state law.

inherent [in HER uhnt] *adj.* natural; innate; inborn
   The survival instinct is an <u>inherent</u> part of human nature.

mode [MOHD] *n.* manner or way of acting
   As a manager, Sam is very excitable and often operates in crisis <u>mode</u>.

piety [PY uh tee] *n.* devotion to religious duties and practices
   Attending church every day, Ms. Ramirez was much respected for her <u>piety</u>.

restricted [ree STRIK tuhd] *v.* limited
   The new law <u>restricted</u> the use of cell phones by people driving a motor vehicle.

semblance [SEM bluhns] *n.* outward form or appearance
   Under a <u>semblance</u> of calm, Sam was terrified.

shun [SHUN] *v.* to avoid consistently; to keep away from
   Because of Brad's dishonesty, many of his classmates decided to <u>shun</u> him.

transmit [tranz MIT] *v.* to send; to convey; to pass along
   We used e-mail to <u>transmit</u> to our friends the news of our arrival in London.

131

Name _____ Date _____

from **Walden** and from **Civil Disobedience** by Henry David Thoreau
Vocabulary Warm-up Exercises

Exercise A *Fill in the blanks, using each word from Word List A only once.*

Writing in the mid-nineteenth century, Thoreau believed that American life was far too

[1] _____, and he urged his readers to "simplify" their lives. We should try

to focus on the [2] _____ important, inner issues, he thought,

rather than on [3] _____ things or material possessions. The

[4] _____ in which one lives don't matter as much as *how* life is lived.

Testing his theories at Walden Pond, Thoreau recognized that such items as fine

clothes, fancy food, and newspapers are really [5] _____, since they don't

help us to live better. In the [6] _____ of what really matters in life, one

wonders what Thoreau would say if he could have [7] _____ the break-

neck pace and technological quality of American life today. How, for example, would he

have reacted to such [8] _____ as the World Wide Web, the space shuttle,

and electric cars?

Exercise B *Decide whether each statement below is true or false. Circle T or F, and explain your answer.*

1. If you act in *conformity* with others, you can be described as unconventional.
   T / F _____

2. Something *inherent* can be described as topical, accidental, or superficial.
   T / F _____

3. Commuter railroad trains are one *mode* of public transportation.
   T / F _____

4. *Piety* is a sign of irreverence or disrespect.
   T / F _____

5. If your privileges are *restricted*, they have been increased or enhanced.
   T / F _____

6. A clever lie may have the *semblance* of truth.
   T / F _____

7. If you *shun* another person's company, you are at pains to seek out him or her.
   T / F _____

8. To *transmit* a message is to revoke it or call it back.
   T / F _____

from **Walden** and *from* **Civil Disobedience** by Henry David Thoreau
Reading Warm-up A

Read the following passage. Pay special attention to the underlined words. Then, read it again, and complete the activities. Use a separate sheet of paper for your written answers.

There were only two days left before the Wilderness Club set out for its annual hike. That night, the leader, Mr. Simms, had everyone come to a meeting at the school gym. To enter the <u>premises</u>, hikers had to bring with them a backpack loaded with everything they thought they would need for the week-long trek through the mountains.

Dennis showed up with a pack full of canned spaghetti, soda, and a portable TV. He had not <u>anticipated</u> how difficult it would be to carry such a heavy pack on his back for seven days. Mr. Simms took one look at his <u>cluttered</u> pack and told him to take everything out and start from scratch.

"The first rule of backpacking is that anything <u>superfluous</u>—anything you don't need—has to be left behind," said Mr. Simms.

Dennis unloaded his pack. He realized how few comforts he would be allowed on this trip. It would not be one of those fun-filled <u>enterprises</u> he was used to, when the trip was made easy by snacks and entertainment. This trip would involve hard days of hiking, crossing rivers, navigating boulder fields, and then pitching a tent in cold weather, possibly even in snow. Mr. Simms went to the blackboard and wrote out a <u>calculation</u> that showed how much weight you could carry on your back, according to how much you weighed. Then, he held up a rectangle of folded-up plastic, a rain poncho, that weighed almost nothing.

"This little item is all you need to protect you from rain, snow, hail: all the <u>external</u> elements that can seep into your skin and your pack on a hike in bad weather."

He had many other words of advice. However, Dennis learned that, <u>essentially</u>, the less you brought, the better.

1. Underline the words in the previous sentence that give a clue to the meaning of <u>premises</u>. Use the word *premises* in an original sentence.

2. Circle the words that give a clue to the meaning of <u>anticipated</u>. What are two synonyms for *anticipated*?

3. Underline the words in this and the previous sentence that give clues to the meaning of <u>cluttered</u>. Name a synonym for *cluttered*.

4. Circle the words that hint at the meaning of <u>superfluous</u>. Use a word meaning the opposite of *superfluous* in a sentence of your own.

5. Circle the words that offer clues to the meaning of <u>enterprises</u>. What is a synonym for *enterprises*?

6. Underline the words that give a clue to the meaning of <u>calculation</u>. Is a *calculation* normally approximate or precise?

7. Circle the words that give a clue to the meaning of <u>external</u>. Use a word meaning the opposite of *external* in a sentence.

8. Underline the words that hint at the meaning of <u>essentially</u>. Use *essentially* in an original sentence.

Name _____ Date _____

from Walden and **from Civil Disobedience** by Henry David Thoreau
Reading Warm-up B

Read the following passage. Pay special attention to the underlined words. Then, read it again, and complete the activities. Use a separate sheet of paper for your written answers.

One of Thoreau's most prominent qualities was his individualism. He felt that it is an <u>inherent</u> duty of human beings to resist <u>conformity</u>. "If a man does not keep pace with his companions," Thoreau wrote in *Walden,* "perhaps it is because he hears a different drummer. Let him step to the music which he hears, however measured or far away."

It was this approach, or <u>mode</u> of thinking, that inspired Thoreau in his essay "Civil Disobedience." Here Thoreau argues that it is not wrong to disobey an unjust law or policy, especially a law that has wrongly <u>restricted</u> or limited human rights.

Few of Thoreau's readers at the time could have anticipated that his philosophy would directly <u>transmit</u> a set of beliefs to two of the most important men of the twentieth century, Mahatma Gandhi and Martin Luther King, Jr. As an Indian lawyer living in South Africa, Gandhi developed a strategy of nonviolent resistance to the government. The authorities were pursuing a racist policy of discrimination. Back in India, Gandhi believed that there could be no shade or <u>semblance</u> of freedom and dignity for his own people if India's British rulers were allowed to arrest and jail Indians without trial. He called on all Indians to <u>shun</u> work, staying away from their jobs in a massive general strike. Gandhi's strategy of nonviolent resistance, shaped by Thoreau's ideas, set India on the road to independence.

Martin Luther King, in turn, was profoundly influenced by the ideas of both Thoreau and Gandhi. He had deep respect for Thoreau, the simple but wise philosopher, and Gandhi, the man of political commitment and deep religious <u>piety</u>. King spent six weeks in India in early 1959, specifically to learn more about Gandhi. King used ideas that can be traced through Gandhi back to Thoreau. He thus made nonviolent resistance a fundamental element of the American civil rights movement.

1. Underline the words in this sentence that give a clue to the meaning of <u>inherent</u>. Use the word *inherent* in an original sentence.

2. Circle the words in the next sentence that give a clue to the meaning of <u>conformity</u>. From what verb is this noun formed?

3. Underline the word in this sentence hinting at the meaning of <u>mode</u>. What is a synonym for *mode*?

4. Underline the word in this sentence that gives a clue to the meaning of <u>restricted</u>. What are two antonyms for *restricted*?

5. Circle the words in this sentence that give a clue to the meaning of <u>transmit</u>. What are two synonyms for *transmit*?

6. Underline the words in this sentence that hint at the meaning of <u>semblance</u>. What is a synonym for *semblance*?

7. Underline the words in this sentence that give a clue to the meaning of <u>shun</u>. Use a word meaning the opposite of *shun* in a sentence of your own.

8. Circle the word in this sentence that hints at the meaning of the word <u>piety</u>. What is an adjective formed from this noun?

from **Walden** and *from* **Civil Disobedience** by Henry David Thoreau
Literary Analysis: Style

Readers should look not only at what a writer has to say but also at how the writer says it. The way a writer puts thoughts into words is called **style.** Following are some important elements of style and some questions useful in analyzing a writer's style.

- **Choice of words:** Does the writer choose simple and direct words or words that are more complex and formal?
- **Length of sentences:** Does the writer make frequent use of long or short sentences? Does the sentence length vary?
- **Type and structure of sentences:** Does the writer use a fair amount of questions or commands? Many simple sentences, or compound-complex sentences? Does the writer always open with the subject of a sentence or vary sentence beginnings?
- **Rhythm:** Does the writer create an internal rhythm by repeating words or ideas from sentence to sentence?
- **Use of literary devices:** Does the writer use vivid imagery and strong similes, metaphors, and other figures of speech?

DIRECTIONS: *Read this passage from* Walden. *Then, on the lines below the passage, analyze the different elements of Thoreau's style.*

To my imagination it retained throughout the day more or less of this auroral character, reminding me of a certain house on a mountain which I had visited the year before. This was an airy and unplastered cabin, fit to entertain a traveling god, and where a goddess might trail her garments. The winds which passed over my dwelling were such as sweep over the ridges of mountains, bearing the broken strains, or celestial parts only, of terrestrial music.

1. Word choice: _____
   _____

2. Sentence length: _____
   _____

3. Sentence type/structure: _____
   _____
   _____

4. Rhythm: _____
   _____

5. Literary devices: _____
   _____
   _____

Name _____ Date _____

from Walden and from Civil Disobedience by Henry David Thoreau

Reading Strategy: Analyze the Author's Implicit and Explicit Philosophical Assumptions

In both *Walden* and **Civil Disobedience,** Thoreau expresses his **philosophical assumptions,** the system of belief and values that guided his life and actions. He expresses these ideas both **implicitly,** merely suggesting them, and **explicitly,** stating them directly. As you read, analyze Thoreau's philosophy. To do this, note his main ideas and the evidence he uses to support these ideas. Then compare his ideas and evidence by comparing them with your own life experiences. Organize your notes in the following chart.

Thoreau's Main Ideas	
Thoreau's Evidence	
My Experiences	
Analysis	

Name _____ Date _____

from **Walden** and *from* **Civil Disobedience** by Henry David Thoreau
Vocabulary Builder

Using the Root -flu-

A. DIRECTIONS: *The root -flu- means "flow." Using that information, write on the line the letter of the choice that best completes each sentence.*

_____ 1. If Laura shows *fluency* in Russian,
    A. she has little knowledge of Russian.
    B. she has studied Russian but cannot master it.
    C. she speaks it easily.

_____ 2. In an *affluent* society,
    A. many people have and spend money.
    B. most people are very poor.
    C. most people earn good money but refuse to spend it.

Using the Word List

> alacrity   dilapidated   expedient   magnanimity   sublime   superfluous

B. DIRECTIONS: *Circle the letter of the choice that best completes each sentence.*

1. The building was so dilapidated that the city wanted to have it
    A. demolished.   B. publicized.   C. photographed.

2. Her novels include a fair amount of superfluous information, making them rather
    A. easy to read.   B. time consuming.   C. melancholy.

3. The city's architecture was absolutely sublime, so viewing it usually inspired
    A. disgust.   B. indifference.   C. awe.

4. When Jill accepted with alacrity the difficult task he gave her, her boss was
    A. annoyed.   B. impressed.   C. furious.

5. When Thoreau calls government an expedient, he means it is a
    A. tool.   B. useless enterprise.   C. bureaucracy.

6. People display magnanimity when they
    A. hold a grudge.   B. give to charity.   C. perform tasks efficiently.

from **Walden** and *from* **Civil Disobedience** by Henry David Thoreau
Support for Writing

As you prepare to write your editorial about the relevance of Thoreau's ideas today, reread the selections. Decide whether you support or reject Thoreau's ideas. Make entries into the chart below that strengthen your position.

Editorial on Simplicity
Why I support or reject Thoreau's ideas of simplicity:
Examples from today's world to support my opinion:
Examples from Thoreau's world to support my opinion:
Direct quotes from Thoreau that strengthen my position:

On a separate page, write a draft of your editorial. Then revise it, and be sure to justify the choice you have made with examples from Thoreau or with examples from today's world. Submit your editorial to the school newspaper.

from **Walden** and *from* **Civil Disobedience** by Henry David Thoreau
Enrichment: Social Studies

Authors of both nonfiction and fiction often respond to important contemporary events. Thoreau was especially concerned with two controversial issues of his day—slavery and the war between the United States and Mexico. He opposed both and even refused to pay taxes to a government that condoned them. His protest led to a night in jail—and to his famous essay on civil disobedience.

DIRECTIONS: *Following are some important events of Thoreau's day. Using your knowledge of his attitudes and writings, decide how Thoreau probably would have felt about each event. On the line before it, write S if you think he would have supported it and O if you think he would have opposed it. Explain why on the lines that follow. Support your answer with an example or detail from one of the selections.*

____ 1. Campaigning for the presidency in 1844, James K. Polk said it was the "manifest destiny" of the United States to expand its boundaries from Texas to the Pacific Ocean.

_____

_____

____ 2. In March of 1846, General Zachary Taylor moved American troops into the Mexican part of Texas.

_____

_____

____ 3. In May of 1846, the United States declared war on Mexico.

_____

_____

____ 4. A young American congressman named Abraham Lincoln challenged President Polk to prove that the land on which American troops were fighting was really American and not Mexican.

_____

_____

____ 5. In 1846, Congressman David Wilmot proposed that slavery should not be permitted in any territory that might be acquired from Mexico.

_____

_____

____ 6. In 1846, a great many people, from Ralph Waldo Emerson to Lieutenant Ulysses S. Grant, condemned the Mexican War as a "shameful theft."

_____

_____

Name _____ Date _____

from **Walden** and *from* **Civil Disobedience** by Henry David Thoreau
Open-Book Test

Short Answer *Write your responses to the questions in this section on the lines provided.*

1. In Thoreau's description of the Holloway farm in the selection from *Walden*, find and read the sentence in which the word *dilapidated* is used. What other words in the sentence give you clues to the meaning of *dilapidated*?

_____

_____

2. In the selection from *Walden*, reread the first part of the paragraph that begins, "I went to the woods because I wished to live deliberately . . . ." What does this passage tell you about Thoreau's philosophy of life?

_____

_____

_____

3. Thoreau states in *Walden*, "As long as possible live free and uncommitted." Then he goes on to compare a farm with jail. Explain what his analogy means. What larger issue does he address?

_____

_____

_____

4. In *Walden*, as part of the construction of his argument for simplicity, Thoreau uses repetition to state what one should do and what one should avoid. Fill in the chart below by listing three "shoulds" and three "should nots" that Thoreau states.

_____	_____
_____	_____
_____	_____

5. At the end of the paragraph in *Walden* in which Thoreau calls for simplicity, he says, "Our life is like a German Confederacy, made up of petty states, with its boundary forever fluctuating . . . ." Reread the rest of this passage, along with the note at the bottom, and describe what Thoreau means by this analogy and how it ties in with his idea of simplicity.

_____

_____

_____

_____

6. In the selection from *Walden*, what does Thoreau mean to suggest when he compares legislators with people who put obstacles on railroad tracks?

_____

_____

_____

7. In *Walden*, Thoreau states, "If a man does not keep pace with his companions, perhaps it is because he hears a different drummer." What can you infer from Thoreau's statement? How does this relate to his comments about the path he has made from the cabin to the pond?

_____

_____

_____

_____

8. In *Civil Disobedience*, what do you think Thoreau means by his statement at the end of the first paragraph, which begins, "Witness the present Mexican war . . ."?

_____

_____

_____

9. In the second to last paragraph in *Civil Disobedience*, what does Thoreau mean by his repetition of the word *It*?

_____

_____

10. According to Thoreau in the final paragraph in the selection from *Civil Disobedience*, who has the right to determine what kind of government people shall form?

_____

_____

Essay

Write an extended response to the question of your choice or to the question or questions your teacher assigns you.

11. Choose one:

In *Walden*, Thoreau says in The Conclusion, "I left the woods for as good a reason as I went there." Reread the rest of the passage and write a brief essay to interpret what Thoreau means in this paragraph and how his meaning is connected to his views on trodding the same path continually.

In *Civil Disobedience*, Thoreau says he agrees with the motto, "That government is best which governs least." What do you think he means by this statement? Write a brief essay to interpret this motto.

12. Choose one:

In the final paragraph before The Conclusion in the selection from *Walden*, Thoreau uses an extended metaphor that begins, "The intellect is a cleaver." Follow this metaphor through the rest of the paragraph and write a brief essay about what things Thoreau is comparing in the metaphor and how these images reflect his view of life.

In the second paragraph of the selection from "*Civil Disobedience*" Thoreau uses a metaphor that compares government to something else. To what does he compare government? What message is he communicating with this metaphor?

13. Choose either *Walden* or *Civil Disobedience*. Decide what Thoreau's basic messages are and write a brief essay about how such ideals are realized in society today. Cite policies and events that you have learned about to support your opinions.

14. **Thinking About the Essential Question: Essential Question: How does literature shape or reflect society?** Henry David Thoreau was an American original. His main ambition was to find a way of life free of conventional ambition— to live as far as possible from the complicating, conformist pressures of a standard career and society. In what respect does he seek to reshape society through his personal example and his overall philosophy as expressed in the excerpts from *Walden* and "Civil Disobedience"? Develop your thoughts in an essay supported by details from the selections.

Oral Response

15. Go back to question 2, 4, 6, or 9 or to the question your teacher assigns to you. Take a few minutes to expand your answer and prepare an oral response. Find additional details *Walden* or *Civil Disobedience* that will support your points. If necessary, make notes to guide your response.

from **Walden** and *from* **Civil Disobedience** by Henry David Thoreau
Selection Test A

Critical Reading *Identify the letter of the choice that best answers the question.*

____ 1. At the beginning of the selection from *Walden*, what does Thoreau allow himself to do through his imagination?
   A. build houses all over his town
   B. buy all the farms in his area
   C. make as much money as he can
   D. collect seeds from nearby places

____ 2. Which of Thoreau's philosophical assumptions is found in this passage from *Walden*?
   > Our life is frittered away by details. An honest man has hardly need to count more than his ten fingers, or in extreme cases he may add his ten toes, and lump the rest.
   A. People should pay attention to details.
   B. People should live life simply.
   C. People should aim for personal honesty.
   D. Working with one's hands is the best kind of life.

____ 3. What is a regular element of Thoreau's style in *Walden*?
   A. to ask questions and then answer them
   B. to state main ideas only once
   C. to jump quickly from idea to idea
   D. to expand on personal experiences

____ 4. Which element of Thoreau's style is shown in these passages from *Walden*?
   > Simplicity, simplicity, simplicity! I say, let your affairs be as two or three, and not a hundred or a thousand . . . Simplify, simplify. Instead of three meals a day, if it be necessary eat but one; instead of a hundred dishes, five . . .
   A. using mathematical examples
   B. using themes from the kitchen
   C. repeating main ideas
   D. using only short sentences

____ 5. Which of Thoreau's philosophical assumptions is expressed in this passage from *Walden*?
   > If a man does not keep pace with his companions, perhaps it is because he hears a different drummer. Let him step to the music which he hears, however measured or far away.
   A. Music should be appreciated.
   B. People should do what others do.
   C. People should live as individuals.
   D. People should have close friends.

____ **6.** What situation caused Thoreau to write *Civil Disobedience*?
   A. trade laws with India
   B. uprisings in California
   C. the Mexican War
   D. President Polk's election

____ **7.** What does Thoreau call for, in terms of government, at the conclusion of this selection from *Civil Disobedience*?
   A. a better government
   B. no government at all
   C. a government run by businesses
   D. a government run by a king

____ **8.** What is Thoreau's central idea in *Civil Disobedience*?
   A. the ability of government to control others
   B. the importance of trade in government
   C. the ability of people to govern themselves
   D. the importance of armies in government

Vocabulary

____ **9.** In which of these sentences is the meaning of the word *superfluous* expressed?
   A. Thoreau imagined himself buying all the farms around his town.
   B. Thoreau wanted to get all unnecessary concerns out of his life.
   C. Thoreau believed governments were best when they governed not at all.
   D. Thoreau believed in the importance of individual action.

____ **10.** Which of the following is *opposite* in meaning from the word *alacrity*?
   A. slowness
   B. laziness
   C. swiftness
   D. bitterness

Essay

11. In *Walden*, Thoreau says, "I left the woods for as good a reason as I went there. Perhaps it seemed to me that I had several more lives to live, and could not spare any more time for that one. It is remarkable how easily and insensibly we fall into a particular route, and make a beaten track for ourselves." What do you think he means by falling into "a particular route"? Why does he see doing the same thing over and over as a problem? Write a brief essay to express your opinions. Use at least two examples from *Walden* to support your opinions.

12. In *Civil Disobedience*, how does Thoreau compare governments to people, in terms of getting things done? Does he think governments are useful? Write a brief essay to express Thoreau's philosophical assumptions about government. Use at least two examples from *Civil Disobedience* to support your ideas.

13. **Thinking About the Essential Question: Essential Question: How does literature shape or reflect society?** Henry David Thoreau was an American original. His main ambition was to find a way of life free of conventional ambition— to live as far as possible from the complicating, conformist pressures of a standard career and society. In what respect does he seek to reshape society through his personal example and his overall philosophy as expressed in the excerpts from *Walden* and "Civil Disobedience"? Develop your thoughts in an essay supported by details from the selections.

***from* Walden** and ***from* Civil Disobedience** by Henry David Thoreau
Selection Test B

Critical Reading *Identify the letter of the choice that best completes the statement or answers the question.*

_____ 1. Which of these statements best reflects Thoreau's philosophical assumption as expressed in *Walden*?
A. Human beings are creatures of great complexity.
B. Building a cabin in the woods is practical and inexpensive.
C. Wealth is desirable, but spiritual happiness is also important.
D. Living a simple life close to nature lets a person concentrate on important things.

_____ 2. Which of Thoreau's philosophical assumptions is found in this passage from *Walden*?
If a man does not keep pace with his companions, perhaps it is because he hears a different drummer.
A. Nature should be loved and valued.
B. Individualism is an important value.
C. People should avoid materialism.
D. Simplicity is the best way of life.

_____ 3. What is Thoreau's main point about time in the paragraph beginning "Time is but the stream I go a-fishing in"?
A. Time is shallow, but eternity remains.
B. Time is elusive; we cannot pin it down.
C. To succeed in life, you must harness time and make it work for you.
D. Time is of the essence.

_____ 4. One aspect of Thoreau's style is to
A. begin a paragraph with a specific event and build to a general truth.
B. avoid repetition of words or ideas.
C. follow each long sentence with a short, punchy sentence.
D. ask a series of rhetorical questions.

_____ 5. How does Thoreau's style reinforce his theme of living with deliberation?
A. by relying on unusually difficult words
B. by instructing the reader to pay attention
C. by imitating a scientific report
D. by repeating his main ideas

_____ 6. What does Thoreau hope to convey with the description of the path his feet had worn to the pondside within a week?
A. Establishing habits makes daily living easier.
B. Human beings fall into dull routines all too readily.
C. Living far away from friends is good discipline.
D. Everyone should march to the same tune.

_____ 7. What message does Thoreau hope to convey with his anecdote of the strong and beautiful bug in the conclusion of *Walden*?
   A. Life can be beautiful, but it can also be dangerous.
   B. Not all bugs are ugly.
   C. Something that appears lifeless can give rise to new life.
   D. Carpenters live simple lives close to nature.

_____ 8. *Walden*'s closing image of the morning star leaves readers feeling
   A. inspired.
   B. hopeless.
   C. exhausted.
   D. argumentative.

_____ 9. What is the central idea of *Civil Disobedience*?
   A. People must overthrow the government.
   B. Trade and commerce should be strictly regulated.
   C. The fewer people who run the government, the better.
   D. Citizens should be willing to act on their opinions.

_____ 10. In *Civil Disobedience*, how does Thoreau support his view that the government is abused by powerful individuals?
   A. He compares American and foreign governments.
   B. He analyzes the structure of America's government.
   C. He cites the example of an unpopular war.
   D. He alludes to several corrupt Massachusetts politicians.

_____ 11. Thoreau's view of the war with Mexico is best described as
   A. patriotic.
   B. indifferent.
   C. critical.
   D. practical.

_____ 12. Which word best describes Thoreau's style in *Civil Disobedience*?
   A. objective
   B. repetitive
   C. scholarly
   D. casual

_____ 13. Based on *Civil Disobedience*, what can you infer about Thoreau's assumptions about political philosophy?
   A. He relies on government leaders for moral guidance.
   B. He feels it is America's destiny to spread to the Pacific Ocean.
   C. He stresses that we must all work together to accomplish great deeds.
   D. He believes that people are politically responsible for themselves.

____ 14. Which of Thoreau's philosophical assumptions is reflected in *Civil Disobedience*?
A. the individual's ability to judge the actions of government
B. nature as a model for governing harmoniously
C. democratic governments, rather than individuals, as the most effective response to people's needs
D. warfare as sometimes the only means by which oppression can be cast off and society changed

Vocabulary

____ 15. What does Thoreau mean when he describes the fences as *dilapidated*?
A. They are under construction.
B. They need to be repaired.
C. There are many fences.
D. The fences are very high.

____ 16. Which word best completes the following sentence?
Sunset in the mountains is a(n)_____ view.

A. expedient
B. sublime
C. magnanimous
D. alacritous

____ 17. Which word below can substitute for the italicized word in this sentence?
Thoreau thinks people spend too much time on *superfluous* concerns.

A. upper-class
B. unnatural
C. unnecessary
D. important

Essay

18. Based on *Walden*, what would you say that living in the woods taught Thoreau about the human spirit and the natural world? Answer this question in a short essay, and support your evaluation with details from the selection.

19. In both *Civil Disobedience* and *Walden*, Thoreau urges people to act. How would Thoreau define taking action? Does action imply physical activity? When does Thoreau think people should take action? What action does he think they should take? Using examples from the selection, write a short essay responding to these questions.

20. **Thinking About the Essential Question: How does literature shape or reflect society?** Henry David Thoreau was an American original. His main ambition was to find a way of life free of conventional ambition—to live as far as possible from the complicating, conformist pressures of a standard career and society. In what respect does he seek to reshape society through his personal example and his overall philosophy as expressed in the excerpts from *Walden* and "Civil Disobedience"? Develop your thoughts in an essay supported by details from the selections.

Unit 2: A Growing Nation
Benchmark Test 3

MULTIPLE CHOICE

Literary Analysis and Reading Skills

Read the selection. Then, answer the questions that follow.

Well, thish-yer Smiley had rat-tarriers, and chicken cocks, and tomcats and all them kind of things till you couldn't rest, and you couldn't fetch nothing for him to bet on but he'd match you. He ketched a frog one day and took him home, and said he cal'lated to educate him; and so he never done nothing for three months but set in his back yard and learn that frog to jump. And you bet you he *did* learn him, too. He'd give him a little punch behind, and the next minute you'd see that frog whirling in the air like a doughnut—see him turn one summerset, or maybe a couple if he got a good start, and come down flat-footed and all right, like a cat. He got him up so in the matter of ketching flies, and kep' him in practice so constant, that he'd nail a fly every time as fur as he could see him. Smiley said all a frog wanted was education and he could do 'most anything—and I believe him.

—from "The Celebrated Jumping Frog of Calaveras County" by Mark Twain

1. Which of these is revealed about the character of Smiley, based on the narrator's description of him?
   A. Smiley can communicate with animals.
   B. Smiley is an easy-going person.
   C. Smiley enjoys betting.
   D. Smiley loves all animals.

2. Which of these best describes the author's style in this passage?
   A. dignified and vivid
   B. comic and rambling
   C. lyrical and formal
   D. journalistic and precise

Read this stanza from a poem by William Shakespeare. Then, answer the question.

> Then to Silvia let us sing,
>   That Silvia is excelling;
> She excels each mortal thing
>   Upon the dull earth dwelling:
> To her let us garlands bring.

3. In the final line of the selection, what are the words *To her*?
   A. a metrical foot
   B. an unstressed syllable
   C. iambic pentameter
   D. a stanza

Read this passage from Edgar Allan Poe's "The Fall of the House of Usher." Then, answer the questions that follow.

During the whole of a dull, dark, and soundless day in the autumn of the year, when the clouds hung oppressively low in the heavens, I had been passing alone, on horseback, through a singularly dreary tract of country, and at length found myself, as the shades of evening drew on, within view of the melancholy House of Usher. I know not how it was—but, with the first glimpse of the building, a sense of insufferable gloom pervaded my spirit. I say insufferable; for the feeling was unrelieved by any of that half-pleasurable, because poetic, sentiment, with which the mind usually receives even the sternest natural images of the desolate or terrible.

4. The "single effect" created by this passage springs from which of the following literary elements?
   A. dialogue
   B. plot
   C. character
   D. setting

5. Which of these details is least relevant to the mood of the passage?
   A. dreary tract of country
   B. clouds hung oppressively low in the heavens
   C. insufferable gloom pervaded my spirit
   D. passing alone on horseback

Read the introduction and the stanzas of the poem. Then, answer the questions that follow.

Eldorado was an imaginary place abounding in gold, thought by sixteenth-century Spaniards to exist in America.

> Gaily bedight,
> A gallant knight,
> In sunshine and in shadow,
> Had journey long,
> Singing a song,
> In search of Eldorado.
>
> But he grew old,
> This knight so bold,
> And o'er his heart a shadow
> Fell as he found
> No spot of ground
> That looked like Eldorado.

—from "Eldorado" by Edgar Allan Poe

6. Which of these does *shadow* most likely symbolize in the first stanza of the poem?
   A. adversity
   B. dreams
   C. protection
   D. hope

7. The journey in this poem is a symbol for life. Which of these best describes this type of symbol in literature?
   A. simile
   B. theme
   C. archetype
   D. diction

8. "Eldorado" is a short poem that tells a story. What kind of poem is it?
   A. a lyric poem
   B. a narrative poem
   C. a dramatic poem
   D. a limerick

Answer the question that follows.

9. What is the defining characteristic of a parable?

   A. It teaches a lesson.
   B. It contains dialogue.
   C. It features animal characters.
   D. It is narrated in the first person.

Read the poem. Then, answer the question that follows.

Dead Men Tell No Tales

THEY say that dead men tell no tales!

Except of barges with red sails
And sailors mad for nightingales;

Except of jongleurs stretched at ease
Beside old highways through the trees;   5

Except of dying moons that break
The hearts of lads who lie awake;

Except of fortresses in shade,
And heroes crumbled and betrayed.

But dead men tell no tales, they say!   10

Except old tales that burn away
The stifling tapestries of day:

Old tales of life, of love and hate,
Of time and space, and will, and fate.

—Haniel Long

10. Which is the best summary of the theme of the poem?

    A. Dead people have no place in the memory of the living.
    B. The dead are more imaginative than the living.
    C. The dead live on in history.
    D. The dead are best forgotten.

Answer the following questions.

11. What figure of speech does the following sentence contain?

    The flower lifted its droopy head and drank eagerly.

    A. simile
    B. metaphor
    C. assonance
    D. personification

12. Which kind of graph would best show how data changes over time?

    A. line graph
    B. bar graph
    C. pictograph
    D. circle graph

13. Which of the following literary elements would be least affected by the historical period of a work of fiction?
    A. characters
    B. plot
    C. setting
    D. style

Read the passage about two sisters, Mary and Martha. Then, answer the questions that follow.

(1) One day, about the middle of November, the sisters were both at home, and sat each by her chosen window, stitching busily. (2) Sometimes Mary would stop for a minute or two, and look out across the country, as if she really took pleasure in seeing the leafless trees against the gray sky, and the band of pale yellow in the southwest, the soft pale brown of the fields and pastures, and a bronzed oak here and there against the blackish-green pine woods. (3) Martha thought it a very bleak, miserable sort of day; her window overlooked the road to the village, and hardly anybody had gone by all the afternoon. . . . (4) Mary, as usual, humbly wondered if her sister were lonely and troubled, and if she herself were half so good and tender as she ought to be to one so dear and kind.

—from "Mary and Martha," by Sarah Orne Jewett

14. When you break down sentence 2 of the selection, what is the core of sentence?
    A. Mary would stop and look out.
    B. Mary would stop and take pleasure.
    C. Mary would look out.
    D. Mary took pleasure.

15. From the details in the selection, what do you infer is a main difference between the two sisters?
    A. Mary, though content in most things, is jealous of her sister Martha's beauty and intellect.
    B. Martha is unhappy with her life; Mary is content, except that she worries about her sister.
    C. Martha loves nature and the great outdoors; Mary prefers indoor activities.
    D. Mary is shy and unfriendly; Martha is more outgoing and easier to please

Read the passage from The Innocents Abroad *by Mark Twain. Then, answer the questions that follow.*

Guides know about enough English to tangle everything up so that a man can make neither head nor tail of it. They know their story by heart—the history of every statue, painting, cathedral, or other wonder they show you. They know it and tell it as a parrot would—and if you interrupt, and throw them off the track, they have to go back and begin over again. All their lives long, they are employed in showing strange things to foreigners and listening to their bursts of admiration. It is human nature to take delight in exciting admiration. It is what prompts children to say "smart" things, and do absurd ones, and in other ways "show off" when company is present. It is what makes gossips turn out in rain and storm to go and be the first to tell a startling bit of news. Think, then, what a passion it becomes with a guide, whose privilege it is, every day, to show to strangers wonders that throw them into perfect ecstasies of admiration! He gets so that he could not by any possibility live in a soberer atmosphere. After we discovered this, we *never* went into ecstasies any more—we never admired anything—we never showed any but impassible faces and stupid indifference in the presence of the sublimest wonders a guide had to display.

16. How might a reader challenge the author's text in this selection?
    A. Evaluate Twain's choice of words in the selection.
    B. Compare Twain's opinion with that of others who have employed guides.
    C. Compare this selection with other works by Twain.
    D. Determine the author's purpose for writing the selection.

17. What detail does the author use to support his philosophy that humans "take delight in exciting admiration"?
    A. Children like to show off.
    B. Guides memorize their stories.
    C. Guides show strange things to others.
    D. People admire what guides show them.

18. Which sentence best summarizes the conclusion of the passage?
    A. The author loses his appreciation for art because of the guide.
    B. The author pities the guide and exaggerates his exclamations of wonder.
    C. The author fails to feel moved by the artwork the guide shows him.
    D. The author withholds his admiration because he questions the guide's motives.

Vocabulary

19. Based on your understanding of the prefix *ex-*, what do you do when you *extract* a tooth?
    A. You drill it.
    B. You fill it.
    C. You clean it.
    D. You pull it out.

20. Based on your understanding of the prefix *mal-*, who would most likely arouse feelings of *malice*?
    A. a friend
    B. a boss
    C. an enemy
    D. a spouse

21. Based on your understanding of the root *-voc-*, what do you do when you *vocalize* a problem?
    A. You solve it.
    B. You hide it.
    C. You speak out about it.
    D. You ignore it.

22. Based on your understanding of the root *-voc-*, what would your *advocate* do?
    A. speak up for you
    B. pay no attention to you
    C. solve your problems
    D. keep your secrets

23. Based on your understanding of the root *-flu-*, what is the meaning of *fluidity*?
    A. in a hurried manner
    B. free of self-consciousness
    C. showing great strength
    D. characterized by a flowing style

24. Based on your understanding of the prefix *ab-*, who would be most likely to *abscond* with the bank's money?
    A. a teller
    B. a thief
    C. a manager
    D. a security guard

Grammar

25. Identify the adjective clause in this sentence.

Nobody knew if it was the girl who had placed first in the race on Sunday.

A. Nobody knew

B. if it was

C. who had placed first in the race on Sunday

D. on Sunday

26. Identify the adverb clause in this sentence.

Because her pies are delicious, Maria makes them for her family on special occasions.

A. Because her pies are delicious

B. Maria makes them

C. for her family

D. on special occasions

27. Which sentence uses a past participle as an adjective?

A. The party planner was arranging a large wedding.

B. My great-great grandparents had an arranged marriage.

C. We arranged the books alphabetically by author.

D. Alyson enjoys arranging cut flowers.

28. What is the infinitive phrase in the following sentence?

Ms. Bell went to the mayor's office to complain about his treatment of the protestors.

A. to the mayor's office

B. to complain

C. about his treatment

D. of the protestors

29. What is the gerund in the following sentence?

Carlene thought that talking in a loud voice would attract Eric's attention.

A. thought   B. attract   C. talking   D. attention

30. Which comparative word or words complete the sentence?

Chimpanzees are _____ than gorillas.

A. more small   B. smallest   C. more smaller   D. smaller

31. Which word completes the sentence?

Of all the accounts of what took place, his is _____ from the truth.

A. further   B. farther   C. farthest   D. furthest

ESSAY

32. Think of a time when you made a difference in someone's life. What did you do? How did it help the person? How did the experience affect you? Write a reflective essay in which you think about this experience and help readers understand why it was important to you.

33. Write a piece of literary criticism on a story that you have read. Include a précis of a story, and then explain what you do and do not like about it.

34. Think of a character from a story or novel that provoked a strong response in you. Write a brief character study that includes a detailed description of the character and an explanation of why you find the character memorable. Write in complete sentences, using a variety of sentence structures.

Vocabulary Warm-up Word Lists

Study these words from the selections. Then, complete the activities.

Word List A

absorb [ab SORB] *v.* to suck up; to take in and incorporate; to assimilate
  It took us hours to <u>absorb</u> all the information from the lengthy chapter.

assignable [uh SYN uh buhl] *adj.* able to be given away
  In her will, she left the <u>assignable</u> parts of her estate to her favorite niece.

keepsakes [KEEP sayks] *n.* souvenirs; mementoes; heirlooms
  Mother has a trunk full of <u>keepsakes</u> in the attic.

leisure [LEE zhuhr] *n.* free time; relaxation
  Timothy uses much of his <u>leisure</u> for reading.

onset [ON set] *n.* approach; beginning
  A tickling in my throat signaled the <u>onset</u> of a cold.

portion [POR shuhn] *n.* part; section
  The dessert was so large that I could eat only a <u>portion</u> of it.

quivering [KWIV uhr ing] *adj.* shivering
  When the dog barked loudly, the cat retreated, <u>quivering</u> with fear.

wrung [RUNG] *v.* squeezed; compressed
  I <u>wrung</u> out the shirt I had washed, squeezing all the water from it.

Word List B

befel [bee FEL] *v.* happened (modern spelling **befell**)
  What fate <u>befell</u> the hero in that novel?

finite [FY nyt] *adj.* limited; able to be calculated or reckoned
  Although the speed of light is unbelievably fast, it is still <u>finite</u>.

immortality [i mor TAL i tee] *n.* eternal life
  The heroes of ancient epics often had <u>immortality</u> as their goal.

majority [muh JOR uh tee] *n.* greater part or larger number; more than half the total
  The <u>majority</u> of voters did not agree with the governor, and he was not re-elected.

strove [STROHV] *v.* tried very hard; struggled
  Each team <u>strove</u> hard for victory, but the outcome of the game was a tie score.

surmised [suhr MYZD] *v.* guessed; made an inference
  From his remarks, we <u>surmised</u> that Keith was not in favor of our proposal.

unveil [un VAYL] *v.* to uncover; to reveal
  The museum director planned to <u>unveil</u> a dramatic new painting.

valves [VALVZ] *n.* gates or devices regulating the flow of a liquid
  The <u>valves</u> in that automobile engine need regular lubrication.

Name _____ Date _____

Emily Dickinson's Poetry
Vocabulary Warm-up Exercises

Exercise A *Fill in the blanks, using each word from Word List A only once.*

Elaine had promised herself that, when she had a day of [1] _____, she

would do some gardening. All winter, she had tried to [2] _____

all the tips she could from gardening magazines. She had carefully charted

each [3] _____ of the ground, calculating what part was

[4] _____ to rose bushes and how much for vegetables and herbs.

On Saturday morning, she gathered her gardening tools, some of which were

[5] _____ left her by her grandmother. The weather was sunny and still:

not a leaf was shaking or [6] _____ on the trees. Elaine worked all day

long—digging, planting, and watering. With the [7] _____ of twilight, she

had the work done. She felt happy but [8] _____ out with fatigue.

Exercise B *Revise each sentence so that the underlined vocabulary word is logical. Be sure to keep the vocabulary word in your revision.*

Example: Because the work was so <u>arduous</u>, we completed it quickly and easily.
Because the work was so <u>arduous</u>, we had a hard time completing it.

1. Two setbacks <u>befell</u> James, and he was relieved to have avoided them.

_____

2. Because our resources are <u>finite</u>, we can pledge any amount of money for that cause.

_____

3. The <u>immortality</u> of the Greek gods was one way in which they resembled humans.

_____

4. The election was close, and the loser received a very small <u>majority</u> of votes.

_____

5. In all his undertakings, Tom <u>strove</u> hard, putting in minimum effort.

_____

6. Unwilling to use an educated guess, Phil <u>surmised</u> the ending from hints in the story.

_____

7. In favor of concealing the new painting, the museum director prepared to <u>unveil</u> it.

_____

8. <u>Valves</u> are used to heat the water in those pipes.

_____

Name _____   Date _____

Emily Dickinson's Poetry
Reading Warm-up A

Read the following passage. Pay special attention to the underlined words. Then, read it again, and complete the activities. Use a separate sheet of paper for your written answers.

Cathy often finished her homework early. Most nights she had an hour or two of <u>leisure</u> before dinner. Sometimes she played with her baby sister Betsy or read stories to the little girl—usually fairy tales that left Betsy <u>quivering</u> with delight.

At other times Cathy would write in her journal. She always reserved a <u>portion</u> of each journal page for notes about subjects for poems. She would fill this section with ideas she had trained herself to <u>absorb</u> during the day, such as sensory images she'd accumulated on the school bus, in the cafeteria, or on the playing field. Cathy also got ideas for poems from short stories she read in English class. She felt that each fictional character she encountered in a story should be <u>assignable</u> to a poem. Perhaps she might use the character in a story poem. Maybe she would write a lyric poem using the character as the speaker.

Now that it was late fall, with the <u>onset</u> of winter not far off, Cathy wanted to increase the rate at which she wrote notes. During the winter, when the weather was bad, she would stay indoors upstairs at her little desk, depending on the notes to create poetry.

Cathy had heard from her mother that her grandmother, Hetty Pierce, had followed this same system. Some of Hetty's poems, scribbled on old envelopes and the back of shopping lists, had survived and were treasured in the family as <u>keepsakes</u>. These poems dated from the days of the Great Depression and World War II, a difficult time when Hetty had <u>wrung</u> beautiful verse out of the challenges of her life experience. Cathy felt as if she were following in Hetty's footsteps. She knew that poetry would always be a close companion, wherever her life might lead.

1. Underline the words in this sentence and the previous one that give a clue to the meaning of <u>leisure</u>. Use the word *leisure* in an original sentence.

2. Circle the words in this sentence that give a clue to the meaning of <u>quivering</u>. What is a synonym for *quivering*?

3. Underline the words in this sentence and the next that give a clue to the meaning of <u>portion</u>. What is a synonym for *portion*?

4. Circle the word that offers a clue to the meaning of <u>absorb</u> here. What are two synonyms for the word *absorb*?

5. Circle the words in this sentence and the next two sentences that offer clues to the meaning of <u>assignable</u>. What are a verb and a noun related to this adjective?

6. Underline the words in this sentence that give a clue to the meaning of <u>onset</u>. What are two synonyms for *onset*?

7. Circle the words in this sentence that give a clue to the meaning of <u>keepsakes</u>. Use the word *keepsakes* in an original sentence.

8. Underline the words in this sentence hinting at the meaning of <u>wrung</u>. What is a synonym for *wrung*?

Name _____ Date _____

Emily Dickinson's Poetry
Reading Warm-up B

Read the following passage. Pay special attention to the underlined words. Then, read it again, and complete the activities. Use a separate sheet of paper for your written answers.

In her poetry, Emily Dickinson <u>strove</u> to create a distinctive style, and most readers will probably agree that she succeeded brilliantly in this effort. What is the hallmark of this style? In the <u>majority</u> of Dickinson's poems, it is the use of surprise. There are very few Dickinson poems that are entirely predictable.

Surprises in Dickinson's poetry come in a number of forms. By combining slant or approximate rhyme with exact rhyme, for example, she keeps the reader guessing about the sound of the poem. Another important Dickinson technique is sudden changes in rhythm. Try reading "Water, is taught by thirst" aloud, for example. If you think you have <u>surmised</u>, or inferred, how the poem ought to unfold, you may be surprised by the unexpected variations Dickinson uses to hold the reader's attention. Dickinson also uses surprising word choices, such as the noun <u>valves</u> in the next-to-last line of "The Soul selects her own Society." This word suggests mechanical devices, as if the soul had water spigots or faucets that could be turned on or off.

Dickinson also exploits surprises in the speaker's point of view. In several of her poems, for example, we learn that death <u>befell</u> the speaker before the poem opens. The emotions the speaker conveys are either linked to the moment of death, or they are given from the perspective of someone approaching the threshold of <u>immortality</u>.

Finally, Dickinson makes extensive use of paradoxes, or apparent contradictions. A good example is the phrase *finite infinity* at the close of "There is a solitude of space." How can unlimited space, time, or distance be <u>finite</u>, or limited? Surprising paradoxes such as this one often help <u>unveil</u>, or reveal, Dickinson's keenly observant themes about human nature and behavior.

1. Underline the words in this sentence that give a clue to the meaning of <u>strove</u>. Use the word **strove** in an original sentence.

2. Circle the words in this sentence and the next that hint at the meaning of <u>majority</u>. Use a word meaning the opposite of **majority** in a sentence of your own.

3. Underline the word in this sentence hinting at the meaning of <u>surmised</u>. What is a synonym for **surmised**?

4. Underline the words in this sentence and the next that give a clue to the meaning of <u>valves</u>.

5. Circle the words in this sentence that give a clue to the meaning of <u>befell</u>. What is a synonym for **befell**?

6. Underline the words in this sentence that hint at the meaning of <u>immortality</u>. Use a word meaning the opposite of **immortality** in an original sentence.

7. Underline the word in this sentence that gives a clue to the meaning of <u>finite</u>. What is a synonym for **finite**?

8. Circle the word in this sentence that hints at the meaning of the word <u>unveil</u>. What are two antonyms for **unveil**?

Name _____ Date _____

Emily Dickinson's Poetry
Literary Analysis: Rhyme and Paradox

Emily Dickinson plays with rhyme in her poetry, using several different types. She uses **exact rhyme,** in which two or more words have the identical vowel and final consonant sounds in their last stressed syllables. For example, *pound* and *sound* rhyme exactly, as do *brain* and *contain.* She also uses **slant rhyme,** in which the final sounds are similar but not identical. For example, *pond* and *sound* are slant rhymes, as are *brain* and *frame.* In addition, Dickinson uses **internal rhyme,** in which words within a single line of poetry rhyme with each other.

Another technique that Dickinson uses to keep her poetry interesting is **paradox,** or seemingly contradictory statements that actually present a truth. For example, when she says "The Brain—is wider than the Sky," it seems impossible. However, when you realize the capacity of the brain, you can see the truth in the statement.

A. DIRECTIONS: *On the lines after each passage from Dickinson's poetry, identify the words that rhyme, and indicate whether the rhymes are exact slant, or internal.*

1. My life closed twice before its close—
   It yet remains to see
   If Immortality unveil
   A third event to me.

   _____

2. Or rather—He passed Us—
   The Dews grew quivering and chill—
   For only Gossamer, my Gown—
   My Tippet—only Tulle—

   _____

3. None may teach it—Any—
   'Tis the Seal Despair—
   An imperial affliction
   Sent us of the Air—

   _____

4. I heard a Fly buzz—when I died—

   _____

B. DIRECTIONS: *Explain the paradox in this passage:*

   My life closed twice before its close—

   _____

   _____

Name _____ Date _____

Reading Strategy: Rereading to Monitor and Repair Comprehension

Emily Dickinson's poetry can sometimes be confusing because she often omits words that are expected to be understood. She also sometimes inverts the usual word order of a sentence. A good way to **monitor and repair your comprehension** of confusing passages is to **reread** the material. As you do so, mentally fill in the words that seem to be missing, or put the words in their usual order. This can lead you to the probable meaning of the passage.

DIRECTIONS: *Complete this chart by writing your interpretation of each passage. The first one is done for you.*

Original Line	Probable Meaning
1. For only Gossamer, my Gown	My gown was made of only gossamer
2. Since then—'tis Centuries—and yet / Feels shorter than the Day / I first surmised the Horses Heads / Were toward Eternity—	
3. The Brain is deeper than the sea— / For—hold them—Blue to Blue—The one the other will absorb / As Sponges—Buckets do—	
4. There is a solitude of space / A solitude of sea / A solitude of death, but these / Society shall be	

Emily Dickinson's Poetry
Vocabulary Builder

Using the Root -finis-

A. DIRECTIONS: *The root -finis-, often shortened to -fin-, means "end" or "limit." On the lines provided, explain how the meaning of the word is conveyed in each of the following words.*

1. define _____
_____

2. refinish _____
_____

3. finale _____
_____

Using the Word List

affliction   ample   eternity   finite   infinity   interposed   surmised

B. DIRECTIONS: *On the line provided, write the word from the Word List that best completes each sentence.*

1. From her expression, I _____ that she was not happy to see me.
2. There had to be an end to the tunnel, but it seemed to stretch into _____.
3. An immortal god or goddess lives for all _____.
4. Only a _____ number of ways existed to solve the problem.
5. After cooking all day, Sophie had _____ amounts of food for her many guests.
6. Don developed asthma at a young age, and this _____ limited his activities.
7. A moth _____ between my eyes and the computer screen.

C. DIRECTIONS: *On the line, write the letter of the pair of words that expresses a relationship most like the pair in capital letters.*

___ 1. FINITE : INFINITY ::
    A. fatal : fate
    B. endless : eternity
    C. mortal : immortality
    D. significant : importance

___ 2. AMPLE : PLENTIFUL ::
    A. much : little
    B. enough : inadequate
    C. food : drink
    D. slight : scarce

___ 3. SURMISED : SPECULATION ::
    A. anticipated : compliment
    B. forewarned : prediction
    C. flattered : insult
    D. pampered : aid

___ 4. AFFLICTION : PNEUMONIA ::
    A. thoughtful : serious
    B. symptom : cough
    C. ancient : old
    D. depressed : jolly

Name _____ Date _____

Emily Dickinson's Poetry
Support for Writing

As you search Emily Dickinson's poetry for references to boundlessness, the infinite, and things without limit, keep track of your findings in the chart below.

Name of Poem	Detail referring to boundlessness, the infinite, or things without limit

On the lines below, write a general statement about Dickinson's views about the infinite. Put a check next to the details in your chart that best support this statement. Then, on a separate page, write a draft of your blog entry. Begin with your general statement, and support that statement with details from the poems. Be sure to punctuate each direct quotation correctly, and cite the poem in which it appears.

_____

_____

Emily Dickinson's Poetry
Enrichment: Art

Poets often explore the same topics and themes in several different poems. Emily Dickinson frequently returns to topics such as nature, solitude, and death. Consequently, some of the images that she found most striking appear in more than one poem. Each time, the image is approached from a different angle or used in a different way. In the poems in your text, Dickinson writes about solitude several times. Here are two examples:

There is a solitude of space
A solitude of sea
A solitude of death, but these
Society shall be
Compared with that profounder site
That polar privacy
A soul admitted to itself—
Finite Infinity.

The Soul selects her own Society—
Then—shuts the Door—
To her divine Majority—
Present no more—. . .

In the first selection, Dickinson writes about solitude as if it were the same as limitless empty space. In the second selection, though, she writes about solitude as if it meant being trapped in a limited space, behind a door.

DIRECTIONS: *Three of the poems by Emily Dickinson in your textbook are accompanied by paintings. Choose two of these paintings. Explain how each painting illustrates an image in the poem it accompanies. Then, consider whether these paintings could be used to illustrate other images in other poems by Emily Dickinson. Write the name of one other poem that each painting might illustrate, and explain how this painting relates to messages and themes that appear throughout Dickinson's work. Use the space below to organize your work.*

1. Name of painting: _____

   Poem it illustrates: _____

   Image the picture illustrates: _____

   Another poem the painting could illustrate: _____

   How the painting relates to Dickinson's messages and themes: _____

   _____

   _____

2. Name of painting: _____

   Poem it illustrates: _____

   Image the picture illustrates: _____

   Another poem the painting could illustrate: _____

   How the painting relates to Dickinson's messages and themes: _____

   _____

   _____

The Poetry of Emily Dickinson
Open-Book Test

Short Answer *Write your responses to the questions in this section on the lines provided.*

1. In "Because I could not stop for Death," Dickinson uses several example of slant rhymes, pairs of words that do not rhyme exactly but rhyme approximately. Cite three examples of pairs of slant rhymes from the poem.

   _____

   _____

2. In the sixth stanza of "Because I could not stop for Death," the poet uses a paradox, a statement that seems contradictory but actually presents a truth. Identify the paradox and explain the truth the poet is communicating.

   _____

   _____

   _____

   _____

3. Reread the final stanza of "Because I could not stop for Death," and find the word *surmised*. Recall all the things the speaker experienced after she got into Death's carriage, and use these as clues to the meaning of *surmised*. Then restate the third line of the stanza using a word with a similar meaning for the word *surmised*.

   _____

   _____

4. Reread "I heard a Fly buzz - when I died." What does the speaker's experience of the fly seem to communicate?

   _____

   _____

5. In "There's a certain slant of light," Dickinson uses a visual image to capture a larger idea. Reread the poem and identify the image. Then explain the meaning the poet communicates with the image.

   _____

   _____

   _____

6. Reread "My life closed twice before its close." Based on the context of the poem, what do you think the poet means by "Parting is all we know of heaven./And all we need of hell?"

   _____

   _____

   _____

7. Choose examples of pairs of slant rhymes (approximate) or exact (precise) rhymes from "The Soul selects her own Society." Enter the slant rhymes on the left side and the exact rhymes on the right side of the graphic organizer below. Then write a sentence to explain why you think a poet uses slant rhymes.

Slant Rhymes	Exact Rhymes

8. Reread "The Brain—is wider than the Sky." Choose one of the three paradoxes in the poem. Why does the paradox seem contradictory? What truth is the poet communicating with the paradox you chose?

_____

_____

_____

_____

9. In "There is a solitude of space," what does Dickinson suggest about the depth of one's soul compared to other experiences of vastness? What is Dickinson's attitude about the soul?

_____

_____

_____

_____

10. In "Water, is taught by thirst," Dickinson constructs her thoughts the same way in each line. How does she communicate her ideas? What is she saying?

_____

_____

_____

Essay

Write an extended response to the question of your choice or to the question or questions your teacher assigns you.

11. Choose one:

   In the poem "Because I could not stop for Death," the poet uses the word *Death* only once. However, there are several images in the poem that imply that she is talking about death. Write a brief essay to discuss how the images in the poem imply a journey to death. Cite at least three specific images.

   What common life experience is going on in "I heard a Fly buzz—when I died"? Write a brief essay to describe what you think is occurring.

12. Choose one:

In "There's a certain slant of light," what is the poet's view of the element of light? Write a brief essay to characterize her view of this element of the natural world and to explain what the image means.

In "The Soul selects her own Society," what does Dickinson seem to be saying about the attitudes of the world and popularity? Write a brief essay to address this question using details from the poem.

13. Reread the background information about Emily Dickinson. With this understanding of her personality in mind, write a brief essay about how her poetry reveals her personality. Choose examples from her poetry to justify your opinion.

14. **Thinking About the Essential Question: What makes American Literature American?** Plain speaking and plain writing are American characteristics going back to Puritan New England. In a brief essay, examine the extent to which Dickinson too employs a plain style in her poetry. Discuss her ideas and the techniques she uses to present them.

Oral Response

15. Go back to question 2, 5, 8, or 10 or to the question your teacher assigns to you. Take a few minutes to expand your answers and prepare an oral response. Find additional details in the selections that will support your points. If necessary, make notes to guide your response.

Emily Dickinson's Poetry
Selection Test A

Critical Reading *Identify the letter of the choice that best answers the question.*

___ 1. Who are some of the important characters in the carriage in "Because I could not stop for Death—"?

    I. Death

    II. the speaker

    III. Children

    IV. A man

  A. I and III

  B. II and IV

  C. I and IV

  D. I and II

___ 2. In "Because I could not stop for Death—", how does the poet represent Death?

  A. as an undertaker in a graveyard

  B. as a teacher at a children's school

  C. as a kind, polite gentleman

  D. as a fast-driving carriage owner

___ 3. In the following stanza from "I heard a Fly buzz—when I died—," which words form a slant rhyme?

> The Eyes around—had wrung them dry— / And Breaths were gathering firm / For that last Onset—when the King / Be witnessed—in the Room—

  A. *dry* and *firm*

  B. *King* and *Room*

  C. *dry* and *King*

  D. *firm* and *Room*

___ 4. Which stage of life does the late-afternoon winter light represent in "There's a certain Slant of light,"?

  A. when a person is newly born

  B. when a person thinks of death

  C. when a person becomes an adult

  D. when a person thinks of family

____ 5. In the following stanza from "The Soul selects her own Society," which pair of words forms a slant rhyme?

> Unmoved—she notes the Chariots—pausing— / At her low Gate— / Unmoved—an Emperor be kneeling / Upon her Mat—

    A. *pausing* and *Gate*

    B. *pausing* and *Mat*

    C. *Gate* and *Mat*

    D. *Gate* and *kneeling*

____ 6. What is the paradox in these lines from "The Brain—is wider than the Sky"?

> The Brain—is wider than the Sky—/For—put them side by side—/The one the other will contain/With ease—and You—beside—

    A. The brain is like an empty space filled with millions of stars.

    B. An intelligent person can describe the constellations in the sky.

    C. The brain can hold and understand ideas bigger than the sky.

    D. The brain may be small, but it is the same shape as the sky.

____ 7. In the following stanza from "The Brain—is wider than the Sky—," which words create an exact rhyme?

> The Brain is deeper than the sea— / For—hold them—Blue to Blue— / The one the other will absorb— / As Sponges—Buckets—do—

    A. *sea* and *Blue*

    B. *Blue* and *absorb*

    C. *Blue* and *do*

    D. *absorb* and *do*

____ 8. After rereading to clarify the elliptical phrasing, what can you conclude is the message of "Water, is taught by thirst"?

    A. Opposites teach about each other.

    B. Thirsty people long for water.

    C. Life has difficult challenges.

    D. Battles and war are unnecessary.

Vocabulary

____ 9. In which sentence is the meaning of the word *oppresses* expressed?

    A. The poet writes about how the death of loved ones weighs on her.

    B. She composes several poems about the nature of death.

    C. The poet has a rich imagination that shows in her poetry.

    D. Though she has few visitors, she is close to her family.

___ 10. In which sentence is the word *surmised* used correctly?

    A. When she started crying, we *surmised* that she was upset.

    B. The poet *surmised* us with her insights.

    C. He *surmised* the report so we did not have to read it all.

    D. The explorers *surmised* the landscape from the mountaintop.

Essay

11. In Dickinson's poem "The Soul selects her own Society," she uses a combination of exact rhyme and slant rhyme. How do you think slant rhyme affects the reader? In a brief essay, analyze the poem explaining the rhymes and how the use of slant rhyme in this poem surprises the reader and emphasizes the poet's meaning.

12. The poem "Water is taught by thirst" uses pairs of opposite words to show the paradox that knowledge of something is gained by knowing its opposite. What other examples could you use to show the value of paradoxical pairs of words? Think about the pairs used in the poem: water and thirst, land and oceans, or peace and battles. Think about how we could not appreciate certain experiences without understanding opposite experiences. Write a brief poem using some of the following pairs to show the paradox of how humans learn. You may also use pairs of your own choosing.

food and hunger
sleep and wakefulness
sorrow and joy
night and sunrise

13. **Thinking About the Essential Question: What makes American literature American?** Individualism means being your own person and not necessarily following the crowd. It is an important American value found in everything from Franklin's *Autobiography* and Thoreau's *Walden* to the stories of western heroes and big-city detectives told in American movies and television. Write a brief essay about the message of individualism in the poems "The Soul selects its own Society" and "There is a solitude of space." Explain what the poems say about individualism, and also explain how these ideas relate to what you have learned about Emily Dickinson's own life.

Emily Dickinson's Poetry
Selection Test B

Critical Reading *Identify the letter of the choice that best completes the statement or answers the question.*

_____ 1. In "I heard a Fly buzz—when I died—," why is there a stillness in the room?
   A. The people in the room have stopped talking in order to listen to the fly.
   B. The people in the room are waiting for the speaker to make her will.
   C. The people in the room are waiting for the speaker's final moment.
   D. The storm outdoors has momentarily ceased its "heaves."

_____ 2. In the following stanza from "I heard a Fly buzz—when I died—," which words create slant rhyme?

   I heard a Fly buzz—when I died— / The Stillness in the Room / Was like the Stillness in the Air— / Between the Heaves of Storm—

   A. *Air* and *Storm*
   B. *Room* and *Storm*
   C. *died* and *Room*
   D. *died* and *Air*

_____ 3. Reread these lines from "Because I could not stop for Death." Which choice below best clarifies the lines?

   The Dews drew quivering and chill—/For only Gossamer, my Gown—/My Tippet—only Tulle—

   A. The dews chilled me and caused shivering, because my gown was only gossamer and my tippet was only tulle.
   B. The dews quivered and chilled my gossamer gown and my tulle tippet.
   C. The dews caused quivering and chill, and I only wore Gossamer and Tulle.
   D. The chill caused dews and made me quiver because of my gossamer gown and tulle tippet.

_____ 4. In "Because I could not stop for Death—," Death is personified as
   A. a polite gentleman.
   B. a rough and harried carriage driver.
   C. a weary gravedigger.
   D. a well-informed tour guide.

_____ 5. Which of these statements best expresses the central message of "My life closed twice before its close—"?
   A. Our lives are divided into three parts, and death is the last one.
   B. Parting is heavenly when you are glad to be rid of someone but hellish when you know you will miss the person.
   C. Parting may be the closest we come in life to understanding death.
   D. Death is followed by immortality.

____ 6. What is the chief effect of the slant rhyme in this final stanza from "The Soul selects her own Society—"?

I've known her—from an ample nation— / Choose One— / Then—close the Valves of her attention— / Like Stone—

A. It creates a harmony that stresses how well the speaker knows the soul.
B. It creates a disharmony that suggests strife in the ample nation.
C. It creates a disharmony that echoes the unsociable actions of the soul.
D. It captures the sound of the running water that the valves imply.

____ 7. Which of these sentences best summarizes "There's a certain Slant of light"?
A. An afternoon church service depresses the speaker.
B. The speaker expresses a wish to die.
C. A winter day reminds the speaker of her mortality.
D. The speaker is too depressed to go outside.

____ 8. What idea does the slant rhyme emphasize in these lines from "I heard a Fly buzz—when I died"?

The Eyes around—had wrung them dry—/And Breaths were gathering firm/For that last Onset—when the King/Be witnessed—in the Room—

A. Death is coming into the room.
B. People have gathered around the death bed.
C. People had cried until their eyes were dry.
D. People are preparing for a visit from the King.

____ 9. Which statement best paraphrases the central comparison in "There is a solitude of space"?
A. Compared to the solitude of death, the solitude of space and sea are like society.
B. Compared to the solitude of a soul admitted to itself, the solitude of space, sea, and death are like society.
C. Compared to the solitude of space, sea, and death, living in society is a more restrictive form of solitude.
D. Compared to the solitude of space and sea, the solitude of death is more profound.

____ 10. What is the paradox in the poem "The Brain—is wider than the Sky—"?
A. The brain is physically larger than any other animal's brain.
B. The brain, though small, can hold ideas bigger than the sky.
C. The brain is like an empty space filled with millions of stars.
D. Although the brain is small, it is as blue as the sea and the sky.

____ 11. In these lines from "Water, is taught by thirst," which words provide slant rhyme?

Water, is taught by thirst. / Land—by the Oceans passed. / Transport—by throe— / Peace—by its battles told— / Love, by Memorial Mold— / Birds, by the Snow.

A. *thirst* and *passed*
B. *throe* and *told*
C. *told* and *Mold*
D. *throe* and *Snow*

_____ 12. In "Water, is taught by thirst," which of the following choices best clarifies the line "Birds, by the Snow"? Reread the title to help you understand this line.
   A. Birds are taught to live by snow.
   B. Birds learn to take bird baths in the snow.
   C. We learn about birds when we see them clearly in the snow.
   D. We learn how birds live by seeing them drink melted snow.

_____ 13. Which of the following poems focuses most strongly on a lesson that can be learned from nature?
   A. "There is a solitude of space"
   B. "Because I could not stop for Death—"
   C. "My life closed twice before its close—"
   D. "There's a certain Slant of light"

Vocabulary

_____ 14. Which word below is the best replacement for *surmised* in the lines "I first *surmised* the Horses Heads / Were toward Eternity—"?
   A. guessed   C. taught
   B. screamed   D. whispered

_____ 15. Where would you most likely see a *cornice*?
   A. on a tulle gown   C. on a carriage
   B. on a building   D. on a gravestone

_____ 16. Which of these is considered an *affliction*?
   A. health.   B. oceans.   C. nature   D. disease

_____ 17. Which word best completes the following sentence?
      Birds need ____ food for the winter.
   A. finite   B. ample   C. infinite   D. oppressed

Essay

18. Consider the three Dickinson poems in your text that focus most on the subject of death: "I heard a Fly buzz—when I died—," "Because I could not stop for Death—," and "My life closed twice before its close—." Do you think Dickinson feared death? Why or why not? Write an essay explaining your answer.

19. Write an essay exploring the identity of the teachers and the lessons being taught in "Water, is taught by thirst." First, identify and compare the "teachers" in the poem. Then analyze the relationship between each teacher and the lesson taught, and determine what makes the relationships analogous to each other. Finally, discuss what you feel is the central message of the poem.

20. **Thinking About the Essential Question: What makes American literature American?** Plain speaking and plain writing are American Characteristics going back to Puritan New England. In a brief essay, examine the extent to which Dickinson too employs a plain style in her poetry. Discuss her ideas and the techniques she uses to present them.

Vocabulary Warm-up Word Lists

Study these words from the selections. Then, complete the activities.

Word List A

applause [uh PLAWZ] *n.* approval or praise, shown by clapping hands
   The audience burst out into loud <u>applause</u> at the end of the play.

astronomer [uh STRAHN uh muhr] *n.* scientist who studies the heavenly bodies
   The <u>astronomer</u>'s specialty was the study of comets.

intermission [in ter MISH uhn] *n.* pause
   Between the play's two acts there was a 15-minute <u>intermission</u>.

lectured [LEK chuhrd] *v.* delivered a talk or analysis in public
   Professor Robinson <u>lectured</u> every Thursday morning to his economics class.

measureless [MEZH uhr luhs] *adj.* without measure or number; infinite
   Before Columbus crossed the Atlantic, the ocean must have seemed <u>measureless</u>.

mechanics [muh KAN iks] *n.* workers skilled in using tools
   Work on the space shuttle requires highly skilled, specialized <u>mechanics</u>.

moist [MOYST] *adj.* slightly wet; damp
   The cushions on the patio were <u>moist</u> this morning from last night's rain.

venturing [VEN churh ing] *v.* undertaking a risk
   The explorers were <u>venturing</u> into unknown territory.

Word List B

abeyance [uh BAY uhns] *n.* temporary suspension
   Our vacation plans are in <u>abeyance</u> due to the airline strike.

filament [FIL uh muhnt] *n.* very slender thread or fiber
   The <u>filament</u> generated by the spider shimmered in the early-morning sunlight.

gossamer [GAHS uh muhr] *adj.* made of very thin, soft, filmy cloth
   The bride wore a <u>gossamer</u> veil, and her face could be seen clearly behind it.

isolated [EYE suh layt uhd] *adj.* solitary; alone
   The air force base was located on an <u>isolated</u> island that had few visitors.

melodious [muh LOH dee uhs] *adj.* tuneful
   At the beginning of the musical, the orchestra struck up a <u>melodious</u> tune.

promontory [PRAHM uhn tor ee] *n.* crag; rocky outcropping
   On the dramatic <u>promontory</u> of the cliff, an eagle stood, surveying the ocean.

unaccountable [un uh KOUNT uh buhl] *adj.* not able to be explained; strange
   Hugo was <u>unaccountable</u> for his actions.

vacant [VAY kuhnt] *adj.* empty
   The apartment building was <u>vacant</u>, awaiting demolition.

Name _____ Date _____

Walt Whitman's Poetry
Vocabulary Warm-up Exercises

Exercise A *Fill in the blanks, using each word from Word List A only once.*

Dr. Conway taught one of the core science courses in the continuing education program
for adults at the state college. A noted [1] _____, he had discovered several comets, and one was even named after him. He realized that many of his students
were [2] _____ into scientific subjects for the first time. Some of them, in
fact, were auto [3] _____, working for credits toward a college degree.
Many of them were probably so nervous that their palms were [4] _____.
So, when he [5] _____, Dr. Conway was careful to keep his delivery simple and clear. He often paused for a(n) [6] _____, to see if any of his
points were unclear. His patience with the students was [7] _____. For
their part, they appreciated his help and concern, and more than one of his lectures
ended with [8] _____.

Exercise B *Decide whether each statement below is true or false. Circle T or F, and explain
your answer.*

1. If you hold a project in *abeyance,* you suspend it temporarily.
   T / F _____

2. A *filament* is a thick strand of fiber.
   T / F _____

3. A garment made of *gossamer* cloth might be transparent.
   T / F _____

4. If people feel *isolated,* they may experience loneliness and sadness.
   T / F _____

5. A *melodious* tune appeals because it can be easily hummed or sung.
   T / F _____

6. A *promontory* may be located by digging deep down into the earth.
   T / F _____

7. If an explanation is *unaccountable,* it is logical and credible.
   T / F _____

8. If none of the motel rooms are *vacant,* it will not be possible to make a reservation.
   T / F _____

Name _____ Date _____

Read the following passage. Pay special attention to the underlined words. Then, read it again, and complete the activities. Use a separate sheet of paper for your written answers.

Sam stayed in his bedroom all afternoon, practicing for a poetry recitation at school. His teacher had assigned him Whitman's poem "When I Heard the Learn'd Astronomer." The more Sam recited the poem, the more he liked it. Still, he knew that poetry recitals were often boring, and he felt he would be nervous, <u>venturing</u> onto a stage with just a poem to keep everyone's attention.

To make matters worse, he kept imagining the situation described in the poem itself. He was the somber <u>astronomer</u> explaining the movements of the planets and stars with a series of charts. Instead of a wonder or mystery, the night sky became like the inside of a car engine, a bunch of objects to be tinkered with by <u>mechanics</u>. As he recited the poem, Sam could feel the atmosphere in the auditorium: the dim light, the air made <u>moist</u> by the breath of a few hundred people. He imagined just sitting there, unable to voice an opinion, as the astronomer <u>lectured</u> the crowd.

Wouldn't everyone feel just as bored tomorrow when Sam gave his reading? He imagined himself onstage, yelling out the words, while his fellow students yawned and waited for <u>intermission</u>, when they could leave the auditorium for a few minutes of fresh air. When he came to the end, they might clap a little, but the <u>applause</u> would be insincere.

How could he get across the real point of the poem, which was that the world and everything in it was fascinating? Inside a school auditorium, would anyone really be able to picture the night sky that the poem described, its mystery and its <u>measureless</u> size?

Probably not, Sam guessed, but when he looked at the poem again, he still liked it. All he could do was let it speak for itself.

1. Underline the words in this sentence that give a clue to the meaning of <u>venturing</u>. Use the word **venturing** in a sentence of your own.

2. Circle the words in this sentence that give a clue to the meaning of <u>astronomer</u>. What is an adjective related to this word?

3. Underline the words that give a clue to the meaning of <u>mechanics</u>. Use this word in an original sentence.

4. Circle the words that offer a clue to the meaning of <u>moist</u> here. Use a word meaning the opposite of **moist** in a sentence of your own.

5. Circle the words in this sentence that offer clues to the meaning of <u>lectured</u>. What is a synonym of **lectured**?

6. Underline the words in this sentence that give a clue to the meaning of <u>intermission</u>. What are two synonyms for **intermission**?

7. Circle the words in this sentence that give a clue to the meaning of <u>applause</u>. Use the word **applause** in an original sentence.

8. Underline the words in this sentence hinting at the meaning of <u>measureless</u>. What are two synonyms for **measureless**?

Name _____ Date _____

Walt Whitman's Poetry
Reading Warm-up B

Read the following passage. Pay special attention to the underlined words. Then, read it again, and complete the activities. Use a separate sheet of paper for your written answers.

Walt Whitman published his landmark work *Leaves of Grass* in 1855. For this poet, however, no work was ever really finished; it was held in <u>abeyance</u>, subject to periodic revision. For nearly forty years, Whitman brought out successive editions of *Leaves of Grass*, and the book became like a <u>filament</u>, a long and winding thread that recorded the poet's stages of development.

Work on *Leaves of Grass* did not leave Whitman <u>isolated</u>, focusing only on one priority. Whitman engaged his numerous talents in many different fields. In late 1862, for example, he heard that his younger brother George had been wounded at the Battle of Antietam; to be near him, Whitman traveled to a Washington hospital.

Civil War hospitals were scenes of <u>unaccountable</u> chaos, confusion, and misery. According to one officer, the Civil War was fought "at the end of the medical middle ages." Knowledge about sanitation, proper nutrition, and the causes of infection was <u>gossamer</u>-thin. Two thousand wounded men a day were pouring into Washington hospitals, and the beds in them were never <u>vacant</u>.

Whitman was so shocked by conditions that he decided to move to Washington to become a hospital volunteer, and for the next two years, he devoted his life to supporting the wounded men. He talked to the soldiers about their battle experiences; indeed, perhaps one of Whitman's most valuable services was as a listener to these lonely, suffering soldiers.

Somehow, Whitman found the inspiration to create tuneful verse out of his hospital work in the often <u>melodious</u> poetry collection *Drum-Taps*, published in 1865. Although he had maintained that "the real war will never get in the books," his Civil War poems reveal him as a prophet, or seer. He sits on a <u>promontory</u>, or rocky outcropping, surveying the battlefields and revealing their glory and terror in a realistic, memorable vision.

1. Underline the words in this sentence that give a clue to the meaning of abeyance. Use the word *abeyance* in an original sentence.

2. Circle the words in this sentence that give a clue to the meaning of filament. Briefly explain the simile the writer uses in this sentence.

3. Underline the words in this sentence hinting at the meaning of isolated. What are two synonyms for the word *isolated*?

4. Underline the words in this sentence that give a clue to the meaning of unaccountable. What is an antonym for this word?

5. Circle the words in this and the previous sentence that give a clue to the meaning of gossamer. Is this word used literally or figuratively here?

6. Underline the words in this sentence that hint at the meaning of vacant. Use a word meaning the opposite of *vacant* in a sentence of your own.

7. Underline the word in this sentence that gives a clue to the meaning of melodious. What is a synonym for *melodious*?

8. Circle the words in this sentence that hint at the meaning of the word promontory.

Name _____ Date _____

Walt Whitman's Poetry
Literary Analysis: American Epic Poetry

Walt Whitman is the inventor of a new brand of poetry: **American epic poetry.** Unlike traditional epic poetry, which features an ambitious and untouchable hero, Whitman's brand celebrates the common person and acknowledges that all human beings have a spiritual kinship with one another. Rather than focusing on the story of a single hero's quest, Whitman focuses on the interconnectedness of all humanity.

DIRECTIONS: *For each of the following passages from Whitman's poetry, explain how it exemplifies American epic poetry.*

1. And what I assume you shall assume, / For every atom belonging to me as good belongs to you. _____
   _____
   _____

2. My tongue, every atom of my blood, formed from this soil, this air, / Born here of parents born here from parents the same, and their parents the same. _____
   _____
   _____

3. I am enamor'd of . . . the builders and steerers of ships and the wielders of axes and mauls, and the drivers of horses, / I can eat and sleep with them week in and week out.
   _____
   _____

4. By the bivouac's fitful flame, / A procession winding around me, solemn and sweet and slow—but first I note, / The tents of the sleeping army _____
   _____
   _____

5. I hear America singing, the varied carols I hear. / Those of mechanics . . . / The carpenter . . . / The mason . . . / The boatman . . . / The shoemaker . . . / The wood-cutter's song . . ."
   _____
   _____

Walt Whitman's Poetry
Reading Strategy: Adjust Reading Rate

Good readers know that they should **adjust** their **reading rate,** depending on the difficulty level of the material they are reading. They slow down when they come to more difficult passages, and they speed up when they come to easier ones. How can you tell when you should slow down? If the lines are long and dense and the vocabulary is relatively abstract, the passage will probably require more study. If the lines are short and the vocabulary is relatively concrete, the passage will probably require less study.

DIRECTIONS: *On the chart below, note three passages from Whitman's poetry that you read slowly. Explain why you slowed down when you came to these passages. Then, explain the meaning of the passage.*

Passage	Why I Slowed Down	Meaning of Passage

Walt Whitman's Poetry
Vocabulary Builder

Multiple Meaning Words

A. DIRECTIONS: *On the line, write the letter of the choice that best defines the underlined word.*

_____1. The <u>stirring</u> bees flitted from flower to flower, gathering pollen.
    A. mixing with a spoon   C. busy
    B. emotional   D. waking up slowly

_____2. The horses ran freely, without <u>check</u>, across the prairie.
    A. restraint   C. a mark of approval
    B. one's bill at a restaurant   D. to examine for accuracy

_____3. After adding the <u>figures</u> in each column, Alex determined the grand total.
    A. diagrams   C. shapes
    B. numbers   D. illustrations

_____4. The soldiers <u>note</u> the positions of the enemy camps.
    A. a musical tone   C. a short letter
    B. a promise to pay   D. observe

Using the Word List

    abeyance   bequeath   effuse   robust   stealthily   stirring

B. DIRECTIONS: *On the lines provided, rewrite each sentence by replacing the italicized word with a simpler word that means the same thing.*

1. I depart as air, I shake my white locks at the runaway sun, I *effuse* my flesh in eddies, and drift it in lacy jags.

_____

2. Creeds and school in *abeyance*, retiring back a while sufficed at what they are, but never forgotten.

_____

3. In the history of earth hitherto the largest and most *stirring* appear tame and orderly to their ampler largeness and stir.

_____

4. I *bequeath* myself to the dirt to grow from the grass I love . . .

_____

5. . . . as I lift my eyes they seem to be *stealthily* watching me.

_____

6. . . . at night the party of young fellows, *robust*, friendly, Singing with open mouths their strong melodious songs.

_____

Walt Whitman's Poetry
Support for Writing

To organize your material to write a Whitman-esque poem (a poem in Whitman's style), enter information in the chart below.

Poem in Imitation of Walt Whitman	
Poem Topic	
Sensory images and details	
arrangement of lines	
Catalogs (long lists)	
anaphora (repetition of phrases or sentences with similar structure or meanings)	
Onomatopoeia (words that sound like their meaning)	

On a separate page, write a draft of your poem. When you revise, be sure you have used a variety of line lengths, sensory images, catalogs, anaphora, onomatopoeia, and lots of enthusiasm.

Walt Whitman's Poetry
Enrichment: Science

Scientists collect knowledge about the world in a careful and systematic way. They use the scientific method, which includes collecting data through observations and experiments, formulating and testing hypotheses, and drawing conclusions. Scientists strive to be objective in their work, trying not to be influenced by their personal beliefs, opinions, and emotions.

Poets, on the other hand, often do not approach the world in a scientific way. Poetry is usually written from a particular, subjective point of view. Poets usually do not do controlled experiments, although they may make observations and draw conclusions. The conclusions that poets draw, however, are different from scientific conclusions, since a poet's conclusions often are philosophical and/or emotional.

Consider Walt Whitman's poetry. Is Whitman more a scientist or a poet? Why do you think so?

DIRECTIONS: *Refer to Whitman's poems "When I Heard the Learn'd Astronomer" and "A Noiseless Patient Spider" to answer the questions below.*

1. What phrases in these poems show that Whitman approaches the stars and the spider more as a poet than as a scientist?

   _____

   _____

2. Does Whitman's approach to the natural world have anything in common with that of a scientist? Explain why or why not.

   _____

   _____

3. What might a scientist want to know about the stars?

   _____

   _____

4. What might a scientist want to know about the spider?

   _____

   _____

5. Choose one of the poems, and rewrite it from the point of view of a scientist.

   _____

   _____

   _____

   _____

   _____

   _____

The Poetry of Walt Whitman
Open-Book Test

Short Answer *Write your responses to the questions in this section on the lines provided.*

1. How do the ideas expressed in the first paragraph of the preface to *Leaves of Grass* act as a helpful support for Whitman's use of free verse in his poetry? Use a detail from the paragraph to support your answer.

   _____

   _____

   _____

   _____

2. The first paragraph of the preface to *Leaves of Grass* is all one sentence. Which reading rate would you use to gain the fullest understanding of this passage, and why?

   _____

   _____

   _____

   _____

3. In the second paragraph of the preface to *Leaves of Grass*, which adjective or adjectives used in the preface could you use to characterize the America which Whitman describes? Give two examples of words from the preface to support your word choices.

   _____

   _____

   _____

   _____

4. In line 10 of "Song of Myself," find the word *abeyance*. Which lines in this section give you clues to the meaning of the word *abeyance*? Explain your answer.

   _____

   _____

   _____

   _____

5. In Section 6 of "Song of Myself," how does Whitman's free verse reflect the way people talk naturally in conversation?

   _____

   _____

   _____

   _____

6. In Section 17 of "Song of Myself," what is Whitman communicating about his relationship with his fellow man? Explain your answer using details from the poem.

_____

_____

_____

7. What or whom does Whitman criticize in "When I Heard the Learn'd Astronomer"?

_____

_____

8. In addition to the free-verse, irregular form of "By the Bivouac's Fitful Flame," what other elements of the poem suggest that you should read the poem slowly?

_____

_____

_____

9. Whitman is fond of listing, or cataloguing, people, things, creatures, and experiences. List the kinds of people he hears singing in "I Hear America Singing" in the graphic organizer below. On the lines below, write a general observation you can make about the occupations of these people.

Working People Whom Whitman Celebrates		

_____

_____

10. What is similar about the speaker and spider in "A Noiseless Patient Spider"?

_____

_____

_____

Essay

Write an extended response to the question of your choice or to the question or questions your teacher assigns you.

11. In his preface to *Leaves of Grass*, Whitman calls America "essentially the greatest poem." To prove his claim, he cites several examples of what he perceives to be the poetic nature of the United States. Write a brief essay exploring examples from either *Leaves of Grass* or "I Hear America Singing" that demonstrate the poetry—the inspiration, the excitement, the largeness of spirit—that Whitman sees in America.

Unit 2 Resources: A Growing Nation
183

12. Choose one:

What does Section 6 of "Song of Myself" demonstrate about Whitman's attitude toward death? Write a brief essay to discuss his philosophy concerning death.

How does Whitman view the natural world and animals? Choose any of his poems that consider this subject, and write a brief essay about Whitman's feelings about the natural world and animals.

13. Choose one:

In the second paragraph of the preface of *Leaves of Grass*, Whitman uses an *anaphora*—a word or phrase repeated at the beginning of successive lines, sentences, or phrases. What is the word and how is it used to add to the meaning of the passage in the preface? Write a brief essay to answer these questions.

In the first four statements of "When I Heard the Learn'd Astronomer," Whitman uses an *anaphora*—a word or phrase repeated at the beginning of successive lines, sentences, or phrases. Which word or phrase does he use, and how does it add to the meaning of the poem? Write a brief essay to answer these questions.

14. **Thinking About the Essential Question: What makes American Literature American?** How does Whitman's poetry reflect his feelings about America and American democracy? Explain his views in a brief essay that cites examples from the introduction to *Leaves of Grass* and at least two of Whitman's poems that appear in your textbook. Include in your discussion not only the contents of the poems but also details about their structure or form.

Oral Response

15. Go back to question 3, 5, 6, or 10 or to the question your teacher assigns to you. Take a few minutes to expand your answers and prepare an oral response. Find additional details in the poetry selections by Walt Whitman that will support your points. If necessary, make notes to guide your response.

Walt Whitman's Poetry
Selection Test A

Critical Reading *Identify the letter of the choice that best answers the question.*

____ 1. Which element contributes most to Whitman's poetry of free verse?
   A. regular metrical feet
   B. fixed-length stanzas
   C. regular speech patterns
   D. exact rhyme schemes

____ 2. What can you conclude about Whitman's epic poetry from these lines from "Song of Myself"?

   I celebrate myself, and sing myself/And what I assume you shall assume,/For every atom belonging to me as good belongs to you.

   A. He thinks he is an epic hero.
   B. He thinks his poetry shows he is better than others.
   C. He thinks humanity is the epic hero.
   D. He uses science to support his idea of the epic poem.

____ 3. Which elements of free verse are found in this passage from "Song of Myself"?

   I, now thirty-seven years old in perfect health begin, / Hoping to cease not till death.

   I.   irregular meter
   II. exact rhyme
   III. natural speech cadence
   IV. irregular line length

   A. I, II, IV
   B. I, II, III
   C. I, III, IV
   D. II, III, IV

____ 4. Which element of Whitman's epic style is best represented in this passage from "Song of Myself"?

   The sharp-hoof'd moose of the north, the cat on the house-sill, the chickadee, the prairie dog,/The litter of the grunting sow as they tug at her teats,/The brood of the turkey hen and she with her half-spread wings,/I see in them and myself the same old law.

   A. anaphora
   B. catalogs
   C. onomatopoeia
   D. fixed meter

_____ 5. How would you adjust your reading rate when reading these lines from "When I Heard the Learn'd Astronomer"?

> When the proofs, the figures, were ranged in columns before me,/When I was shown the charts and diagrams, to add, divide and measure them,/When I sitting heard the astronomer where he lectured with much applause in the lecture room . . .

    A. read more carefully

    B. read quickly to understand the rhythm

    C. read slowly

    D. have someone read them aloud

_____ 6. Why does the poet leave the lecture in "When I Heard the Learn'd Astronomer"?

    A. He wants to check the astronomer's facts for accuracy.

    B. He has fallen ill and must go outside to get some air.

    C. He wants to see the stars instead of hearing about them.

    D. He thinks the speaker does not deserve all the applause.

_____ 7. Based on "I Hear America Singing," how does Whitman seem to feel toward the people in the poem?

    A. unfriendly

    B. annoyed

    C. bored

    D. kindly

_____ 8. What class of workers does Whitman focus on in "I Hear America Singing"?

    A. singers

    B. laborers

    C. housewives

    D. athletes

Vocabulary

_____ 9. In which sentence is the meaning of the word *effuse* expressed?

    A. Whitman's poetry symbolizes America for many readers.

    B. His poems pour out feelings for both the human and natural world.

    C. Whitman worked as a nurse in a hospital during the Civil War.

    D. One of his poems expresses grief at the death of Lincoln.

____ 10. In which sentence is the word *stealthily* used correctly?
   A. Whitman believed in living stealthily.
   B. The astronomer behaved stealthily when he spoke at the meeting.
   C. The lion moved stealthily through the tall grass.
   D. Nature appears stealthily in the night sky.

Essay

11. Whitman's Preface to the 1855 Edition of *Leaves of Grass* communicates his belief that America benefits from all the different nationalities that make up its population. America was different from many other countries that had people from similar backgrounds. Write a brief essay that gives examples from your personal experience or reading that support Whitman's beliefs.

12. Readers of Whitman's poetry see him as a poet who celebrated life. Do you think this is true? Write a brief essay stating whether you think Whitman's poetry celebrates life and is positive in its approach. Give at least two examples from his poetry to support your opinion.

13. **Thinking About the Essential Question: What makes American Literature American?** Central to the American vision is the idea of a democracy in which the citizens' views are represented and citizens from all walks of life are valued members of society. How does Whitman's poetry reflect his feelings about American democracy? Answer this question in an essay that cites examples from at least two of Whitman's poems that appear in your textbook.

Walt Whitman's Poetry
Selection Test B

Critical Reading *Identify the letter of the choice that best completes the statement or answers the question.*

_____ 1. When Whitman states, in the preface to the 1855 edition of *Leaves of Grass*, that "The United States themselves are essentially the greatest poem," he supports his opinion by citing
   A. the vitality and diversity of Americans.
   B. the rhythmic speech patterns of Americans.
   C. American respect for literary traditions.
   D. his own popularity as a poet.

_____ 2. Based on the following passage from the preface to the 1855 edition of *Leaves of Grass*, what can you infer about Whitman's attitude toward the past?

   America does not repel the past or what it has produced under its forms or amid other politics or the idea of castes or the old religions . . . accepts the lesson with calmness . . . is not so impatient as has been supposed that the slough still sticks to opinions and manners and literature while the life which served its requirements has passed into the new life of the new forms.

   A. Whitman does not think Americans have anything to learn from the past.
   B. Whitman thinks Americans should study the past for its own sake.
   C. Whitman wishes Americans would follow past traditions more carefully.
   D. Whitman is pleased Americans learn from the past while making a new way of life.

_____ 3. What element makes Whitman's poem "Song of Myself" epic poetry?
   A. Its use of free verse.
   B. Its variety of line length and irregular meter.
   C. Its range of structural elements.
   D. Its theme of humanity as an epic hero.

_____ 4. How would you adjust your reading rate to help you when reading the following lines from "Song of Myself"?

   My tongue, every atom of my blood, formed from this soil, this air,/Born here of parents born here from parents the same, and their parents the same,/I, now thirty-seven years old in perfect health begin,/Hoping to cease not till death.

   A. Read slowly to understand the poet's complicated ideas about human parentage.
   B. Read silently and slowly, stopping to consult a dictionary when necessary.
   C. Read rapidly so that the final short line has the maximum impact.
   D. Read rapidly aloud to appreciate the rhythmic repetitions and rhythm of the verse.

_____ 5. What can you infer about the poet's attitude about humanity from these lines in "Song of Myself"?

> These are really the thoughts of all men in all ages and lands, they are not original with me, / If they are not yours as much as mine they are nothing, or next to nothing. . . .

    A. Whitman is pleased to acknowledge that he borrowed ideas in "Song of Myself" from other epic heroes.
    B. Whitman believes that his observations are, in some sense, universally shared.
    C. Whitman believes that he can predict what people who read his poetry in the future will think.
    D. Whitman thinks that his poetry is worthwhile only if readers agree with him.

_____ 6. Which element of Whitman's epic style is represented in the phrase "barbaric yawp" in "Song of Myself"?
    A. rhythmic cadence   C. onomatopoeia
    B. anaphora   D. catalog

_____ 7. Based on the details in "Song of Myself" and "I Hear America Singing," what can you infer about Whitman's attitude toward other people?
    A. He feels affectionate toward other people.
    B. He does not like to be around people.
    C. He is bossy and likes to control the people around him.
    D. He thinks that most people are very foolish.

_____ 8. "The singing" the speaker hears in "I Hear America Singing" is
    A. the language of different ethnic groups in the American melting pot.
    B. the songs from foreign lands brought to America by immigrants.
    C. the poetry of Whitman and other American poets.
    D. the individuality of Americans in different walks of life.

_____ 9. What can you conclude about Whitman's epic poetry in "I Hear America Singing"?
    A. Long, repetitive sentences are what make his poetry epic.
    B. The common person is the epic hero of his poetry.
    C. Whitman considers himself one of poetry's epic heroes.
    D. Only those who work with their hands can be epic heroes.

_____ 10. Why would you read slowly when reading these lines from "When I Heard the Learn'd Astronomer"?

> When the proofs, the figures, were ranged in columns before me,/When I was shown the charts and diagrams, to add, divide and measure them,/When I sitting heard the astronomer where he lectured with much applause in the lecture room . . .

    A. The ideas are extremely complex.   C. Reading slowly helps you
    B. The lines are long and dense.   understand rhythm.
                                  D. The rhyme is difficult to identify.

_____ 11. Free verse is especially suited to "A Noiseless Patient Spider" because it reflects
    A. the spider's noiselessness.
    B. the spider's patience.
    C. the spider's activity of launching forth filament.
    D. the isolation of the spider and the soul.

____ 12. From the details in "A Noiseless Patient Spider," you can infer that Whitman admires the spider for its ability to
A. use its body to explore its surroundings.
B. quietly and patiently capture the insects it will eat.
C. create beautiful silken web patterns.
D. move from place to place without being noticed.

____ 13. Which of these was *not* a prime reason why Whitman chose to write in free verse?
A. to express his individuality
B. to celebrate democracy
C. to convey a sense of freedom
D. to imitate earlier poets he admired

____ 14. Based on his poetry, what can you infer about Whitman's attitude toward nature?
I. He admires nature.
II. He learns from nature.
III. He considers himself to be part of nature.
IV. He likes to spend time outdoors.
A. I and II only
B. II and III only
C. I, III, and IV only
D. I, II, III, and IV

Vocabulary

____ 15. What does the speaker in "Song of Myself" mean when he says that he holds "creeds and schools in *abeyance*"?
A. He goes to school regularly.
B. He has temporarily let go of philosophies he learned in school.
C. He detests creeds and schools.
D. He thinks that Americans of all creeds should spend more time in school.

____ 16. What is the meaning of the word *stealthily* in these lines from "By the Bivouac's Fitful Flame"?

Like a phantom far or near an occasional figure moving,/The shrubs and trees, (as I lift my eyes they seem to be stealthily watching me,)/While wind in procession thoughts, O tender and wondrous thoughts . . .

A. carefully
B. curiously
C. secretively
D. occasionally

Essay

17. Suppose Whitman had written "I Hear America Singing" today. How would the poem be different? Write an essay describing the differences.

18. Use the information in "Song of Myself" to infer Whitman's attitude toward death. Then, write an essay explaining his attitude. Be sure to cite examples of language and details that point to the general attitude you describe.

19. Write an essay about Whitman's view of nature that draws supporting details from "Song of Myself" and at least one other Whitman poem in your textbook. Also explain why you think Whitman called his poetry *Leaves of Grass* and what grass seems to represent for him.

20. **Thinking About the Essential Question: What makes American Literature American?** Write an essay explaining Whitman's feeling about American democracy. Cite examples from the introduction of *Leaves of Grass* and at least two poems in your textbook. Include in your discussion not only the poem's contents but also details about their structure or form.

Writing Workshop—Unit 2
Narration: Reflective Essay

Prewriting: Narrowing Your Topic
Use the chart below to focus your writing on a specific event and the insight you gained.

List a moment from your life that you want to explore.	
What is an insight you gained from your experience?	
Did you learn something new about yourself? What?	
Did you see the world in a different light? How?	
Write a sentence that identifies the event and the lesson learned.	

Drafting: Providing Elaboration
Use the diagram below to help you add details to your essay to make your essay more substantial.

Thoughts you had during the event	→	
Feelings you experienced during the event	→	
Sensory images you remember from the event	→	

Writing Workshop—Unit 2
Reflective Essay: Revising Your Sentences

Vary Your Sentences

Even though your reflective essay is about an event that happened to you, avoid beginning every sentence with *I*. **Vary sentence beginnings** to make your writing more interesting. You may need to combine some sentences to avoid a string of short, simple sentences that begin the same way.

Boring:	I remember the door. I remember it was locked. I remember being curious.
More interesting:	The door was locked, and I remember being curious.
Boring:	I walked into the room. I looked around. I saw a piano.
More interesting:	When I walked into the room, I looked around and saw a piano.

Fixing Problem Sentences

DIRECTIONS: *Rewrite each passage to create varied sentence beginnings. You may need to combine some sentences.*

1. I heard the wind. I heard it howling. I heard the front door suddenly slam. I heard the windows rattling.

   _____

   _____

   _____

2. Making choices is hard. Making choices is important. Making choices is part of growing up.

   _____

   _____

   _____

3. My big sister is my best friend. My big sister really listens to me. My big sister gives me advice when I ask for it. My big sister usually lets me make my own decisions.

   _____

   _____

   _____

   _____

Name _____ Date _____

Delivering a Persuasive Speech

Choose a topic, purpose, and audience for a persuasive speech. Then use the form to help you develop your arguments and list persuasive techniques to use in your speech.

Topic: _____

Intended audience: _____

Purpose: _____

Thesis: _____
_____

Reasoning: _____
_____
_____

Facts: _____
_____
_____

Possible Opposing Arguments/Answers: _____
_____
_____

Persuasive Language
—*Level of language:* Informal expressions? _____
                     Technical language? _____
—*Rhetorical questions:* _____
_____
—*Parallel structures:* _____
_____
—*Figurative language:* _____
_____

Presentation Techniques
—*Hand gestures* Where to use? _____
—*Tones of voice* Where to vary tone: _____
_____
—*Visual aids* Which and where to use? _____
_____

Unit 2 Vocabulary Workshop
Etymology of Political Science and History Terms

Knowing the meanings of roots, prefixes, and suffixes can help you determine the meanings of many English words. For example, when you recognize the Latin root *bellum* (war) and you see the prefix *re-* (again) attached to it, you can figure out that a *rebellion* means someone is making war again.

A. DIRECTIONS: *For each item, identify the word parts and explain how the meanings of the word parts help you define the word.*

Example: confederacy
Prefix: *con-* (together) Root: *foedus* (league) Suffix: *-acy* (condition)
A *confederacy* is the situation or condition that results when people come together to form a league.

1. constitution

Prefix: Root: Suffix:

_____

2. unanimous

Prefix: Root: Suffix:

_____

3. demographics

Prefix: Root: Suffix:

_____

4. Politics

Prefix: Root: Suffix:

_____

B. DIRECTIONS: *Write a definition for each of the following words based on the meanings of their roots and affixes.*

1. meritocracy

_____

2. nationalism

_____

3. convention

_____

4. expedition

_____

Name _____ Date _____

Essential Questions Workshop—Unit 2

In their stories, poems, and nonfiction, the writers in Unit Two express ideas that relate to the three Essential Questions framing this book. Review the literature in the unit. Then, for each Essential Question, choose an author and at least one passage from his or her writing that expresses a related idea. Use this chart to complete your work.

Essential Question	Author/Selection	Literary Passage
How does literature shape or reflect society?		
What is the relationship between place and literature?		
What makes American literature American?		

Diagnostic Tests and Vocabulary in Context
Use and Interpretation

The Diagnostic Tests and Vocabulary in Context were developed to assist teachers in making the most appropriate assignment of *Prentice Hall Literature* program selections to students. The purpose of these assessments is to indicate the degree of difficulty that students are likely to have in reading/comprehending the selections presented in the *following* unit of instruction. Tests are provided at six separate times in each grade level—a *Diagnostic Test* (to be used prior to beginning the year's instruction) and a *Vocabulary in Context,* the final segment of the Benchmark Test appearing at the end of each of the first five units of instruction. Note that the tests are intended for use not as summative assessments for the prior unit, but as guidance for assigning literature selections in the upcoming unit of instruction.

The structure of all Diagnostic Tests and Vocabulary in Context in this series is the same. All test items are four-option, multiple-choice items. The format is established to assess a student's ability to construct sufficient meaning from the context sentence to choose the only provided word that fits both the semantics (meaning) and syntax (structure) of the context sentence. All words in the context sentences are chosen to be "below-level" words that students reading at this grade level should know. All answer choices fit *either* the meaning or structure of the context sentence, but only the correct choice fits *both* semantics and syntax. All answer choices—both correct answers and incorrect options—are key words chosen from specifically taught words that will occur in the subsequent unit of program instruction. This careful restriction of the assessed words permits a sound diagnosis of students' current reading achievement and prediction of the most appropriate level of readings to assign in the upcoming unit of instruction.

The assessment of vocabulary in context skill has consistently been shown in reading research studies to correlate very highly with "reading comprehension." This is not surprising as the format essentially assesses comprehension, albeit in sentence-length "chunks." Decades of research demonstrate that vocabulary assessment provides a strong, reliable prediction of comprehension achievement— the purpose of these tests. Further, because this format demands very little testing time, these diagnoses can be made efficiently, permitting teachers to move forward with critical instructional tasks rather than devoting excessive time to assessment.

It is important to stress that while the Diagnostic and Vocabulary in Context were carefully developed and will yield sound assignment decisions, they were designed to *reinforce*, not supplant, teacher judgment as to the most appropriate instructional placement for individual students. Teacher judgment should always prevail in making placement—or indeed other important instructional—decisions concerning students.

Diagnostic Tests and Vocabulary in Context Branching Suggestions

These tests are designed to provide maximum flexibility for teachers. Your *Unit Resources* books contain the 40-question **Diagnostic Test** and 20-question **Vocabulary in Context** tests. At *PHLitOnline*, you can access the Diagnostic Test and complete 40-question Vocabulary in Context tests. Procedures for administering the tests are described below. Choose the procedure based on the time you wish to devote to the activity and your comfort with the assignment decisions relative to the individual students. Remember that your judgment of a student's reading level should always take precedence over the results of a single written test.

Feel free to use different procedures at different times of the year. For example, for early units, you may wish to be more confident in the assignments you make—thus, using the "two-stage" process below. Later, you may choose the quicker diagnosis, confirming the results with your observations of the students' performance built up throughout the year.

The **Diagnostic Test** is composed of a single 40-item assessment. Based on the results of this assessment, make the following assignment of students to the reading selections in Unit 1:

Diagnostic Test Score	Selection to Use
If the student's score is 0–25	more accessible
If the student's score is 26–40	more challenging

Outlined below are the three basic options for administering **Vocabulary in Context** and basing selection assignments on the results of these assessments.

1. For a one-stage, quicker diagnosis using the *20-item* test in the *Unit Resources:*

Vocabulary in Context Test Score	Selection to Use
If the student's score is 0–13	more accessible
If the student's score is 14–20	more challenging

2. If you wish to confirm your assignment decisions with a *two-stage* diagnosis:

Stage 1: Administer the 20-item test in the *Unit Resources*	
Vocabulary in Context Test Score	Selection to Use
If the student's score is 0–9	more accessible
If the student's score is 10–15	(Go to Stage 2.)
If the student's score is 16–20	more challenging

Stage 2: Administer items 21–40 from *PHLitOnline*	
Vocabulary in Context Test Score	Selection to Use
If the student's score is 0–12	more accessible
If the student's score is 13–20	more challenging

3. If you base your assignment decisions on the full 40-item **Vocabulary in Context** from *PHLitOnline:*

Vocabulary in Context Test Score	Selection to Use
If the student's score is 0–25	more accessible
If the student's score is 26–40	more challenging

Unit 2 Resources: A Growing Nation

Grade 11—Benchmark Test 3
Interpretation Guide

Skill Objective	Test Items	Number Correct	Reading Kit
Literary Analysis			
Characterization	1		pp. 52, 53
Meter	3		pp. 154, 155
Single Effect	4		pp. 234, 235
Narrative Poem	8		pp. 160, 161
Parable	9		pp. 164, 165
Symbol	6		pp. 254, 255
Archetypes	7		pp. 34, 35
Theme	10		pp. 260, 261
Figurative Language	11		pp. 112, 113
Author's Style	2		pp. 42, 43
Reading Skill			
Summarize	18		pp. 254, 255
Analyze/evaluate information from graphs and charts	12		pp. 102, 103
Evaluate social influences of historical period	13		pp. 100, 101
Breaking Down Long Sentences	14		pp. 46, 47
Drawing Inferences About Meaning	15		pp. 84, 85
Relevant Details	5		pp. 218, 219
Challenging the Text	16		pp. 54, 55
Evaluate a Writer's Message or Philosophy	17		pp. 96, 97
Vocabulary			
Latin Prefixes: ab-, ex-, mal-	19, 20, 24		280, 281, 284, 285
Latin Root: -voc-, -radi-, -flu-, -finis-	21, 22, 23		308, 309, 312, 313
Grammar			
Adjective Clauses	25		pp. 346, 347
Adverb Clauses	26		pp. 348, 349
Participles	27		pp. 378, 379
Gerunds	29		pp. 366, 367
Infinitives	28		pp. 368, 369
Comparative and superlative adjectives and adverbs	30, 31		pp. 356, 357
Writing			
Reflective Essay	32		pp. 442, 443
Literary Criticism	33		pp. 436, 437
Character Study	34		pp. 422, 423

ANSWERS

Unit 2 Introduction

Names and Terms to Know, p. 2

Sample Answers

A. 1. The Louisiana Purchase was a large tract of North American land that Napoleon sold to America.

2. Andrew Jackson was the seventh U.S. President and champion of the average citizen.

3. The Trail of Tears was the trek of more than a thousand miles that the Cherokee were forced to make from their home in Georgia to Oklahoma.

4. Henry Wadsworth Longfellow was the best-known Fireside Poets, popular nineteenth-century American poets whose works were read by the fireside.

5. The "barbaric yawp" was Whitman's description of his distinctly American voice.

6. The Seneca Falls Convention was a women's rights convention organized in 1848 in New York State.

B. 1. Technology brought new inventions that improved farm and factory productivity and made America more prosperous; steamships, canals, and other improvements made transportation easier and faster, and the telegraph, which improved communication.

2. As geographic expansion brought white settlers to more and more areas, the government forced many Indians to leave their traditional lands and move further west.

3. Transcendentalism, shaped by Ralph Waldo Emerson and Henry David Thoreau, provided a backbone for the American belief in the individual's ability to rise about brute reality to a higher ideal.

Essential Question: What is the relationship between place and literature? p. 3

Sample Answers

A. 1. a. the natural wonders and expanse of their country.

b. Examples include waterfalls, mountains, canyons, fertile plains, and forests.

2. a. They found many resources to develop for economic gain

b. It inspired reverence and awe.

3. a. Frontier or rural areas, with forests, mountains, and rivers were the usual setting for the "new American mythology.

b. They included Nathaniel Hawthorne, Herman Melville, Edgar Allan Poe, Ralph Waldo Emerson, Henry David Thoreau, Walt Whitman, and Emily Dickinson.

c. Artists included the naturalist John James Audubon, Thomas Cole and other artists of the Hudson River School and Frederick Law Olmsted, who designed New York City's Central Park.

B. 1. My English teacher inspires me with awe.

2. He or she would probably speak in elegant sentences with elevated Vocabulary.

3. Yes, an expansion means that more good were sold.

Essential Question: How does literature shape or reflect Society? p. 4

Sample Answers

A. 1. a. Examples include steamships, cotton gins, and the telegraph.

b. to ease and speed communication and transportation and make farms and factories more productive

c. Poorer people got more political power under Jackson

d. women and African Americans

e. Southern states that had built their economy around slavery did not welcome Northerns agitating against it

2. a. the antislavery novel Uncle Tom's Cabin and poetry by Henry Wadsworth Longfellow

b. Charles Dickens and Sir Walter Scott were extremely popular.

3. a. They wanted to improve American Society, spread democracy, and define, "public self" for Americans.

b. Hawthorne, Melville, Poe, and Irving, among others

c. real truths lie outside sensory experience

B. 1. something about the writer's life and feeling

2. we saw amazing national parks

3. confidently, without the help of others

Essential Question: What makes American literature American? p. 5

Sample Answers

A. 1. a. informality, colorlful vocabulary, use of slang, and lack of elaborate diction

b. Examples include "sit for a spell" and "take a fork in the road."

c. He wrote in a "barbaric yawp" that sounded conversational, using both plain and elegant and both foreign and native words.

2. a. James Fenimoer Cooper's Leatherstocking Tales and legends about real-life American Daniel Boone and Davy Crockett

b. Melville's Captain Ahab and Hawthorne's Hester Prynne

c. He or she was an individualist who tried to reach a feeling of oneness with all that is beautiful and good.

3. a. It means moving west with the frontier.

b. It expressed optimism, or a belief in human goodness.

c. It expressed the view that human being are often driven toward self-destructiveness, guilt, and cruelty.

d. It fostered confidence and encouraged writers and other artists to persist against all odds to form a new culture.

B. 1. It makes it easier to communicate and travel.
2. the right to free speeech
3. They are likely to be optimistic and materialistic.

Following-Through Activities, p. 6

A. Students should complete the chart with concepts appropriate to the period and groups associated with these concepts.

B. Students should complete the chart with answer that will help them to research a form of spoken literature.

"The Devil and Tom Walker"
by Washington Irving

Vocabulary Warm-up Exercises, p. 8

A. 1. indifference
2. zeal
3. meager
4. notorious
5. prone
6. prior
7. consequence
8. elapsed

B. Sample Answers
1. F; A statement is a contradiction if it opposes, not agrees with, another.
2. T; For a fierce competitor, winning is the uppermost, or primary, concern.
3. T; A nurse performs steadfastly, without change, by remaining with a patient all night.
4. T; Someone who is squeamish would be unable to eat slimy things.
5. T; Using a seatbelt is a precaution, or care taken in advance.
6. F; If a sport is too strenuous, it takes too much energy.
7. F; A letter that disclosed the truth revealed it.
8. F; A disease that is prevalent is common among people.

Reading Warm-up A, p. 9
Sample Answers
1. (enthusiasm); Students may say that they play sports, dance, or read with zeal.
2. celebrate, [not] harmless and obscure; Students may say that someone may be notorious for crime, ignorance, or bad fashion.
3. (tending to); I am prone to believe anyone who is a good storyteller.
4. scarce; Students may say that there may be a meager supply of food, clothes, or ideas.
5. (the overall effect of the satires was very scattered and random); Students may say that one possible

consequence of winning the lottery is quitting one's job or buying a new house.
6. such a short time; Students may say that twenty-four hours have elapsed since their last English class.
7. (not caring at all); Students may say that they feel only indifference toward a certain sport, award show, or art form.
8. before; Prior to lunch, students may wash their hands or have gym.

Reading Warm-up B, p. 10
Sample Answers
1. reveal; Students may note that the identity of a spy or the cause of an accident was recently disclosed.
2. (opposing, opposing, opposing); "Contra" in contradiction indicates being against.
3. existed widely; Students may say that one prevalent attitude in school is that the cafeteria food needs improving.
4. An antonym for uppermost is lowermost.
5. Efforts had to be strenuous, requiring great effort, just to survive starvation, harsh winters, disease, and conflict with Native Americans; vigorous, energetic.
6. (care); One common precaution is to look both ways before crossing the street.
7. (too sensitive); Students may say that many people are squeamish about watching a gory movie or about cleaning up after pets.
8. with firm resolve; Despite a series of failures, the director of the project continued steadfastly to encourage the team.

Literary Analysis: Characterization, p. 11
1. H; 2. A; 3. F; 4. B; 5. C; 6. E 7. D; 8. G

Reading Strategy: Evaluate Social Influences of the Historical Period, p. 12
Sample Answers
1. In the early 1700s, husbands and wives apparently shared the household as common property.
2. Intolerance of religious attitudes was prevalent during this era, an era that also saw many Americans engaged in the slave trade and some involved in witch hunts—all behavior that Irving considers "of the devil."
3. People believed that God used nature to punish them, as in earthquakes.
4. Greed was very much a part of life in New England, at least in Irving's eyes. Irving is warning them in this story about Tom Walker.

Vocabulary Builder, p. 13
A. 1. export; 2. extrovert; 3. exhale; 4. exoskeleton.
B. 1. A; 2. D; 3. C; 4. B; 5. B; 6. A

Enrichment: Narrative Point of View, p. 15

Students should indicate three scenes from "The Devil and Tom Walker." For each scene, students should describe a technique or techniques they would use to film it, keeping the viewpoint of the omniscient narrator in mind. For example, if students choose the scene in which the Devil first confronts Tom, they might decide to open the scene with close-up views of thick, foreboding foliage, from Tom's point of view. Blinks could be represented by quick, black frames. They could look down on the stick, and the skull that is uncovered. Until this point, only "nature" sounds would be heard and a soft "Humph" from Tom. All of a sudden a loud, booming voice says, "Let that skull alone!"

"The Devil and Tom Walker"
by Washington Irving

Open-Book Test, p. 16
Short Answer

1. The writer is foreshadowing the appearance of the Devil.
   Difficulty: *Average*   **Objective:** *Interpretation*

2. He uses direct characterization. He describes her directly as the teller of the story.
   Difficulty: *Easy*   **Objective:** *Literary Analysis*

3. The two of them even try to cheat each other.
   Difficulty: *Easy*   **Objective:** *Interpretation*

4. Irving uses indirect characterization to reveal the Devil's character. The Devil uses his own words to tell the reader about his character and what he thinks of himself.
   Difficulty: *Average*   **Objective:** *Literary Analysis*

5. Tom wants to find his wife not because he misses her as a person, but because she has taken some of their valuables with her. When he finds the bundle, but not his wife, he is overjoyed because he thinks the valuables will be in the bundle.
   Difficulty: *Challenging*   **Objective:** *Interpretation*

6. "cautiously," "precarious foot holds," "pacing carefully"
   Difficulty: *Average*   **Objective:** *Vocabulary*

7. Women were considered less important than men in these times. A woman was identified by her relation to a husband, son, or parents. Women were often referred to as simply "someone's wife, daughter, mother," etc.
   Difficulty: *Average*   **Objective:** *Reading Strategy*

8. bold, brave, arrogant; unafraid of the Devil: IC
   takes advantage of people in need, drives hard bargain: DC
   greedy, always wanting more, undoubtedly dishonest: IC
   Difficulty: *Challenging*   **Objective:** *Literary Analysis*

9. Sample answer: People wanted money in whatever way they could get it. They were wildly putting their money into unreliable ventures.; There was a "rage for

speculating," "people had run mad with schemes" a great "speculating fever . . . raged," etc.
   Difficulty: *Easy*   **Objective:** *Reading Strategy*

10. They were superstitious and believed in witches, goblins, tricks of the Devil, etc. But they were used to these events and were not particularly frightened by them. They just got on with their lives.
    Difficulty: *Challenging*   **Objective:** *Reading Strategy*

Essay

11. Students' essays should state that Tom refuses to "fit out a slave ship," which means he refuses to become a slave trader. Students may note that this refusal reflects Irving's and the Puritans' disapproval of slavery and their likely sympathy with abolitionist ideals and actions.
    Difficulty: *Easy*   **Objective:** *Essay*

12. Students' essays should mention any three of these actions taken by Tom: He starts going regularly to church; he prays loudly; he makes other members of the congregation look remiss by comparison; he judges his neighbors on their sins; he calls for the repression of sects of which he and the community disapprove; he carries a small Bible in his coat pocket and keeps a larger one on his business desk Students should cite the fact that these activities do not change Tom's dealings with his customers; he still cheats them as much as he can.
    Difficulty: *Average*   **Objective:** *Essay*

13. Some students' essays might say that the two are evenly matched. They are both greedy, they are each willing to yell and shout and argue as loudly as the other, and they are each willing to use physical force against each other. Other students may say that they are not evenly matched, that Tom's wife is more like his shadow, that she has no name of her own, that much of the story is not about her but about Tom, and that the reader never learns what happens to her in the woods.
    Difficulty: *Challenging*   **Objective:** *Essay*

14. Students' essays might reflect the Puritans' conflicted views of money and greed. On the one hand, the story makes it clear that Tom is punished by death and hell for being greedy and cheating people. On the other hand, the Puritan characters in the story are quick to take advantage of any financial plan that will make them rich, and many of them do not appear to suffer from this need for great wealth. Accept whichever choice students make as long as they support their opinion with material from the story.
    Difficulty: *Average*   **Objective:** *Essay*

Oral Response

15. Oral responses should be clear, well organized, and well supported by appropriate examples from the selections.
    Difficulty: *Average*   **Objective:** *Oral Interpretation*

Selection Test A, p. 19

Critical Reading

1. ANS: D   DIF: Easy   OBJ: Literary Analysis
2. ANS: B   DIF: Average   OBJ: Reading Strategy
3. ANS: A   DIF: Easy   OBJ: Interpretation
4. ANS: C   DIF: Easy   OBJ: Comprehension
5. ANS: B   DIF: Easy   OBJ: Reading Strategy
6. ANS: C   DIF: Easy   OBJ: Reading Strategy
7. ANS: C   DIF: Easy   OBJ: Interpretation
8. ANS: B   DIF: Easy   OBJ: Literary Analysis

Vocabulary

9. ANS: D   DIF: Easy   OBJ: Vocabulary
10. ANS: D   DIF: Easy   OBJ: Vocabulary

Essay

11. Students' essays should reflect that Tom and his wife are one-dimensional characters. Their chief motivation at the beginning of the story is greed, and they continue to be greedy until their respective deaths. They change only in the way that they seek to be rich. Tom's wife originally hopes that Tom will make a pact with the Devil and make them both rich. When he does not, she goes off to try to make a deal for herself. Tom makes different decisions about how he will become rich, but his greed remains constant.

    Difficulty: *Easy*

    Objective: *Essay*

12. Students who believe Tom deserved his fate may say that he was greedy, unpleasant, and made money as a moneylender. Also, he made a pact with the Devil, so he knew what he was doing. Students who don't believe Tom deserved his fate may say that no one deserves to be taken to hell, and that Tom was only trying to get rich like everyone else. Moneylending may have been unpopular in the days when this story was written, but today people lend money, and it is not considered evil.

    Difficulty: *Easy*

    Objective: *Essay*

13. Students' essays might reflect the Puritans' conflicted views of money and greed. On the one hand, the story makes it clear that Tom is punished by death and hell for being greedy and cheating people. On the other hand, the Puritan characters in the story are quick to take advantage of any financial plan that will make them rich, and many of them do not appear to suffer from this need for great wealth. Accept whichever choice students make as long as they support their opinion with material from the story.

    Difficulty: *Average*

    Objective: *Essay*

Selection Test B, p. 22

Critical Reading

1. ANS: A   DIF: Challenging   OBJ: Interpretation
2. ANS: B   DIF: Average   OBJ: Comprehension
3. ANS: D   DIF: Average   OBJ: Interpretation
4. ANS: D   DIF: Average   OBJ: Comprehension
5. ANS: A   DIF: Average   OBJ: Interpretation
6. ANS: C   DIF: Challenging   OBJ: Interpretation
7. ANS: D   DIF: Average   OBJ: Interpretation
8. ANS: B   DIF: Average   OBJ: Reading Strategy
9. ANS: B   DIF: Average   OBJ: Reading Strategy
10. ANS: D   DIF: Challenging   OBJ: Literary Analysis
11. ANS: C   DIF: Average   OBJ: Literary Analysis
12. ANS: A   DIF: Challenging   OBJ: Reading Strategy
13. ANS: C   DIF: Challenging   OBJ: Literary Analysis

Vocabulary

14. ANS: D   DIF: Easy   OBJ: Vocabulary
15. ANS: B   DIF: Easy   OBJ: Vocabulary
16. ANS: C   DIF: Average   OBJ: Vocabulary
17. ANS: A   DIF: Average   OBJ: Vocabulary

Essay

18. Students should realize that the tree was the one with Tom Walker's name carved on it. They should cite details that suggest that the Devil carves on the trees the names of the souls he owns and, upon their death, destroys the tree by burning.

    Difficulty: *Easy*

    Objective: *Essay*

19. Students may point out that the use of an omniscient narrator allows Irving to make clear the motives and desires of the different characters and also to make general comments on the morals of the characters and the times. Students should give examples that illustrate different characters' thoughts and perceptions and the narrator's general comments. Students should make clear that without an omniscient narrator, some of these important story elements would be absent; others would have to be revealed indirectly, through dialogue and action.

    Difficulty: *Average*

    Objective: *Essay*

20. Students will probably hypothesize that the possessions disappeared or were destroyed because the Devil took back his wealth, perhaps out of spite or to use again on another victim. Information about the Devil's craftiness should be used in the explanation.

    Difficulty: *Challenging*

    Objective: *Essay*

21. Students' essays might reflect the Puritans' conflicted views of money and greed. On the one hand, the story makes it clear that Tom is punished by death and hell for being greedy and cheating people. On the other hand, the Puritan characters in the story are quick to take advantage of any financial plan that will make them rich, and many of them do not appear to suffer from this need for great wealth. Accept whichever choice students make as long as they support their opinion with material from the story.

Difficulty: *Average* **Objective:** *Essay*

Primary Sources Worksheet, p. 25

Sample Answers

1. Lewis says: "This morning I . . . dispatched Drewyer and the Indian down the river." This fulfills Jefferson's statement that "The object of your mission is to explore the Missouri river."

2. Lewis describes a meeting between Sah-ca-ga-we-ah and an Indian woman, both of whom had been taken prisoner by the Minnetares. This tells us that some tribes took women as prisoners and that some women were able to escape, fulfilling Jefferson's order that Lewis find out about the Indians' "relations with other tribes or nations."

3. Lewis describes a fork in the river with a "level smooth bottom covered with a fine turf of green-sward." This fulfills Jefferson's order to "take observations . . . at all remarkable points on the river."

4. Lewis describes a meeting with some Indians, in which he "apprised them of the strength of our government and its friendly dispositions towards them." This fulfills Jefferson's order to "make them acquainted with the position, extent, character, peaceable and commercial dispositions of the United States; of our wish to be neighborly, friendly, and useful to them."

Vocabulary Builder, p. 26

Sample Answers

A. 1. B; 2. C; 3. A
B. 1. practicable
2. latitude, longitude
3. discretion
4. dispatched
5. conspicuous
6. prospect
7. conciliatory
8. membrane
9. celestial

Selection Test, p. 27

1. ANS: B	DIF: Easy	OBJ: Reading Strategy
2. ANS: D	DIF: Average	OBJ: Comprehension
3. ANS: A	DIF: Challenging	OBJ: Comprehension

4. ANS: B	DIF: Average	OBJ: Interpretation
5. ANS: C	DIF: Easy	OBJ: Comprehension
6. ANS: C	DIF: Challenging	OBJ: Interpretation
7. ANS: C	DIF: Easy	OBJ: Literary Analysis
8. ANS: A	DIF: Average	OBJ: Comprehension
9. ANS: B	DIF: Challenging	OBJ: Interpretation
10. ANS: B	DIF: Average	OBJ: Reading Strategy
11. ANS: B	DIF: Average	OBJ: Reading Strategy

12. Students' essay will differ. However, whichever element they choose, their essays should note that explorers must document, describe, and experience as much about a new place as is possible, to know what each region offers in terms of dangers, resources, people, commercial interests, etc.

Difficulty: *Average* **Objective:** *Essay*

"The Song of Hiawatha" and "The Tide Rises, The Tide Falls" by Henry Wadsworth Longfellow
"Thanatopsis" by William Cullen Bryant
"Old Ironsides" by Oliver Wendell Holmes

Vocabulary Warm-up Exercises, p. 30

A. 1. blight
2. communion
3. musings
4. palisades
5. eyries
6. vales
7. moors
8. insensible

B. Sample Answers

1. If you efface a name from a monument, you completely remove it, so it would not be legible.

2. A pensive person is thinking seriously about something, so he definitely has something on his mind.

3. Reverberations are sounds that re-echo after a first, loud sound, so you would expect each repetition of the sound to grow quieter.

4. A summons is an order that must be obeyed, so you cannot decline if you are not in the mood.

5. No, a new coat would not be threadbare, or worn and shabby.

6. No, a vanquished candidate would have been defeated in the election.

7. No, if a dog's obedience is unfaltering, it never wavers or fails.

8. If a snack sustained you, it supported and strengthened you enough to last until dinnertime.

Reading Warm-up A, p. 31

Sample Answers

1. they shared their impressions, trail information, and their general thoughts and musings; The opposite of *communion* would be a situation in which each person in a group remained silent, keeping his or her thoughts private.

2. (thoughts); He abandoned his sober *musings* at the table and joined us on the dance floor.

3. nests; It makes sense for eagles to build their *eyries* in high places in order to help protect their eggs and chicks from predators.

4. (valleys); I have traveled through *vales* without much vegetation, lying between bare, rocky mountains, in a dry desert area.

5. to keep out bears; A fence for a dog, around the perimeter of a yard, is another use for *palisades*.

6. (his bowl of oatmeal); *Insensible* means having no awareness, and no ability to hear, taste, see, smell, or touch.

7. rolling, open, grassy; Because there were few trees, we could see for a great distance when we tramped over the grassy *moors*.

8. (dampening or withering your spirits); A synonym for *blight* is rot, mold, withering, or mildew.

Reading Warm-up B, p. 32

Sample Answers

1. wipe away; Time cannot *efface* a great historical accomplishment, an artistic masterpiece, or true love.

2. ragged, full of holes; When Aaron's mother saw his *threadbare* pants, she knew he needed new clothes.

3. (commanded); A *summons* is a request that, by law, must be obeyed, while an invitation is an optional request that you may decline if you wish.

4. keep echoing; The sound of the bell bounced off the buildings and sent *reverberations* around the village square.

5. (silent) (thought); A *pensive* person will be quietly keeping to himself or herself and appear to be absorbed in thought or staring into space.

6. (defeated); Synonyms for *vanquished* include *beaten, crushed, trampled,* and *conquered*.

7. (unwavering); Many inspiring teachers display *unfaltering* devotion to ensuring the success of their students by giving them extra help and guidance during lunch or after school.

8. supporting; Situations might include a parent, relative, or coach who *sustained* a student by offering material, financial, or moral support to help a student realize a dream or accomplish a goal.

Literary Analysis: Meter, p. 33

The metrical pattern has lines of iambic tetrameter alternating with lines of iambic trimeter.

Oh, bet|ter that| her shat|tered hulk
  Should sink| beneath| the wave;
Her thun|ders shook| the might|y deep,
  And there| should be| her grave;
Nail to| the mast| her hol|y flag.
  Set eve|ry thread| bare sail,
And give| her to| the god| of storms
  The light|ning and| the gale!

Reading Strategy: Summarizing to Repair Comprehension, p. 34

Sample Answers

1. Death unites all people no matter their status in life.

2. It would be better if she (the ship "Old Ironsides") were sunk at sea with dignity by a storm.

Vocabulary Builder, p. 35

A. 1. C; 2. A; 3. B

B. Replacement words are underlined.

1. The valleys were blanketed in a <u>pensive</u> quietness.

2. The old man was knowledgeable and <u>venerable</u>.

3. The ravages of time will soon <u>efface</u> the letters on the monument.

4. The speaker's <u>eloquence</u> moved the audience to tears.

Enrichment: Science p. 37

Students should complete the chart with information about curlews and four other birds of the Northeast. Examples of birds that live in the Northeast: American black duck, black-capped chickadee, mallard, northern goshawk, purple finch, ruffed grouse, and saw-whet owl. For each fact, students should say how the fact could be used to help establish a mood.

"The Song of Hiawatha" and "The Tide Rises, The Tide Falls" by Longfellow; "Thanatopsis" by Bryant; "Old Ironsides" by Holmes

Open-Book Test, p. 38

Short Answer

1. In Stanza 1 the speaker wonders if readers have ever asked about the source of Native American legends and traditions.

   In Stanza 2 the speaker answers that the stories come from the lands and people of the Ojibways, Dacotahs and other Native Americans.

   In Stanza 3 the speaker assumes that readers love the land, too, and will wish to listen to the Song of Hiawatha.

   In Stanza 4, the speaker calls on readers to listen to the stories of Indian Legend that are both sung and spoken.

   Difficulty: *Average*   **Objective:** *Reading Strategy*

2. / u / u / u / u
    Listen to these wild traditions,
    / u / u / u / u
    To this Song of Hiawatha!
    Difficulty: *Easy*   **Objective:** *Literary Analysis*

3. The repetition of "The tide rises, the tide falls" suggests that no matter what other life activities are going on, the movement of the sea continues at its own pace and is eternal.
    Difficulty: *Average*   **Objective:** *Literary Analysis*

4. *erase, wipe out, destroy, wash away,* etc.
    Difficulty: *Average*   **Objective:** *Vocabulary*

5. The calling of the sea is the call to death. The waves are the natural, repetitive events that continue through time. They wipe out everything that has gone before and lead us into the end of our lives.
    Difficulty: *Challenging*   **Objective:** *Interpretation*

6. Students may choose from the following: the last bitter hour; shroud; pall; breatless darkness; the narrow house; cold ground; pale form; tears; eternal resting place; sepulcher; tomb; last sleep; rest; destiny; innumerable caravan; mysterious realm; chamber, silent halls; grave. Students may cite other words or phrases.
    Difficulty: *Average*   **Objective:** *Interpretation*

7. All humans, including the reader, will die.
    Difficulty: *Easy*   **Objective:** *Interpretation*

8. Death is not to be feared as if one were going to prison, but embraced as if one were about to lie down for a long rest.
    Difficulty: *Challenging*   **Objective:** *Reading Strategy*

9. The mood is one of anger. The poet is angry at the proposed destruction of the ship. The meter contributes to the mood by using short metric feet that suggest the sound of movement or protest.
    Difficulty: *Challenging*   **Objective:** *Literary Analysis*

10. The poet does not want the ship to be torn apart or disrespected. He thinks it would be more fitting to turn her loose on the seas and let her battle the storms until she sinks. He perhaps sees this as a more fitting death for a "warrior."
    Difficulty: *Average*   **Objective:** *Interpretation*

Essay

11. "The Tide Rises, The Tide Falls": Students should note that the context of the poem is the constant movement of the seas, the tide rising and falling at daybreak and evening. In this context the curlew represents the evening, and the horses represent the morning.

    "Old Ironsides": Students should note that the context of the poem is the poet's anger that the ship is to be torn apart and left to rot. The harpies of the shore represent those who would destroy the ship and her history. The eagle of the sea is the ship - a strong, fierce bird of prey.
    Difficulty: *Easy*   **Objective:** *Essay*

12. Sample answers: "The Song of Hiawatha": Students may note that the poet calls on all who love nature in all its forms, from violent storms to meadow sunshine. He asks that they listen to the stories of the people who live in this natural world and who have traditions based upon its beauties.

    "Thanatopsis": Students may note that the poet sees the natural world as an unchanging setting for all who will die and lie beneath the ground. It is ancient and outlasts all who live on the earth.
    Difficulty: *Average*   **Objective:** *Essay*

13. "The Tide Rises, The Tide Falls": Students' essays should note that the poet does not determine whether death is to be feared or welcomed, only that it is inevitable, as is the constant movement of the sea. Students may choose their own citations.

    "Thanatopsis": Students' essays should note that the poet communicates a view of death that is not fearful, but accepting. Death comes to everyone, king and commoner alike, and we will share the earth with many, many others. Students may choose their own citations.
    Difficulty: *Challenging*   **Objective:** *Essay*

14. Sample answers: These are main idea responses. Students' essays should fill in more details.

    "Hiawatha" - American history as it began with native Americans; love of the natural world as the source for this history.

    "Old Ironsides" - American history from a specific viewpoint - the ship was crucial to the winning of the War of 1812 and the poet wants to save it as an important part of the history of America.
    Difficulty: *Average*   **Objective:** *Essay*

Oral Response

15. Oral responses should be clear, well organized, and well supported by appropriate examples from the selections.

Selection Test A, p. 41

Critical Reading

1. **ANS:** A	**DIF:** Average	**OBJ:** Comprehension
2. **ANS:** B	**DIF:** Average	**OBJ:** Reading Strategy
3. **ANS:** D	**DIF:** Average	**OBJ:** Literary Analysis
4. **ANS:** D	**DIF:** Easy	**OBJ:** Comprehension
5. **ANS:** B	**DIF:** Easy	**OBJ:** Literary Analysis
6. **ANS:** C	**DIF:** Easy	**OBJ:** Interpretation
7. **ANS:** B	**DIF:** Easy	**OBJ:** Reading Strategy
8. **ANS:** C	**DIF:** Easy	**OBJ:** Literary Analysis
9. **ANS:** C	**DIF:** Easy	**OBJ:** Literary Analysis

Vocabulary

10. **ANS:** C	**DIF:** Easy	**OBJ:** Vocabulary
11. **ANS:** A	**DIF:** Easy	**OBJ:** Vocabulary

Essay

12. Students' essays should reflect the view that Bryant believes that people are buried without respect to their class or importance in human society. Poor people will be buried in the same places as kings, with people of all kinds from different times. Bryant may be suggesting by this that the ways in which people are classified during life make no difference after death. We all end up together, in the same earth.

    Difficulty: *Easy*

    Objective: *Essay*

13. Students' essays should reflect that Bryant's attitude toward death is not fearful, but accepting. He advises people facing death to take comfort from nature, and to realize that all creatures who have lived, or who will live, will die and be buried in the same earth. He says that when death comes, people should trust the experience in the same way they trust that they will have pleasant dreams when they go to sleep at night.

    Difficulty: *Easy*

    Objective: *Essay*

14. Sample answers: These are main idea responses. Students' essays should fill in more details.

    "Hiawatha" - American history as it began with Native Americans; love of the natural world as the source for this history.

    "Old Ironsides" - American history from a specific viewpoint - the ship was crucial to the winning of the War of 1812 and the poet wants to save it as an important part of the history of America.

    Difficulty: *Average*   **Objective:** *Essay*

Selection Test B, p. 44

Critical Reading

1. ANS: C	DIF: Average	OBJ: Reading Strategy
2. ANS: B	DIF: Challenging	OBJ: Comprehension
3. ANS: A	DIF: Easy	OBJ: Comprehension
4. ANS: D	DIF: Challenging	OBJ: Comprehension
5. ANS: C	DIF: Easy	OBJ: Literary Analysis
6. ANS: A	DIF: Easy	OBJ: Comprehension
7. ANS: B	DIF: Average	OBJ: Interpretation
8. ANS: A	DIF: Average	OBJ: Interpretation
9. ANS: D	DIF: Average	OBJ: Interpretation
10. ANS: D	DIF: Average	OBJ: Reading Strategy
11. ANS: B	DIF: Average	OBJ: Literary Analysis
12. ANS: C	DIF: Challenging	OBJ: Literary Analysis

Vocabulary

13. ANS: A	DIF: Average	OBJ: Vocabulary
14. ANS: C	DIF: Challenging	OBJ: Vocabulary
15. ANS: B	DIF: Average	OBJ: Comprehension

Essay

16. Most students will probably feel that the poem would be more influential than an editorial. Students may cite examples of Holmes's use of rhythm, rhyme, vivid descriptions, and emotional exclamations—none of which would ordinarily appear in an editorial.

    Difficulty: *Easy*

    Objective: *Essay*

17. Student responses may discuss how "Thanatopsis" uses nature to build a sense of something larger than the individual and to give a sense of comfort and belonging; how "Old Ironsides" uses images of stormy seas to describe the trials that the ship has undergone and stress its value to the American nation.

    Difficulty: *Challenging*

    Objective: *Essay*

18. Sample answers: These are main idea responses. Students' essays should fill in more details.

    "Hiawatha" - American history as it began with Native Americans; love of the natural world as the source for this history.

    "Old Ironsides" - American history from a specific viewpoint - the ship was crucial to the winning of the War of 1812 and the poet wants to save it as an important part of the history of America.

    Difficulty: *Average*   **Objective:** *Essay*

"The Minister's Black Veil"
Nathaniel Hawthorne

Vocabulary Warm-up Exercises, p. 48

A. 1. apprehensive
2. averse
3. intellect
4. instinctive
5. iniquity
6. amiss
7. ostentatious
8. refrain

B. Sample Answers
1. Meg was charmed by Ben's <u>amiable</u> behavior.
2. Mike's greatest <u>attribute</u> was loyalty, which was deeply ingrained in his personality.
3. Before punishing him, the principal made remarks in <u>censure</u> of Jay's conduct.
4. Inez did an <u>energetic</u> workout, performing her routines rapidly and enthusiastically.
5. Through the telescope on a clear night, we could see a <u>multitude</u> of twinkling stars.
6. The dog had a <u>placid</u> disposition, lying quietly and appearing to smile at visitors.

7. Mr. Lindgren <u>retained</u> a large part of his fortune, giving only a little money to charity.

8. A <u>venerable</u> advisor has given reliable counsel for many years.

Reading Warm-up A, p. 49

Sample Answers

1. <u>fearful</u>; The rock climber was *fearless.*

2. (has indulged in sin); *virtue*

3. <u>but he has behaved . . . and has lost all his money</u>; *correct, accurate*

4. *showy, flashy*; Paul was *ostentatious* in his taste, favoring brightly colored ties and jackets.

5. (hardly . . . to recovering their lost youth); *opposed to*

6. <u>uttered again and again</u>; repeated

7. (rivalries get the better of them); *instinct*

8. <u>may find this story hard to accept</u>; *mind*

Reading Warm-up B, p. 50

Sample Answers

1. <u>one of those ancient bits of wisdom that everyone accepted</u>; *elderly, ancient, aged*

2. (Ever since her earliest childhood . . . Marcy had . . .); Even after listening to Tad's explanation, I *retained* some doubts about his honesty.

3. <u>like a face . . . a person's identity</u>; *characteristic, trait*

4. <u>the head cheerleader, a peppy . . . girl</u>; *listless, lethargic*

5. (disapproval); *praise*

6. (the crowd); After the interesting lecture, excited audience members posed a *multitude* of questions.

7. <u>who valued quiet thoughtfulness</u>; *quiet, tranquil, peaceful, calm*

8. <u>encouraging smile</u>; The coach's discouraging remarks depressed the team.

Literary Analysis: Parable and Symbol, p. 51

Sample Answers

1. The simple description of the villagers sounds like people everywhere: The children behave like most children, and the bachelors behave like most bachelors.

2. No name is given to the deceased. The point is not *who* the deceased was, but the way that the other people responded to her death.

3. The language of this excerpt focuses on the veil and speaks of it in strong and symbolic language.

Reading Strategy: Draw Inferences to Determine Essential Meaning, p. 52

1. Students may know that wearing a veil like this is not normal, and that a minister is assumed to be close to God. As a result, students may infer that the veil represents a division between Hooper and God.

2. Students will probably understand how busybodies like to interfere with other people's lives. As a result, they may infer that something very significant has happened to make Hooper different and unapproachable about the veil.

Vocabulary Builder, p. 53

Sample Answers

A. 1. Pathology is concerned with the causes, prevention, and treatment of disease.

2. No, I would not. If I felt antipathy toward another person, I would dislike that person intensely.

3. If a friend suffered a terrible disappointment, I would show that I was sympathetic by putting a comforting arm around him or her.

B. 1. Because of Megan's obstinacy, she was never willing to change her mind—not even if there were good reasons.

2. Everyone had great respect for the venerable old man.

3. The inanimate object stayed in one place, not moving.

4. The audience was moved to tears at the pathos in the play.

5. The impertinent child showed no respect to his elders.

6. The sound of the hummingbird's wings was imperceptible from twenty feet away.

Grammar and Style: Using Adjective and Adverb Clauses, p. 54

A. 1. <u>As the people approached the meetinghouse</u>, the sexton tolled the bell.
adverb clause modifying the verb *tolled*

2. Mr. Hooper, <u>who walked slowly toward the meeting-house,</u> was wearing a veil.
adjective clause modifying the noun *Mr. Hooper*

3. Mr. Hooper gave a powerful sermon <u>while the parishioners wondered about the veil</u>.
adverb clause modifying the verb *gave*

4. The veil, <u>which was made of black crape</u>, covered most of Mr. Hooper's face.
adjective clause modifying the noun *veil*

5. <u>After he performed the wedding ceremony</u>, Mr. Hooper raised a glass to his lips.
adverb clause modifying the verb *raised*

B. Sample Answers

1. When the visitors were seated in Mr. Hooper's home, they felt very uncomfortable.
adverb clause modifying the verb *felt*

2. Elizabeth, who had been engaged to him for some time, asked him to remove the veil.
adjective clause modifying the noun *Elizabeth*

3. As she hinted at the rumors surrounding the veil, Elizabeth began to cry.
adverb clause modifying the verb *began*

4. The guilt that Mr. Hooper suffered caused him great sorrow.
adjective clause modifying the noun *guilt*

5. The veil, which he refused to remove, was buried with him.
   adjective clause modifying the noun *veil*

Enrichment: Art, p. 56

Sample Answers

1. The colors of the painting are neutral—gray-blue, black, gray, dark brown, yellow beige. They are not joyful colors. The people are dressed mainly in dark colors. The contrasting whiteness of the snow adds no warmth and little light to the painting—everything seems dark and washed out. The mood produced by this lack of color is somber and sad, harsh and unforgiving, very much like the mood of the story.

2. A wintry scene is appropriate to the text because the events that Hawthorne narrates have a darkness, an emotional coldness, and a starkness about them that seem wintry. The characters seem imprisoned in the grip of a spiritual terror and isolation that suggests winter with no possibility of spring.

3. The light background of the snow makes everything seem darker in hue, just as the minister's veil drains life and color from everything that it confronts. The white door of the church, with its contrasting black window above, repeats the snowy, bleak landscape of the whole picture rather than inviting the viewer to a warm and cheerful interior. The same is true of the white curtains in the black windows of the houses. Nothing in this painting suggests cheer.

4. The church dominates the landscape of the picture, as it does the setting of the story, but it is set to one side. The wintry track of the road takes center stage and fades to nothing at the horizon. The trees are lifeless. There is a lack of hope here. In a similar way, Hawthorne's tale seems to suggest a lack of hope for human lives. Although some of the people are grouped in the picture, there is a separateness about them. We don't know how the groups relate to each other or how the individuals in each group do. The fence in the foreground also hints at separation. Perhaps the most arresting figure is the one near the center of the picture. It is solitary and silhouetted—utterly alone. As in the story, the picture seems to stress our separation from, and lack of knowledge about, each other.

5. The painting is an appropriate accompaniment to the story in the importance that it puts on religion, as shown by the church. It also reflects the themes of human isolation and lack of hope that are found in the story. Its chilling bleakness is similarly appropriate.

"The Minister's Black Veil"
by Nathaniel Hawthorne

Open-Book Test, p. 57

Short Answer

1. Hawthorne is trying to show that ignorant and superstitious poeple become frigntened, upset, and suspicious when faced with the unknown. The minister's veil makes him a strange and frightening being, even though they can see and hear that he's the same person under the veil.
   Difficulty: *Average* **Objective:** *Literary Analysis*

2. The veil makes it possible for them to be conscious of their own wrongdoing. They feel their misdeeds are revealed. They feel guilty and overwhelmed by their own sense of sin.
   Difficulty: *Easy* **Objective:** *Interpretation*

3. They believe that the minister's black veil permits him to view the afterlife and allows the dead to see him.
   Difficulty: *Challenging* **Objective:** *Reading Strategy*

4. The word *living* has a contrasting meaning.
   Difficulty: *Easy* **Objective:** *Vocabulary*

5. Sample answers: They jump to conclusions; they are judgmental; they lack courage; they act in silly ways in response to the black veil; they are superstitious, they are narrow-minded; they see things that are not there, etc. Students may cite other faults with support from the text.
   Difficulty: *Easy* **Objective:** *Literary Analysis*

6. Sample answers: She believes that two people who plan to spend their lives together should not have secrets between them. She values honesty above all else.
   Difficulty: *Average* **Objective:** *Interpretation*

7. The clue phrase is "did he resist all her entreaties." Sample synonyms: stubbornness, inflexibility, determination
   Difficulty: *Average* **Objective:** *Vocabulary*

8. The veil symbolizes Mr. Hooper's sins, which keep him from seeing the holy page with clear eyes.
   The veil symbolizes the gulf between Mr. Hooper and the townspeople, meaning that as long as he wears it he cannot communicate honestly with them.
   The veil symbolizes the fact that no one can ever know another person completely, not even those who are engaged to be married.
   Difficulty: *Challenging* **Objective:** *Literary Analysis*

9. Sample answer: The beneficial effect is that sinners feel able to talk to the minister, which may be Hawthorne's way of saying that people are only able to admit to their wrongs in secret.
   Difficulty: *Challenging* **Objective:** *Interpretation*

10. Sample answer: She is loyal. She still loves him. To Elizabeth, Mr. Hooper is someone who is ill, not someone who is to be feared or shunned.
    Difficulty: *Average* **Objective:** *Reading Strategy*

Essay

11. Students' essays should note that the veil of eternity is the one that separates the time of life from the time of death. Mr. Hooper is near death, and the reverend

wants him to remove the veil. But even though Mr. Hooper is dying, he refuses.

Difficulty: *Easy* **Objective:** *Essay*

12. Sample answers: Hawthorne repeatedly refers to Mr. Hooper as "good Mr. Hooper," but this statement may be ironic. Some may think that Mr. Hooper has willingly taken on all the evilness of the townspeople, and becomes a mirror that reflects the evil back to them. But this does not help most of them, so Mr. Hooper can at least be said to be a bad, or ineffective minister. However, he continually tries to fulfill his normal responsibilities as a parson even in the midst of dealing with this difficult new role. Other students may question why Mr. Hooper would do something that alienates himself so completely from the people he is supposed to counsel. He knows the superstitious nature of his parishioners, so why would he do something that often makes communication with them impossible? Some students may suggest that the character of Mr. Hooper is not what is most important to Hawthorne. What Hawthorne is trying to do is show that when people step out of their expected roles in any way, they upset a society that is ignorant, judgmental, and superstitious.

Difficulty: *Average* **Objective:** *Essay*

13. Sample answer: Students' essays should note that this paragraph and other parts of the selection convey the message that all people hide behind some kind of "veil," whether it is physical or otherwise, to keep people from knowing them or their secrets. The minister's veil is visible, and he judges the townspeople for not being willing to communicate with the man he still is under the veil. Yet, he says, they are all veiled themselves.

Difficulty: *Challenging* **Objective:** *Essay*

14. Students' essays should discuss the important role of a minister as a community leader in a small Puritan village; the shock the small community must at first feel at the Reverend Mr. Hooper's wearing of the veil; the significance of faith in Puritan thought, which may inspire Mr. Hooper's donning of the veil.

Difficulty: *Average* **Objective:** *Essay*

Oral Response

15. Oral responses should be clear, well organized, and well supported by appropriate examples from the selections.

Difficulty: *Average* **Objective:** *Oral Interpretation*

Selection Test A, p. 60

Critical Reading

1. ANS: C	DIF: Easy	OBJ: Literary Analysis
2. ANS: B	DIF: Easy	OBJ: Interpretation
3. ANS: D	DIF: Easy	OBJ: Reading Strategy
4. ANS: A	DIF: Easy	OBJ: Reading Strategy
5. ANS: C	DIF: Easy	OBJ: Interpretation
6. ANS: C	DIF: Easy	OBJ: Comprehension

7. ANS: D	DIF: Easy	OBJ: Literary Analysis
8. ANS: B	DIF: Easy	OBJ: Literary Analysis

Vocabulary and Grammar

9. ANS: B	DIF: Easy	OBJ: Vocabulary
10. ANS: D	DIF: Easy	OBJ: Grammar

Essay

11. Students' essays should reflect that according to the story, dying sinners are changed because of the example of the minister and his black veil. However, the other members of the parish, including his own beloved fiancée, are isolated from him, through fear, lack of understanding, or general uneasiness. In these cases, people may have been less likely to listen to his sermons and other religious statements. They may have been less likely to accept his religious teachings. So perhaps his wearing of the veil is a powerful statement, but it does not have the effect he wishes.

Difficulty: *Easy*

Objective: *Essay*

12. Some students may suggest that the minister is confronting the people at his deathbed by asking them why they are so fearful of the black veil he wears. Don't they understand that they all wear black veils, too? He suggests that they are as sinful or as hopeful of hiding their shame as he is. In asking these questions, he may be admitting that his lifelong wearing of the veil has been unsuccessful, since his parishioners do not understand his message that, with or without a physical veil, they are all still sinners.

Difficulty: *Easy*

Objective: *Essay*

13. Students may observe that the theme is illustrated mainly by contrasting Hooper with the townspeople in each of the encounters listed. In each case, his ambiguity is played off against their rigidity and absolutism, and Hawthorne clearly sides with the minister every time.

Difficulty: *Average*

Objective: *Essay*

14. Students' essay should discuss the important role of a minister as a community leader in a small Puritan village; the shock the small community must at first feel at the Reverend Mr. Hooper's wearing of the veil; the significance of faith in Puritan life and/or the centrality of sin in Puritan life, and/or the centrality of faith in Puritan life; and/or the centrality of sin in Puritan thought, which may inspire Mr. Hooper's donning of the veil.

Difficulty: *Easy*

Objective: *Essay*

Selection Test B, p. 63

Critical Reading

1. ANS: B	DIF: Average	OBJ: Comprehension

2. ANS: D	DIF: Easy	OBJ: Comprehension
3. ANS: C	DIF: Average	OBJ: Interpretation
4. ANS: D	DIF: Easy	OBJ: Literary Analysis
5. ANS: C	DIF: Challenging	OBJ: Literary Analysis
6. ANS: A	DIF: Average	OBJ: Literary Analysis
7. ANS: B	DIF: Challenging	OBJ: Literary Analysis
8. ANS: C	DIF: Average	OBJ: Literary Analysis
9. ANS: B	DIF: Average	OBJ: Interpretation
10. ANS: C	DIF: Average	OBJ: Reading Strategy
11. ANS: D	DIF: Average	OBJ: Reading Strategy

Vocabulary and Grammar

12. ANS: A	DIF: Easy	OBJ: Vocabulary
13. ANS: B	DIF: Average	OBJ: Vocabulary
14. ANS: B	DIF: Easy	OBJ: Vocabulary
15. ANS: D	DIF: Average	OBJ: Grammar
16. ANS: A	DIF: Challenging	OBJ: Grammar

Essay

17. Some students may feel that Hooper's veil is confession of general wrongfulness stemming from the belief that all human beings are sinners in the wake of the Fall of Man (original sin in the Garden of Eden) or is a confession of more specific wrongdoing, even of some particularly terrible sin, the details of which Mr. Hooper is hiding. Others may feel that he is making a statement and is less concerned with confessing his own sins than with giving his congregation a terrible reminder of their own sins, or of the belief that human beings are all sinners. Some students may say that the veil can function in both ways at the same time.

Difficulty: *Easy*

Objective: *Essay*

18. Students will probably recognize that Hawthorne's Puritans are close-knit in their small communities and that their lives center around the church, making the pastor an important figure. They are concerned with religion and sin to a great degree. Some students may mention that Hawthorne is stressing the Puritans' hypocrisy, despite their concern with religion and sin. On the other hand, they may note that Hawthorne does make the Puritans seem human: they admire each other, they gossip, they celebrate happy events, the children make merry. Some students may feel that Hawthorne is fond of Hooper, whom he shows as a gentle soul; others may feel that he sees Hooper's veil as an extreme, even harmful, gesture, and may mention his behavior toward Elizabeth as particularly extreme and cruel.

Difficulty: *Average*

Objective: *Essay*

19. Students should mention that objects need not be strange or unique in themselves to acquire symbolic power. Rather, they become symbolic because of their particular setting, the events of which they are a part, and the people who use them. So a veil on the bonnet of a woman may be purely decorative or may symbolize ornamentation or proper dress; a veil worn by a nun or a Moslem woman may symbolize purity or piety; a veil worn by a widow may symbolize grief. When such a veil is taken out of that common context and used in a more bizarre way, it becomes a potent symbol, with power beyond the ordinary to cause an emotional reaction in all who see it.

Difficulty: *Challenging*

Objective: *Essay*

20. Students may identify Hawthorne's major theme as the ambiguity of moral absolutes, and they may observe that this is illustrated mainly by contrasting it with the strict, black-and-white standards of Puritan New England. Some features of that culture may include the people's sense of their own moral rectitude; their intolerance of things or people they don't understand; their "speechless, confused" and guiltily uneasy reaction to his presumed judgment on them; the moral cowardice of the deputies when they fail to ask him about the veil; the "fable" that the stares of dead people motivated the veil; rumors that he had committed a "great crime"; his whole life becoming "shrouded in dismal suspicions," and so on. In short, the guiding vision of the story is Hooper's nonconformity in a society of enforced conformity.

Difficulty: *Average*

Objective: *Essay*

"The Fall of the House of Usher" and "The Raven" by Edgar Allan Poe

Vocabulary Warm-up Exercises, p. 67

A. 1. maturity
   2. alternately
   3. similarly
   4. enchantment
   5. somber
   6. sinister
   7. boon
   8. ghastly

B. Sample Answers
   1. T; *Acuteness* connotes keenness, accuracy, and reliability.
   2. F; A person exhibiting *apathy* would typically be indifferent.
   3. F; *Demeanor* relates to outer appearance and behavior.
   4. T; A *gradual* scenario would unfold over time.
   5. F; An *inaccessible* office would not be easy to locate and would probably be closed.
   6. F; *Sensibility* implies an awareness of the feelings of others.

7. F; *Solace* connotes comfort and a decrease in sorrow or suffering.

8. F; *Succumbed* means "yielded" or "surrendered."

Reading Warm-up A, p. 68

Sample Answers

1. gloomy; Lane's *somber* expression indicated that he was feeling sad and depressed.

2. (a special sign of favor); an advantage

3. fascination; positive connotations

4. (terrifying); *horrible, frightful, grim*

5. (adult); *childhood, infancy*

6. the two species are . . . sooty-colored; *comparably, likewise*

7. *by turns;* At summer camp, Stan was *alternately* upbeat and homesick.

8. grim and . . . spreading confusion; *ominous, threatening*

Reading Warm-up B, p. 69

Sample Answers

1. with which a reader keenly experiences this effect; Tom had studied hard, and he answered the exam questions with unusual *acuteness* and accuracy.

2. (with many interruptions from start to finish); We were not prepared for the sudden change.

3. for the characters and situation

4. actual indifference; *concern, caring*

5. (ruled out the impact of a single effect); The new walkway made the park more *accessible.*

6. yielding all of his or her attention; *conquered, vanquished*

7. outward

8. (comfort); *consolation*

Edgar Allan Poe: Author in Depth, p. 70

Sample Answers

A. Part I Summary: Alone in the world, Poe was taken in by the family of John Allan, living with them in England till age eleven.

Suggested visual: Poe and the Allan family on a ship that is coming into port in England

Part II Summary: After joining the army at age 18, Poe published two volumes of poetry. His military career ended when he was expelled from West Point for bad grades.

Suggested visual: Poe in an army uniform writing poetry by candlelight

Part III Summary: Unable to make much money from his poetry, he turned to fiction and literary criticism. His work began to gain him some recognition.

Suggested visual: The window of an 1840s bookstore with Poe's works on display

Part IV: Summary: Poe's final years were marked by poverty, depression, and madness. He died two years after the death of his beloved wife, Virginia.

Suggested visual: Poe, distraught, tending to his sick wife

B. 1. Being raised by people who never adopted me made me feel like an outsider, as did being expelled from West Point. These feelings come out in my work. Many of my characters do not have normal human relationships.

2. I think that any reader who enjoys mysteries, vivid imagery, unusual characters, and gothic literature will be drawn to my stories and poems.

3. Distinctly American qualities include an independent spirit and an openness to new experiences. My writing shows both, for I invented the detective story, and my psychological thrillers are like no others.

Literary Analysis: Single Effect, p. 71

Sample Answers

1. A. high, narrow, pointed windows
   B. feeble light
   C. "an atmosphere of sorrow"

2. A. the oppressive air
   B. its darkness, dampness, and depth
   C. the grating door

3. A. the light of the storm and of the moon
   B. the widening fissure
   C. the sound of its cracking

4. A. his unusual appearance
   B. his feverish conversation
   C. his odd books

5. A. her pathetic illness
   B. her ghastly passage through Usher's room
   C. her bloodied appearance

Literary Analysis: Gothic Style, p. 72

Sample Answers

A. 1. Setting: a cemetery in 1850

2. Character: a man who is mourning the death of his wife

3. Events: The distraught husband visits the grave of his wife, who had been buried earlier that day. In his grief, he throws himself across the gravesite. As he lies there on the ground, he hears a faint sound from below. It sounds like a scratching. He convinces himself that she is still alive in the coffin, scratching at the lid. He digs up the earth with his bare hands and opens the coffin. It turns out she'd been in a coma so deep that it looked like death (to a doctor in 1850 whose technology didn't measure faint signs of life) and has just revived.

4. Phrases: pounding heart, frantic digging, bloody fingernails

B. 1. An air of "irredeemable gloom hung over and pervaded all."

2. "it was in the bleak December"

3. the lady Madeline being put alive into the tomb

4. The narrator has a "soul with sorrow laden."

Reading Strategy: Break Down Long Sentences, p. 73

1. Suggested core sentence: I had been passing alone through a singularly dreary tract of country and found myself within view of the melancholy House of Usher.

   Sample clarification: Traveling alone through a dreary area, I came within view of the melancholy House of Usher.

2. Suggested core sentence: I reined my horse and gazed down upon the inverted images of the gray sedge, and the ghastly tree stems, and the vacant and eyelike windows.

   Sample clarification: I reined my horse and looked at the gloomy reflection [in the tarn] of the house and landscape.

3. Suggested core sentence: He admitted that much of the peculiar gloom which thus afflicted him could be traced to the severe and long-continued illness—indeed to the evidently approaching dissolution—of a tenderly beloved sister.

   Sample clarification: He admitted that a lot of his gloom was caused by the fatal illness of his beloved sister.

4. Suggested core sentence: Our books were in strict keeping with this character of phantasm.

   Sample clarification: Our books were consistent with our eerie state.

Vocabulary Builder, p. 74

A. Sample Answers

1. When you *advocate* something, you use your voice in support of it.

2. *Vocabulary* refers to the words we know and speak.

3. Something *evocative* calls forth memories or images in our minds.

B. 1. C; 2. A; 3. C; 4. C; 5. C; 6. B

Grammar and Style: Comparative and Superlative Adjectives and Adverbs, p. 75

A. 1. superlative; 2. superlative; 3. comparative;

4. comparative

B. Sample Answers

1. more difficult

2. most surprising

3. dreariest

4. more cheerful

5. most peculiar

6. bleakest

7. more loudly

8. most ominously

9. most frightening

10. more effective

Enrichment: Film Versions of Edgar Allan Poe Stories, p. 77

Students' scripts should reflect their notes on descriptions of setting, characters, camera shots, and special visual and sound effects.

"The Fall of the House of Usher" and "The Raven" by Edgar Allen Poe

Open-Book Test, p. 78

Short Answer

1. He is striving for an effect of impending doom. Something awful is going to happen. The reader does not know what, but words such as *melancholy, desolate, terrible, insufferable gloom,* etc., foreshadow something terrible to come.

   Difficulty: *Easy*   **Objective:** *Literary Analysis*

2. Sample answer: I recognized the carvings on the ceilings, the wall tapestries, the black floors, and the fantastic, rattling suits of armor. At first I did not want to admit how familiar they all were to me. I had seen them in my childhood. Even so, now they represented new and frightening images to me.

   Difficulty: *Challenging*   **Objective:** *Reading Strategy*

3. Usher is sick, in both body and spirit. His physical appearance, his movements, his speech, and his ideas all suggest that he is a man on the edge of insanity, if not already insane.

   Difficulty: *Easy*   **Objective:** *Interpretation*

4. "repeated deeds," "charity"

   Difficulty: *Average*   **Objective:** *Vocabulary*

5. Usher fears the *effect of fear* on his sanity. The reader may have been expecting that Usher fears a real danger, but he fears only his emotional response - terror - to upcoming events. Students may or may not be surprised by Usher's fears. Accept both responses.

   Difficulty: *Challenging*   **Objective:** *Interpretation*

6. The narrator values reason. He constantly analyzes his reactions to the frightening situation. He tries to find a reason for all his impressions, and to shake off feelings of superstition and dread.

   Difficulty: *Average*   **Objective:** *Interpretation*

7. Sample answer: The narrator is studying his books late one night. He has almost fallen asleep when he hears tapping on his bedroom door. He assumes it is a visitor, nothing more.

   Difficulty: *Easy*   **Objective:** *Reading Strategy*

8. Sample answers: "Nevermore" could mean many things: the realization that the narrator will never see Lenore again, never learn where she is, never learn why the

Unit 2 Resources: A Growing Nation
© Pearson Education, Inc. All rights reserved.
212

Raven has come, etc. The word can also symbolize fate, hopelessness, despair, etc. Students may respond with different effects, as long as they can justify them in terms of the poem.

Difficulty: *Average*   **Objective:** *Literary Analysis*

9. Sample answer: The bird's behavior changed my sadness into a smile. I pulled over a chair and sat before him, trying to figure out what he wanted. I wondered why this strange and threatening-looking bird kept saying, "Nevermore." What could he mean by it?

Difficulty: *Average*   **Objective:** *Reading Stradegy*

10. Sample responses: The narrator is staring into the darkness, wondering what is out there and having fantasies no one has ever had before: single effect: fear

The narrator whispers the name of his lost love into the darkness. An echo brings her name back to him. But she does not appear. The single effect: mystery

The narrator is sick of the bird coming into his life and causing him heartbreak. He tells the raven to leave. The raven says, "Nevermore." Single effect: Fate, helplessness

Difficulty: *Challenging*   **Objective:** *Literary Analysis*

Essay

11. Sample answers: "The Fall of the House of Usher": Students' essay may suggest that Roderick's long solitude has affected his mind and that he may have an ill sister, or he may have imagined her to give himself a companion. In any case, his solitary nature means that he is much more subject to fantasies - images of things that are not really there - than someone surrounded by people and noise all day long would be. Students might infer that Roderick's long solitude means that even when the narrator is present and willing to read, listen to music, and otherwise engage with him, these make no difference because Usher is already too mentally distressed. Students may cite any number of examples from the text to support the opinion that Roderick is severely ill.

"The Raven": Students' essays may suggest that the speaker's loss of his love Lenore has forced him into solitude, where he spends time with his books instead of people. The Raven, whether real, imagined, or representing a part of himself, can be seen as a way for him to relate to someone outside himself. If the Raven is his own mind and/or soul, however, this is a terrible realization, because he is only talking to himself about things to which he already knows the answers. Lenore is gone and he is alone. Students may cite examples from the text to show the speaker's solitude.

Difficulty: *Easy*   **Objective:** *Essay*

12. Sample answers: The narrator has come to Roderick Usher's home in response to a pleading letter from his friend. Usher says he is both physically and mentally ill and he hopes that the presence of his old friend will help cure him. The narrator tries: he listens to Usher worry about his sister Madeline, he reads with Usher,

he plays and listens to music with his friend, and he helps Usher bury his sister when she dies. After all of this, he is unable to help his friend when Usher becomes convinced that Madeline has returned from the grave. The narrator flees this house of horror, and as he looks back on the events, he must wonder what more he could have done for his friend. He must also wonder whether the things he describes really happened, or whether he was drawn into his friend's mental illness.

Students' essays should note that the repeated word "Nevermore," which strikes such terror into the speaker, is matched with several rhyming words throughout the poem - *lore, door, floor, more,* etc. The repetition of the *-or* sound in conjunction with the word "Nevermore," which deprives the speaker of all hope, contribute to the feeling of doom. Poe also uses phrases with alliteration and rhyme to suggest the speaker's feelings: "weak and weary," "beating . . . repeating," ". . . wondering, fearing,/doubting, dreaming. . . ", and so forth.

Difficulty: *Average*   **Objective:** *Essay*

13. Sample answers: "The Fall of the House of Usher"

Students' essays may suggest that the House of Usher symbolizes Roderick Usher himself, or at least his mind. The outside of the house is rotting, and the inside contains two very ill individuals, or perhaps one very ill and disturbed man and his fantasy sister. When Roderick's mind finally goes, the house disappears into the swamp, and the narrator barely escapes with his life.

Students may make other arguments for what the house symbolizes as long as they can justify their opinions with material from the poem.

"The Raven"

Students' essays may suggest that the Raven symbolizes the speaker's soul, or his longing for his lost love, Lenore. He believes that the bird is real and is there to give him a message, but the Raven says nothing but "Nevermore" in response to all the speaker's questions. It is important to note that the speaker already knows the answers to the questions he asks the Raven. He knows Lenore is lost forever, that he will never see her again. Some students may suggest that the Raven does not leave because the Raven is part of the speaker's being.

Students may make other arguments for whom or what the Raven symbolizes as long as they can justify their opinions with material from the poem.

Difficulty: *Challenging*   **Objective:** *Essay*

14. "Fall of the House of Usher": Students' essays should remark on the negative effect the setting of the House of Usher has on its owner. He is seriously disturbed by what he sees and hears, or what he thinks he sees and hears. There is nothing in the landscape or the house to give joy. Students should also recognize the seemingly supernatural relationship between the house and those in it—they perish, and the house falls down.

"The Raven" - Students' essays should note that the setting of the poem is bleak, dark, and stormy. They should recognize that midnight is an eerie time often associated with the supernatural and that December is a winter month with shortdays a long, cold nights.

Difficulty: *Average*   **Objective:** *Essay*

Oral Response

15. Oral responses should be clear, well organized, and well supported by appropriate examples from the selections.

    Difficulty: *Average*   **Objective:** *Oral Interpretation*

Selection Test A, p. 81

Critical Reading

1. ANS: B	DIF: Easy	OBJ: Literary Analysis
2. ANS: C	DIF: Easy	OBJ: Reading Strategy
3. ANS: C	DIF: Easy	OBJ: Comprehension
4. ANS: B	DIF: Average	OBJ: Literary Analysis
5. ANS: D	DIF: Easy	OBJ: Reading Strategy
6. ANS: D	DIF: Average	OBJ: Literary Analysis
7. ANS: B	DIF: Easy	OBJ: Comprehension
8. ANS: B	DIF: Easy	OBJ: Interpretation

Vocabulary and Grammar

9. ANS: D	DIF: Average	OBJ: Vocabulary
10. ANS: D	DIF: Average	OBJ: Grammar

Essay

11. Students' essays should reflect the realization that both the owners and the house are dying or decaying. Madeline is dying of a disease. Roderick is dying of fear and torment. He is no longer a part of the living world but only of his fantasies. The house is decaying because it has not been kept up. Students may even suggest that the siblings and the house are parts of the same reality, so that when Roderick and Madeline die, the house dies with them.

    Difficulty: *Easy*

    Objective: *Essay*

12. Students' essays should reflect that in this poem, the bird is not a symbol of hope, freedom, or light. It is a symbol of darkness, of the loss of hope. The raven symbolizes the poet's refusal to accept the death of Lenore, the woman he loved. Some students may suggest that the raven represents the part of the poet that knows the truth but will not accept it.

    Difficulty: *Easy*

    Objective: *Essay*

13. Students may conclude that an air of doom, disaster, and otherworldly menace is created by Poe's gothic descriptions. Specific examples may include the following:

    • The "bleak walls" of the house
    • The "vacant eyelike windows"

    • "rank sedges" (dead vegetation)
    • "decayed trees"
    • A "black and lurid tarn"
    • "gray walls and turrets"
    • The burial chamber, "immensely long," "at an exceeding depth below the surface of the earth," lit by "a flood of intense rays" that "bathed the whole in a ghastly and inappropriate splendor."
    • "gray stones" of the house, with "fungi that overspread them"
    • The wild storm
    • The "distinctly visible gaseous exhalation which hung about and enshrouded the mansion"

    Difficulty: *Easy*

    Objective: *Essay*

14. "Fall of the House of Usher": Students' essays should remark on the negative effect the setting of the House of Usher has on its owner. He is seriously disturbed by what he sees and hears, or what he thinks he sees and hears. There is nothing in the landscape or the house to give joy. Students should also recognize the seemingly supernatural relationship between the house and those in it—they perish, and the house falls down.

    "The Raven" - Students' essays should note that the setting of the poem is bleak, dark, and stormy. They may recognize that midnight is an eerie time, often associated with the supernatural and that December is a winter month with short days and long, cold nights..

    Difficulty: *Easy*   **Objective:** *Essay*

Selection Test B, p. 84

Critical Reading

1. ANS: C	DIF: Easy	OBJ: Literary Analysis
2. ANS: D	DIF: Average	OBJ: Comprehension
3. ANS: A	DIF: Average	OBJ: Interpretation
4. ANS: A	DIF: Easy	OBJ: Literary Analysis
5. ANS: D	DIF: Easy	OBJ: Reading Strategy
6. ANS: C	DIF: Average	OBJ: Interpretation
7. ANS: B	DIF: Challenging	OBJ: Comprehension
8. ANS: A	DIF: Challenging	OBJ: Interpretation
9. ANS: B	DIF: Easy	OBJ: Comprehension
10. ANS: D	DIF: Easy	OBJ: Interpretation
11. ANS: A	DIF: Average	OBJ: Reading Strategy
12. ANS: D	DIF: Challenging	OBJ: Interpretation
13. ANS: C	DIF: Average	OBJ: Reading Strategy

Vocabulary and Grammar

14. ANS: D	DIF: Average	OBJ: Vocabulary
15. ANS: D	DIF: Average	OBJ: Grammar
16. ANS: D	DIF: Challenging	OBJ: Vocabulary
17. ANS: B	DIF: Easy	OBJ: Grammar

Essay

18. Students might mention feelings such as surprise, fear, dislike, curiosity, or even pleasure in their encounter with the raven. They may say that they would respond to the raven less dramatically and more scientifically than the speaker does. They might take the bird's appearance less personally. They may be less likely to see it as a supernatural messenger and may suggest that the word "Nevermore" has no real significance and is simply the only word it learned from a former master.

Difficulty: *Easy*
Objective: *Essay*

19. Students who agree with this interpretation should note that just about everything Usher does is unrelated to any existence outside his house or mind. They should mention such things as Usher's strange creations in all areas of art, especially his abstract paintings; the painful acuteness of his senses; and his absorption in fantasy literature. Students who disagree may say that Usher represents anyone completely isolated from others, not just a creative artist. Some students may point to Usher's affluence, rather than his creativity, as the root of his problem. They may cite evidence such as his large estate, servants, and lack of gainful employment to suggest that wealth and privilege without purpose may be destructive. Some students may see in Usher a member of a doomed family whose weaknesses through several generations lead to destruction, or they may place more emphasis on supernatural causes, such as a family curse, as the root of his problems.

Difficulty: *Average*
Objective: *Essay*

20. Student essays may comment on the parallelism that Poe creates between the Usher mansion and the medieval castle of the poem. Fantastic elements and their real-world counterparts include the following:

Palace	Mansion
"two luminous windows"	"vacant eyelike windows"
"evil things"	Madeline's premature burial
a "cracking and ripping sound"	"the very cracking and ripping sound" in "a very remote part of the mansion"
the "dragon's unnatural shriek"	"the exact counterpart" of this in the narrator's mind
the clanging of the fallen shield	a metallic sound "as if a shield . . . had fallen. . . ."
the "coppered archway of the vault"	the immensely long, deep vault at Usher
the "breaking of the hermit's door"	the self-opening door at the moment of Madeline's appearance

Difficulty: *Challenging*
Objective: *Essay*

21. "Fall of the House of Usher": Students' essays should remark on the negative effect the setting of the House of Usher has on its owner. He is seriously disturbed by what he sees and hears, or what he thinks he sees and hears. There is nothing in the landscape or the house to give joy. Students should also recognize the seemingly supernatural relationship between the house and those in it—they perish, and the houe falls down.

"The Raven" : Students' essays should note that the setting of the poem is bleak, dark, and stormy. They should recognize that midnight is an eerie time often associated with the supernatural and that December is a winter month with short days and long, cold nights.

Difficulty: *Average*
Objective: *Essay*

Literary Analysis: Comparing Gothic Literature p. 87

Students should note that both passages describe aspects of the exterior of a residence. Both discuss features that show deterioration. They are different in that the Poe excerpt describes the outside of a building that is in a state of disrepair, and the Oates excerpt describes a swing set that is in disrepair.

Vocabulary Builder, p. 88

A. 1. B; 2. C; 3. A; 4. B
B. 1. B; 2. C; 3. D; 4. D; 5. A

Selection Test, p. 90

Critical Reading

1. ANS: A	DIF: Easy	OBJ: Literary Analysis
2. ANS: D	DIF: Average	OBJ: Comprehension
3. ANS: D	DIF: Average	OBJ: Interpretation
4. ANS: C	DIF: Easy	OBJ: Literary Analysis
5. ANS: C	DIF: Easy	OBJ: Reading Strategy
6. ANS: C	DIF: Average	OBJ: Interpretation
7. ANS: B	DIF: Challenging	OBJ: Comprehension
8. ANS: B	DIF: Challenging	OBJ: Interpretation
9. ANS: B	DIF: Easy	OBJ: Comprehension

from **Moby-Dick** by Herman Melville

Vocabulary Warm-up Exercises, p. 93

A. 1. accumulated
2. cringing
3. outrageous
4. dislodged
5. foreboding
6. acquiescence
7. downcast
8. imperial

B. Sample Answers

1. F; *Admonitions* are warnings.
2. T; A *haughty* attitude might easily lead to arrogant behavior.
3. F; Heroism is related to virtue and courage, not to deceit.
4. T; An *inscrutable* person would be hard to analyze.
5. F; If you *intercept* a message, you are in possession of it.
6. T; *Pagan* means "heathen."
7. F; By definition, a *specific* argument is detailed and particular, not vague or general.
8. T; *Vengeance* involves retribution or retaliation.

Reading Warm-up A, p. 94

Sample Answers

1. he had . . . such a record of good conduct; Iris had begun to save three months before, and by now she had accumulated a sizable reserve fund.
2. (couldn't refuse); *agreement*
3. gray and ominous . . . as if a violent storm might erupt . . .; Greg was full of *foreboding*, feeling that something bad was about to happen.
4. (her . . . face showing her nervousness); *happy, cheerful*
5. (the boat . . . itself from the dock and set out for the open sea); The opposite of *dislodged* is *attached*.
6. she sat gripping the edge of her seat . . . with anxiety; *shrinking*
7. (to go to all this trouble and not even see a tail or a fin); If your behavior in school is *outrageous*, you may be sent home for a few days.
8. dominated the whole ocean . . . enormous power; *figuratively*

Reading Warm-up B, p. 95

Sample Answers

1. that had won fame in rough and challenging quests; Dr. Martin Luther King, Jr., led a *heroic* campaign for social justice and equality of opportunity.
2. (mysterious); *obscure, incomprehensible*
3. privateers . . . damage British ships; *interrupt*
4. ignored British . . . to stop these raids; Nathan didn't heed his parents' *admonitions* to dress warmly, and as a result, he caught a cold on the ski trip.
5. (when the Americans ignored . . . the British sought . . . they burned New Bedford); *revenge, requital, retribution, retaliation*
6. display of arrogance; Despite her talents, the violinist was humble.
7. detailed; *vague, general*
8. (ruled by no caring divinity but by the hostile forces of nature)

Literary Analysis: Symbol, p. 96

Sample Answers

1. Starbuck may represent the voice of reason and religious faith; both are overridden by Ahab's obsession.
2. The sea may represent the overwhelming forces of nature that overpower humanity and its efforts, represented by the ship; the sea may represent Ahab's fanatical, irrational obsession (or fanaticism or obsessive behavior in general), which destroys human society or the spirit of community, represented by the ship.
3. The sky hawk may represent heavenly faith and innocence, which like the crew is destroyed by Ahab's fanatical, obsessive behavior.

Reading Strategy: Identify Relevant Details, p. 97

Sample Answers

1. the "peculiar mark" of his walk, his "ribbed and dented brow" with its "still stranger footprints" of "his one unsleeping, ever-pacing thought"
2. thought; a warped nature; brooding; obsession; vengeance
3. his footprints; the imprints of his one good leg and one ivory peg
4. comparing the planks with those prints to geological stones; calling the mark of his walk "peculiar," connecting the imprints on the planks to the imprint on his mind "of his one unsleeping, ever-pacing thought" (of vengeance against the whale)
5. obsession; vengeance; Ahab's warped, obsessive nature

Vocabulary Builder, p. 98

A. 1. D; 2. B; 3. B; 4. A; 5. C
B. 1. D; 2. C; 3. A; 4. B; 5. F; 6. E

Grammar and Style: Using Participles, Gerunds, and Infinitives, p. 99

A. 1. infinitive phrase
2. participial phrase
3. participial phrase
4. gerund phrase
5. infinitive phrase
6. participial phrase

B. Sample Answers

1. Standing on the deck, Ahab was a formidable figure. (participial phrase)
2. Ahab's sole purpose was pursuing the whale. (gerund phrase)
3. Ahab wanted to take revenge. (infinitive phrase)

Enrichment: Art, p. 101

Sample Answers

1. The picture reveals Ahab's inflexibility in his stance—legs spread apart, firmly bracing him, head lifted almost defiantly, gazing out over the sea. The shadow cast by Ahab strengthens the image. The shadow of his good leg forms a triangle with his legs, an additional brace. The shadows on his figure make it seem substantial and three-dimensional. Though his face is white, shadows define his hard, craggy features.

2. The feeling conveyed by the picture of Moby-Dick leaping from the sea is one of great, even frightening, power. Two-thirds of his body protrudes vertically from the water. The water from his mighty spout slashes across the picture, indicating rapid movement. He is truly fearsome—almost supernatural in his might—and triumphant. The white body of the whale adds to the effect of power. It is almost without shadows—only a few to mark its ear and "wrinkled brow." It is solid, reminding the viewer of "that wall, shoved near to me" that Ahab mentions. Moby-Dick's body contrasts totally with the sky and sea. It seems to be its own source of light, like the stars it appears to reach for. Like them, too, the whale is an overwhelming force of nature. The stars also help the viewer place Moby-Dick, showing that he has risen above the ocean's surface.

3. The picture of the whale and the boat expresses the insignificance of humans in the face of the brute force of nature. The variation in size is one way the picture makes this point. Only the huge tail of Moby-Dick is shown. The composition emphasizes that it is as long as a boat that holds several men. The men themselves are tiny in comparison. Flung high into midair along with their equipment, they are puny and helpless. The height of the boat above the tail is stark evidence of its power. Yet, there is something almost calm about the tail itself that contrasts with the chaos of the tossed boat. It suggests the ease with which natural forces can destroy the work of humans.

4. Some students might find the use of black and white appropriate because it would emphasize the stark power and opposition of the antagonists, Ahab and Moby-Dick. They may also see symbolism of good and evil in these colors. Students who like black-and-white illustrations may also mention the simplicity and clarity they give to the events and issues. Others may feel that full color makes the events seem more natural and adds reality to the complex events.

from **Moby-Dick** by Herman Melville

Open-Book Test, p. 102

Short Answer

1. Ahab is pacing back and forth, he is knitting his brow into wrinkles, and he is deep in thought. These actions symbolize his obsession with Moby-Dick. He can do nothing except pace and worry and plot about how to hunt and kill the whale.

   Difficulty: *Easy*   **Objective:** *Literary Analysis*

2. Ahab needs the crew's help in finding Moby-Dick. He knows they do not share his obsession, so he tries to make it financially worthwhile for them to help him. He polishes the coin to make it glitter more brightly in the eyes of the crew.

   Difficulty: *Average*   **Objective:** *Interpretation*

3. Ahab compares Moby-Dick to a prison wall. He asks how a man can escape except by punching through the wall. This suggests that Ahab believes he will never be free until he destroys Moby-Dick.

   Difficulty: *Challenging*   **Objective:** *Reading Strategy*

4. The men see Moby-Dick as they see any whale—as a creature to be hunted, killed, and turned into whale oil to sell to pay their wages. Unlike Ahab, they do not feel any need for revenge on Moby-Dick.

   Difficulty: *Easy*   **Objective:** *Interpretation*

5. The men drink with Ahab to show that they will join him in the hunt for Moby-Dick. This symbolizes the theme of men working to conquer nature.

   Difficulty: *Average*   **Objective:** *Interpretation*

6. To Ahab, the wind represents a strong force of nature, but one which in many cases is helpful to him and his ship. He refers to the wind as "glorious and gracious," "strong and steadfast," "these same trades that so directly blow my good ship on;" and so forth.

   Difficulty: *Average*   **Objective:** *Reading Strategy*

7. No, the dog would not be surprised because "prescient" means knowing ahead of time. The vultures and sharks in Moby-Dick are described as also having prescient behavior.

   Difficulty: *Average*   **Objective:** *Vocabulary*

8. Sample answers: Ahab is saying that his life has been lonely and his death will be lonely, too, but that his hate for Moby-Dick is so great that he will fight him to the death.

   Ahab is suggesting that when man and nature clash, sometimes both are destroyed.

   Difficulty: *Challenging*   **Objective:** *Interpretation*

9. The sharks symbolize danger - a warning that if Ahab persists, he will die and his ship will be destroyed. They also symbolize that nature prevails against the will of humans, even when humans are enraged. Melville uses descriptions such as "maliciously snapped at the blades of the oars," "sharks following them in the same prescient way as vultures," "the unpitying sharks accompanied him," etc.

   Difficulty: *Average*   **Objective:** *Literary Analysis*

10. Ahab feels at one with the ship. If parts of the ship are destroyed, he feels that parts of himself are destroyed, too.

    Difficulty: *Easy*   **Objective:** *Interpretation*

Essay

11. Sample answers: the sinking ship (the destruction of men by nature), the shroud of the sea covering it (the

sea as a huge coffin for both men and other creatures) and the amount of time during which the sea has been rolling onward (the sea as timeless, older than mankind and able to outlive mankind).

Difficulty: *Easy*   **Objective:** *Essay*

12. Students' essays should note that Tashtego is trying to keep the ship's flag in position by nailing it to a remaining spar, even as the ship is being destroyed. His action symbolizes the persistence of the human will to survive, even in the face of death.

Difficulty: *Average*   **Objective:** *Essay*

13. Students' essays might note that the sky hawk symbolizes the same greediness that afflicts the men who go along with Ahab. The men want financial reward and the hawk wants food. Such greediness will result in death, both for the men and for the hawk. The larger theme is that all living things are ultimately powerless in the face of the whims and strength of nature.

Difficulty: *Challenging*   **Objective:** *Essay*

14. Students might suggest that Ahab's quest of vengeance and conquest represents key aspects of the American experience: When the colonists first arrived here, they faced a wild, unknown continent, inhabited by unknown peoples, and through brute force and determination overcame both the native population and the wilderness to create a new society. To this extent, Ahab's quest can be seen as symbolic of the American experience. Students might note that persistence and determination have been traits of human beings throughout history.

Difficulty: *Average*   **Objective:** *Essay*

Oral Response

15. Oral responses should be clear, well organized, and well supported by appropriate examples from the selections.

Difficulty: *Average*   **Objective:** *Oral Interpretation*

Selection Test A, p. 105

Critical Reading

1. ANS: B	DIF: Easy	OBJ: Comprehension
2. ANS: D	DIF: Easy	OBJ: Comprehension
3. ANS: B	DIF: Easy	OBJ: Literary Analysis
4. ANS: D	DIF: Easy	OBJ: Comprehension
5. ANS: A	DIF: Easy	OBJ: Reading Strategy
6. ANS: C	DIF: Easy	OBJ: Literary Analysis
7. ANS: C	DIF: Easy	OBJ: Literary Analysis
8. ANS: D	DIF: Easy	OBJ: Reading Strategy

Vocabulary and Grammar

9. ANS: B	DIF: Easy	OBJ: Vocabulary
10. ANS: C	DIF: Easy	OBJ: Grammar

Essay

11. Students may suggest that Ahab symbolizes the eternal struggle between humans and creatures, or humans

and the natural world, or life and death, and so on. Accept any argument that a student can support with material from the selection.

Difficulty: *Easy*

Objective: *Essay*

12. Students' essays should reflect that in some ways, Ahab seems to be a free person. He has his own business, and he can sail wherever he likes. But students should also see that his obsession, which ultimately kills him, imprisons him even while he is alive. He can neither act nor think freely, because both his actions and thoughts are ruled by his feelings of vengeance and helplessness against a stronger rival.

Difficulty: *Easy*

Objective: *Essay*

13. Students' essays might note that the sky hawk symbolizes the same greediness that afflicts the men who go along with Ahab. The men want financial reward and the hawk wants food. Such greediness will result in death, both for the men and for the hawk. The larger theme is that all living things are ultimately powerless in the face of the whims and strength of nature.

Difficulty: *Average*

Objective: *Essay*

14. Students might suggest that Ahab's quest of vengeance and conquest represents key aspects of the American experience: When the colonists first arrived here, they faced a wild, unknown continent, inhabited by unknown peoples, and through brute force and determination overcame both the native population and the wilderness to create a new society. To this extent, Ahab's quest can be seen as symbolic of the American experience. Students might note that persistence and determination have been traits of human beings throughout history.

Difficulty: *Average*

Objective: *Essay*

Selection Test B, p. 108

Critical Reading

1. ANS: A	DIF: Easy	OBJ: Comprehension
2. ANS: C	DIF: Easy	OBJ: Comprehension
3. ANS: C	DIF: Average	OBJ: Comprehension
4. ANS: D	DIF: Easy	OBJ: Interpretation
5. ANS: B	DIF: Average	OBJ: Interpretation
6. ANS: D	DIF: Challenging	OBJ: Interpretation
7. ANS: C	DIF: Challenging	OBJ: Interpretation
8. ANS: A	DIF: Easy	OBJ: Reading Strategy
9. ANS: D	DIF: Average	OBJ: Reading Strategy
10. ANS: C	DIF: Easy	OBJ: Literary Analysis
11. ANS: C	DIF: Challenging	OBJ: Literary Analysis
12. ANS: A	DIF: Challenging	OBJ: Literary Analysis
13. ANS: B	DIF: Average	OBJ: Literary Analysis

Vocabulary and Grammar

14. ANS: D	DIF: Easy	OBJ: Vocabulary
15. ANS: A	DIF: Average	OBJ: Vocabulary
16. ANS: D	DIF: Easy	OBJ: Grammar
17. ANS: C	DIF: Easy	OBJ: Grammar

Essay

18. Ahab's good points could include the leadership ability that helps him unite and motivate the crew, his apparent liking and respect for his men, his generosity with money, and his physical bravery. Bad points should include his abandonment of the business of the voyage, his obsessive personality, and, most important, his willingness to endanger the lives of his crew to fulfill his own ends.

Difficulty: *Easy*
Objective: *Essay*

19. Students should recognize that these words apply well to Ahab. He is a ship's captain and thus, at sea, has a great deal of power with almost no external restraints. He also seems to lack the constraints that religious faith or fear of physical danger might provide. Thus, there is nothing to keep him from being driven by his innermost necessities—hatred and vengefulness for Moby-Dick. Students may even say that without external restraints, Ahab is a victim of his inner self. They may also see in Starbuck the opposite of Ahab: the external restraints of his position on the ship—he must obey Ahab—keep him from being driven by his inner recognition that Ahab's mission is wrong.

Difficulty: *Average*
Objective: *Essay*

20. Students may say that the scene is a good way of clarifying Ahab's motivation dramatically, through his own words and actions, rather than by having Ishmael merely summarize them. Students may also say that to make the idea of the mission against Moby-Dick believable, Melville had to show the great psychological power that Ahab exerts over his crew, whom he must persuade to give up their usual business and follow him, and without whose willing help Ahab cannot hope to succeed. In addition, the scene explores Ahab's obsession in his confrontation with Starbuck, tells us about reactions of some other characters to the quest and to Ahab, and establishes the reality of Moby-Dick outside the mind of Ahab. With its high drama and ritualistic events, the scene, despite clear elements of foreshadowing, catches the reader up in Ahab's passion.

Difficulty: *Challenging*
Objective: *Essay*

21. Students' essays might note that the sky hawk symbolizes the same greediness that afflicts the men who go along with Ahab. The men want financial reward and the hawk wants food. Such greediness will result in death, both for the men and for the hawk. The larger theme is that all living things are ultimately powerless in the face of the whims and strength of nature.

Difficulty: *Challenging*
Objective: *Essay*

22. Students might suggest that Ahab's quest of vengeance and conquest represents key aspects of the American experience: When the colonists first arrived here, they faced a wild, unknown continent, inhabited by unknown peoples, and through brute force and determination overcame both the native population and the wilderness to create a new society. To this extent, Ahab's quest can be seen as symbolic of the American experience. Students might note that persistence and determination have been traits of human beings throughout history.

Difficulty: *Average*
Objective: *Essay*

---

from Nature, *from* Self-Reliance, and "Concord Hymn"
by Ralph Waldo Emerson

Vocabulary Warm-up Exercises, p. 112

A. 1. resides
2. embattled
3. brink
4. melancholy
5. misunderstood
6. testify
7. exhilaration
8. harmony

B. Sample Answers
1. Their habitual smiles showed us that our cousins had a blithe outlook on life.
2. Otis was not afraid to contradict the boss by saying that he completely disagreed with her.
3. Morris invited us to his perennial holiday party, which he held every year.
4. Hercules was thought to be immortal since he lived forever.
5. Sam gladly imparted the news by revealing every detail of the story.
6. Known for her integrity, Mayor Zeiss never faced a corruption inquiry.
7. If an event is described as an occurrence, it has definitely happened.
8. The sea seemed tranquil, with gentle waves lapping the shoreline.

Reading Warm-up A, p. 113

Sample Answers
1. (sad); An antonym for *melancholy* is *cheerful* or *happy*.
2. the ultimate responsibility for such matters in a school; The responsibility to go to school every day and complete my homework *resides* with me.
3. peaceful agreement; Alyssa and her brother played together in *harmony*.

4. (Serena's work); Peter *misunderstood* the math problem, so he calculated the wrong answer.

5. to explain that her writing and art were intended to poke fun . . . and not meant to criticize; A person might have to *testify* at a trial in a courtroom.

6. (*Tattler* staff); The *embattled* senate candidate won over voters with his new ad campaign.

7. the edge; A person might be on the *brink* of deciding whether to pursue a college degree after high school or to enter the workforce.

8. (great joy); An antonym for *exhilaration* is *dejection* or *despair*.

Reading Warm-up B, p. 114

Sample Answers

1. (peaceful); *stormy, turbulent*
2. an utterly honest goal; *Corruption* ruined the business.
3. what the majority of his fellow men pursued at the time—a life of increasing prosperity and ease; A synonym for *contradict* is *oppose*, or *deny*.
4. (or natural event); The launch of the first space shuttle was a landmark *occurrence*.
5. shared his experiences; A synonym for *imparted* is *conveyed*, or *passed on*.
6. year after year; At Sandy's Ice Cream Shop, the hot fudge sundae is a *perennial* favorite on the menu; customers order them at every visit.
7. The residents of Brook Farm hoped to live in *blithe* and peaceful harmony; Antonyms for *blithe* include *anxious* and *unhappy*.
8. existed only six years so it was hardly, but its name lives on; A synonym for *immortal* is *deathless*, *undying*, or *eternal*.

Literary Analysis: Figurative Language, p. 115

1. metaphor; 2. imagery or synecdoche; 3. imagery;
4. metaphor; 5. synecdoche; 6. imagery;
7. synecdoche; 8. description.

Reading Strategy: Challenging, or Questioning, the Text, p. 116

Sample Answers

1. Society is the enemy of individualism; society forces people to conform.
2. Students should recognize that, following the opening sentence of the paragraph, the next three sentences constitute evidence. They will probably feel that these sentences do not offer strong support because they consist merely of additional assertions and are basically restatements of the opening assertion in different words.
3. Support: laws that limit freedoms; peer pressure to conform

   Refute: laws that protect freedoms; notice and sometimes admiration given those who are different

Vocabulary Builder, p. 117

A. Sample Answers

1. away from what is sensible
2. away from what is normal
3. away from what is concrete
4. retrained from deciding or voting
5. away from a place; not here

B. 1. C; 2. B; 3. C; 4. D; 5. C; 6. A; 7. A

Enrichment: Local Landmarks p. 119

Students should provide clear and detailed answers. If students are having trouble finding a monument, suggest that they consult a local library or a historical society in the area.

from Nature, *from* Self-Reliance, and "Concord Hymn" by Ralph Waldo Emerson

Open-Book Test, p. 120

Short Answer

1. He says, "In the woods, too, a man casts off his years, as the snake his slough, and at what period soever of life is always a child." This figurative statement says that man sheds years, or becomes younger, as the snake sheds its skin, and when in the woods he is always a child.

   Difficulty: *Average*   **Objective:** *Literary Analysis*

2. He experiences it basically through sight. When he says that there is no calamity that nature cannot repair, he makes an exception of his eyes, which suggests that being able to see the natural world is more important to him than being able to experience it with his other senses.

   Difficulty: *Average*   **Objective:** *Interpretation*

3. He is saying that he is no longer himself, but has become an eye, or a way to reflect all of nature through him.

   Difficulty: *Easy*   **Objective:** *Literary Analysis*

4. Sample answer: Emerson says nature can be beautiful and sad, to suit either mood. Students may agree by saying that nature does suit either mood. They may disagree by saying that nature does not always match one's feelings.

   Difficulty: *Easy*   **Objective:** *Reading Strategy*

5. Emerson writes a metaphor, a comparison of two unlike things. He compares the air with a cordial, which is drink or food that gives pleasure and energy.

   Difficulty: *Challenging*   **Objective:** *Literary Analysis*

6. Students will probably agree with Emerson, saying that society does value "names and customs" rather than "realities and creators," and "Whosoever would be a man must be a nonconformist."

   Difficulty: *Average*   **Objective:** *Reading Strategy*

7. Sample answer: Each person's success is determined by the effort he or she puts into the task given to him or her by God: "A man is relieved and gay when he has put his heart into his work." But if he or she does not have the courage to live up to his or her potential, "His genius deserts him."

    Difficulty: *Challenging* **Objective:** *Interpretation*

8. Sample answers: Self-reliance is the opposite of conformity. Self-reliance is disliked by conformists. Self-reliance is the enemy of conformity. People who are self-reliant dislike conformity.

    Difficulty: *Average* **Objective:** *Vocabulary*

9. The members of both sides, the enemy and the victor, are now dead and sleep in silence.

    Difficulty: *Easy* **Objective:** *Interpretation*

10. The poet hopes the monument will keep alive the memory of the brave deeds done at this site, long after the men who participated and the generations that follow dead and gone.

    Difficulty: *Average* **Objective:** *Interpretation*

Essay

11. Students will have a variety of examples from which to choose, but whichever selection they choose, they should note that the importance of each individual is paramount for Emerson. In *Nature*, the individual is best served by observing and reflecting nature, and living in harmony with it. In *Self-Reliance*, the individual must struggle against society's continual demands for conformity.

    Difficulty: *Easy* **Objective:** *Essay*

12. Sample answers: "Concord Hymn": Students' essays should recognize that "fired the shot heard round the world" is a synecdoche. The *shot* stands for the Revolutionary War itself, and the poem celebrates the farmers who began it in Lexington and Concord. The "shot heard round the world" is a figurative way of saying that the Revolutionary War was an event that was important to and affected many people in the world.

    Nature: Students' essays should note that Emerson says that the experience of nature has as much to do with the spirit of the person observing it as it does with the objective state of the natural world. Nature may appear "[dressed] in holiday attire" to someone who is happy, but may inspire only contempt in someone who is grieving the loss of a friend.

    Difficulty: *Average* **Objective:** *Essay*

13. *Self-Reliance*: The metaphor in the paragraph is the beginning of the sentence "Society is a joint-stock company . . . ." Emerson compares a society of humans with a corporation. He says that for each human member of the corporation to have food to eat, all members must give up their liberty and culture, or conform. This metaphor states exactly what Emerson believes about the need for individuals to resist conformity.

Nature: Emerson is suggesting in this paragraph that all living things are related to one another. He is related to the vegetables, the trees, the leaves, and so forth. This vision is one that Emerson states in different ways throughout the essay - the importance of nature to humans and the Earth.

    Difficulty: *Challenging* **Objective:** *Essay*

14. Students might note that in "Self-Reliance," Emerson is quite clear about his distaste for the conformist pressures of society and the need to resist them. He writes. "Society everywhere is in conspiracy against the manhood of every one of its members." His prescribed answer to this pressure is to trust and believe in oneself alone: "Whoso would be a man must be a nonconformist." This spirit of self-reliance extends to his view of nature, which Emerson views, in "Nature," as always wearing "the colors of the spirit"—as serving as an inspiration for the individual's goals. The poem "Concord Hymn" celebrates and encourages just this spirit of independence, paying tribute to the soldiers of the American Revolution whose sacrifices made possible the freedom of their descendants. In all these works, Emerson seeks to inspire his reader to find his or her own path.

Oral Response

15. Oral responses should be clear, well organized, and well supported by appropriate examples from the selections.

    Difficulty: *Average* **Objective:** *Oral Interpretation*

Selection Test A, p. 123

Critical Reading

1. ANS: A	DIF: Easy	OBJ: Reading Strategy
2. ANS: B	DIF: Easy	OBJ: Literary Analysis
3. ANS: B	DIF: Easy	OBJ: Interpretation
4. ANS: C	DIF: Easy	OBJ: Interpretation
5. ANS: C	DIF: Easy	OBJ: Literary Analysis
6. ANS: C	DIF: Easy	OBJ: Literary Analysis
7. ANS: D	DIF: Easy	OBJ: Comprehension
8. ANS: B	DIF: Easy	OBJ: Literary Analysis

Vocabulary

9. ANS: C	DIF: Easy	OBJ: Vocabulary
10. ANS: D	DIF: Easy	OBJ: Vocabulary

Essay

11. Students' essays should reflect that Emerson does not respect the expectations of society. He calls it a "conspiracy" against its members. He says it is a "joint-stock company," which expects each shareholder to give up his or her independence and individuality in order to prosper. He is against conformity and consistency, and

recommends that people contradict themselves regularly if they believe different things on different days.

Difficulty: *Easy*

Objective: *Essay*

12. Emerson is suggesting that all living things are related to one another. He indicates that he is related to the vegetables, the trees, the leaves, and so forth. Students should cite additional ideas and examples from throughout the essay, recognizing that this vision is one that Emerson states in different ways all through the essay—the importance of nature to humans and the Earth.

Difficulty: *Easy*

Objective: *Essay*

13. Students might note that in *Self-Reliance*, Emerson is quite clear about his distaste for the conformist pressures of society and the need to resist them. He writes, "Society everywhere is in conspiracy against the manhood of every one of its members." His prescribed answer to this pressure is to trust and believe in oneself alone: "Whoso would be a man must be a nonconformist." This spirit of self-reliance extends to his view of nature, which Emerson views, in *Nature* as always wearing "the colors of the spirit"—as serving as an inspiration for the individual's goals. The poem "Concord Hymn" celebrates and encourages just this spirit of independence, paying tribute to the soldiers of the American Revolution whose sacrifices made possible the freedom of their descendants. In all these works, Emerson seeks to inspire his reader to find his or her own path.

Difficulty: *Easy*

Objective: *Essay*

Selection Test B, p. 126

Critical Reading

1. **ANS:** C	**DIF:** Challenging	**OBJ:** Literary Analysis
2. **ANS:** B	**DIF:** Easy	**OBJ:** Comprehension
3. **ANS:** C	**DIF:** Easy	**OBJ:** Reading Strategy
4. **ANS:** D	**DIF:** Challenging	**OBJ:** Literary Analysis
5. **ANS:** A	**DIF:** Average	**OBJ:** Reading Strategy
6. **ANS:** D	**DIF:** Average	**OBJ:** Comprehension
7. **ANS:** A	**DIF:** Challenging	**OBJ:** Literary Analysis
8. **ANS:** B	**DIF:** Average	**OBJ:** Interpretation
9. **ANS:** D	**DIF:** Average	**OBJ:** Interpretation
10. **ANS:** B	**DIF:** Easy	**OBJ:** Literary Analysis
11. **ANS:** A	**DIF:** Average	**OBJ:** Interpretation
12. **ANS:** C	**DIF:** Challenging	**OBJ:** Interpretation
13. **ANS:** D	**DIF:** Average	**OBJ:** Reading Strategy

Vocabulary

14. **ANS:** D	**DIF:** Average	**OBJ:** Vocabulary
15. **ANS:** B	**DIF:** Easy	**OBJ:** Vocabulary
16. **ANS:** B	**DIF:** Average	**OBJ:** Vocabulary
17. **ANS:** A	**DIF:** Easy	**OBJ:** Vocabulary

Essay

18. Students should cite or summarize lines from *Nature* that focus on the relationship between nature and the human spirit; for example, "In the woods is perpetual youth. Within these plantations of God, a decorum and sanctity reign"; "Standing on the bare ground—my head bathed by the blithe air and uplifted into infinite space—all mean egotism vanishes. I become a transparent eyeball: I am nothing: I see all: the currents of the Universal Being circulate through me: I am part or parcel of God"; and "Nature always wears the colors of the spirit."

Difficulty: *Easy*

Objective: *Essay*

19. The feelings and attitudes evoked are admiration for Minutemen in facing a foe, recognition of the overwhelming odds they faced, and appreciation for their courage and for the importance of their stand. The image of a "rude bridge" shows that they were willing to stand in defense of their land; the image of a flag flying implies their patriotism and willingness to stand up to their foes; the phrases "embattled farmers" and "shot heard round the world" show their courage and the importance of the stand they took.

Difficulty: *Average*

Objective: *Essay*

20. Emerson is suggesting that all living things are related to one another. He indicates that he is related to the vegetables, the trees, the leaves, and so forth. Students should cite additional ideas and examples from throughout the essay, recognizing that this vision is one that Emerson states in different ways all through the essay—the importance of nature to humans and the Earth.

Difficulty: *Challenging*

Objective: *Essay*

21. Students might note that in *Self-Reliance*, Emerson is quite clear about his distaste for the conformist pressures of society and the need to resist them. He writes, "Society everywhere is in conspiracy against the manhood of every one of its members." His prescribed answer to this pressure is to trust and believe in oneself alone: "Whoso would be a man must be a nonconformist." This spirit of self-reliance extends to his view of nature, which Emerson views, in *Nature*, as always wearing "the colors of the spirit"—as serving as an inspiration for the individual's goals. The poem "Concord Hymn" celebrates and encourages just this spirit of independence, paying tribute to the soldiers of the American Revolution whose sacrifices made possible the freedom of their descendants. In all these works, Emerson seeks to inspire his reader to find his or her own path.

Difficulty: *Average*

Objective: *Essay*

Contemporary Commentary

Gretel Ehrlich Introduces *Walden* by Henry David Thoreau, p. 129

1. She grew up on the central California coast.
2. Examples include Thoreau's opinions about land and home ownership, about the relative importance of wealth or poverty, and about life lived on a moment-by-moment basis.
3. A. Details include the changing weather, changing human relationships, physical changes in our bodies, and the cycle of natural change.
   B. Sample responses: Yes, because nature is always developing, growing, and changing; no, because human beings ought to hold onto certain fundamental principles that do not change.
4. Thoreau would have us simplify, slow down, become quiet, and try to reach the heart of things.
5. He means the fresh, dawn-like character of things—in other words, their essence in the here and now.
6. Sample responses: Yes, because our individuality is our most precious asset; no, because cooperation, harmony, and interdependence are sometimes essential.
7. Sample questions: Was Thoreau ever apprehensive or agitated when he was living at Walden Pond? What happened to Thoreau after his stay at Walden Pond was over?

Gretel Ehrlich

Listening and Viewing, p. 130

Segment 1: Gretel Ehrlich believes that, since we come from super-materialistic America, we may not have a concept of what other people are like. Traveling provides insight into the way others live and deal with hardships and, most important, helps an individual develop compassion. Students may suggest that these experiences afforded them opportunities to learn about different people and places and gain a new understanding of humanity.

Segment 2: Gretel Ehrlich structured her book that describes her experiences in Greenland like Thoreau's *Walden:* the book chronicles the writer's experiences during the four seasons. Ehrlich also lived off the land in Greenland and Wyoming for many years, much the way Thoreau lived close to nature at Walden Pond.

Segment 3: Gretel Ehrlich thinks that writing is a fresh rendition of an experience, character, or observation; it is crucial to take notes in order to have details to expand into a story. Students may say they use scraps of paper, notebooks, journals, outlines, computers, etc.

Segment 4: Gretel Ehrlich believes that the writer must contribute something to society that is worth reading and has universal appeal and value. Students may suggest that by reading anthropological books, they would appreciate the common bonds of humanity and learn to tolerate the differences.

from Walden and **from *Civil Disobedience*** by Henry David Thoreau

Vocabulary Warm-up Exercises, p. 132

A. 1. cluttered
2. essentially
3. external
4. premises
5. superfluous
6. calculation
7. anticipated
8. enterprises

B. Sample Answers
1. F; Someone acting in *conformity* would be considered conventional.
2. F; *Inherent* means "innate" or "inborn," so something *inherent* would not be superficial.
3. T; Commuter trains are a means, or method, of public transportation.
4. F; *Piety* means "devotion."
5. F; *Restricted* means "limited" or "curbed," not "increased" or "enhanced."
6. T; A clever lie could have the appearance, or simulation, of truth.
7. F; *Shun* means "to avoid."
8. F; *Transmit* means "to send, convey, or pass along."

Reading Warm-up A, p. 133

Sample Answers
1. the school gym; A sign clearly stated that it was illegal to distribute flyers on the *premises.*
2. (how difficult it would be); *expected, forecast, predicted*
3. such a heavy pack . . . take everything out and start from scratch; *crowded, congested*
4. (anything you don't need); A coat is *necessary* in this cold weather.
5. (on this trip . . . it would not be one of those fun-filled . . . he was used to); *undertakings, ventures*
6. that showed how much weight you could carry on your back, according to how much you weighed; *precise*
7. (rain, snow, hail: all the . . . elements that can seep into your skin and your pack); *Internal* injuries may not be noticed.
8. . . . learned that . . . the less you brought, the better; Numismatics may be defined, *essentially,* as the study of coins.

Reading Warm-up B, p. 134

Sample Answers
1. duty of human beings; Each person has an *inherent* right to equal protection under the law.
2. (keep pace with his companions); *conform*

3. <u>approach</u>; *manner, way*
4. <u>limited</u>; *increased, enlarged, augmented*
5. (directly . . . a set of beliefs to two of the most important men of the twentieth century); *convey, pass along, send*
6. <u>shade</u>; *appearance*
7. <u>staying away</u>; Please *accept* our invitation.
8. (reverence); *pious*

Literary Analysis: Style, p. 135

Sample Answers

1. Word choice: Thoreau uses fairly simple words sprinkled with an occasionally complex, formal term, such as *auroral, terrestrial, celestial.*
2. Sentence length: Thoreau uses fairly long sentences in this passage.
3. Sentence type/structure: Thoreau tends to use long simple or compound sentences lengthened by several verbal and prepositional phrases. He varies sentence beginnings by opening one sentence with a prepositional phrase.
4. Rhythm: Thoreau achieves a quiet, regular rhythm in this descriptive passage.
5. Literary devices: Thoreau uses fairly vivid images and figurative language, such as "airy and unplastered cabin," "broken strains . . . of terrestrial music", and the comparison of the cabin to a place "where a goddess might trail her garments."

Reading Strategy: Analyze the Author's Implicit and Explicit Philosophical Assumptions, p. 136

Students may cite some of the following main ideas: Simplify your own life and concentrate on what is truly meaningful. Value your own life, no matter how poor it may seem. Dare to be a nonconformist. Be wary lest you serve only the needs of the few. Use civil disobedience, if necessary, to make your government more responsive to individual needs.

Students should cite or summarize different portions of the selections to support each main idea and then list personal experiences that support or refute the main idea. Analysis of each main idea should take into account students' personal experiences.

Vocabulary Builder, p. 137

A. 1. C; 2. A
B. 1. A; 2. B; 3. C; 4. B; 5. A; 6. B

Enrichment: Social Studies, p. 139

Sample Answers

1. O; 2. O; 3. O; 4. S; 5. S; 6. S

Students should support their answers with details from the selections.

from Walden and *from* Civil Disobedience
by Henry David Thoreau

Open-Book Test, p. 140

Short Answer

1. The clues are "the gray color and the ruinous state of the house and barn."
   Difficulty: *Average*   **Objective:** *Vocabulary*
2. Thoreau wanted to live deliberately, to be conscious of everything he was doing, so that he would not die with the feeling that he had not lived. He wanted to determine what was essential for life and live in that way.
   Difficulty: *Challenging*   **Objective:** *Reading Strategy*
3. Thoreau compares a farm to a jail because a farm burdens a farmer with responsibilities that limit his freedom, just as a prisoner loses his or her freedom. As a larger issue, Thoreau resists anything in life that keeps a person from being free.
   Difficulty: *Challenging*   **Objective:** *Literary Analysis*
4. Sample answers: Shoulds: Count only your fingers and toes.

   Let your affairs be two or three.

   Keep your half-dozen accounts on a thumbnail.

   Eat one meal a day

   Have five dishes.

   Should nots: Concern yourself not with a hundred or thousand affairs.

   Don't have a million accounts.

   Don't eat three meals a day.

   Don't have a hundred dishes.

   Difficulty: *Easy*   **Objective:** *Interpretation*
5. He means that many people's lives are divided into many compartments, in fact, too many compartments. In the same way, the German Confederacy is made up of too many individual states. Life is cluttered with things and activities that are unnecessary. The analogy reflects Thoreau's main values about simplicity.
   Difficulty: *Easy*   **Objective:** *Literary Analysis*
6. Legislators lay barriers to block people from carrying on trade and commerce, just as vandals block or wreck trains by putting barriers on railroad tracks.
   Difficulty: *Average*   **Objective:** *Literary Analysis*
7. He says that the path he made from the cabin to the pond very quickly became a rut and a path that others used. He says he had several more lives to live and suggests that people march to the drummer they hear, not the drummer that others hear (the path others have trod).
   Difficulty: *Challenging*   **Objective:** *Interpretation*
8. Thoreau believes the policies of the government should reflect the will of a great number of people, not just the

will of few. He believes the American people would not have consented to the war with Mexico.

Difficulty: *Average*   **Objective:** *Interpretation*

9. He means the government.

Difficulty: *Easy*   **Objective:** *Interpretation*

10. "every man," or everyone

Difficulty: *Average*   **Objective:** *Reading Strategy*

Essay

11. Sample Answers: *Walden*: Students' essay should note that Thoreau goes on to say that he has several more lives to live. He does not want to fall into the rut of taking the same path every day, but wanted to walk different paths and see what else life had to offer.

Civil Disobedience: Students' essays should note that Thoreau appears to subscribe to the political view that government should take charge of as few affairs of people as is possible. He thinks individuals know what is good for them much better than the government does.

Difficulty: *Easy*   **Objective:** *Essay*

12. Sample answers: *Walden*: Students' essay may suggest any one or more of the following, or other interpretations that make sense given the passage: When Thoreau compares the intellect to a cleaver, he is saying that the mind is capable of cutting through reality to get at the truth. Next he compares the mind, or head, with his hands and feet and clearly thinks that his best abilities are found in his mind. Finally, he compares his intellect, or mind, with the burrowing snout and paws that some creatures use to dig into the earth looking for food. In this extended metaphor, Thoreau suggests that one's mind can act in all the ways other organs can act in order to find the truth of life.

Civil Disobedience: Students' essays should note that Thoreau believes that an individual man has more vitality and force than the government. In his comparison, he compares government to a wooden gun. His view of government is that it is as useless as this wooden gun, which would fall apart if fired.

Difficulty: *Average*   **Objective:** Essay

13. Sample answers: *Walden*: Students' essays might note any of the following as well as any application they can justify based on the selection: Thoreau's ideas on simplicity are necessary today in a world which needs to consume less in order to save the planet. His ideas would appear to be the basis for the concentration on recycling and reusing of materials. Also, his ideas about how there is too much of everything is the basis for many people's returning to a simpler life today. Or, his ideas on following the sound of one's own drummer could oppose the focus on conformism that society forces on us.

Civil Disobedience: Students' essays might note any of the following as well as any application they can justify based on the selection. Thoreau's judgment of President Polk's war on Mexico without the consent of the American public

could be compared with many war-policy decisions made by current and past presidents without the agreement of much of the nation. His ideas about government getting in the way of people and their lives has much to say about the ways in which the administration and legislators attempt to regulate people's private lives. Thoreau's willingness to practice civil disobedience in defense of a larger value applies to all movements for social justice throughout history, for example the Abolitionist Movement, the Civil Rights Movement, the Women's Suffrage movement, and so forth.

Difficulty: *Challenging*   **Objective:** *Essay*

14. In *Walden*, Thoreau explains his motives for wanting to retreat into a small cabin in the woods for an extended period: "I wanted to live deep and suck out all the marrow of life, to live so sturdily and Spartanlike as to put to rout all that was not life." He felt that he had to do this because a life in society is "frittered away by detail," by the unnecessary and maddening complications of day-to-day life; his motto was "Simplify, simplify." By this example and outlook he hoped to inspire people to examine their inner lives more closely, undistracted by the pressures of normal careers and superficial social attachments. "Civil Disobedience" preaches a similar message, but on a less personal, more political and social level: He advises people that they should deliberately refuse to obey laws that violate their personal principles. On a personal and political level, Thoreau tries to reshape society by urging people to pay less attention to external pressures and more to their inner spirit.

Difficulty: *Average*   **Objective:** *Essay*

Oral Response

15. Oral responses should be clear, well organized, and well supported by appropriate examples from the selections.

Difficulty: *Average*   **Objective:** *Oral Interpretation*

Selection Test A, p. 143

Critical Reading

1. ANS: B	DIF: Easy	OBJ: Comprehension
2. ANS: B	DIF: Easy	OBJ: Reading Strategy
3. ANS: D	DIF: Easy	OBJ: Literary Analysis
4. ANS: C	DIF: Easy	OBJ: Literary Analysis
5. ANS: C	DIF: Easy	OBJ: Reading Strategy
6. ANS: C	DIF: Easy	OBJ: Comprehension
7. ANS: A	DIF: Easy	OBJ: Comprehension
8. ANS: C	DIF: Easy	OBJ: Reading Strategy

Vocabulary

9. ANS: B	DIF: Easy	OBJ: Vocabulary
10. ANS: A	DIF: Easy	OBJ: Vocabulary

Essay

11. Students' essays should reflect that Thoreau seems to be saying that too much time spent in one activity or way of life does not lead to greater skill or understanding but only to unthinking habit. He apparently thinks that people should attempt to learn from different ways of life, or different occupations. Some students may remember that Thoreau says earlier in the selection that he went to the woods because he wished to live "deliberately," meaning with a purpose. Now, he says he left the woods for the same reason. He wants to explore other ideas and actions.

    Difficulty: *Easy*

    Objective: *Essay*

12. Students' essays should reflect that Thoreau believes in the saying, "That government is best which governs least." He believes that governments get in the way of people behaving in socially useful ways. He blames the Mexican war on the actions of a few people, and says the majority of the people do not want the war. He believes governments find it easy to convince people that they need a government. Thoreau's beliefs support the actions of people, not governments.

    Difficulty: *Easy*

    Objective: *Essay*

13. In *Walden*, Thoreau explains his motives for wanting to retreat into a small cabin in the woods for an extended period: "I wanted to live deep and suck out all the marrow of life, to life so sturdily and Spartanlike as to put to rout all that was not life." He felt that he had to do this because a life in society is "frittered away by detail," by the unnecessary and maddening complications of day-to-day life; his motto was "Simplify, simplify." By this example and outlook he hoped to inspire people to examine their inner lives more closely, undistracted by the pressures of normal careers and superficial social attachments. "Civil Disobedience" preaches a similar message, but on a less personal, more political and social level: He advises people that they should deliberately refuse to obey laws that violate their personal principles. On a personal and political level, Thoreau tries to reshape society by urging people to pay less attention to external pressures and more to their inner spirit.

    Difficulty: *Average*

    Objective: *Essay*

Selection Test B, p. 146

Critical Reading

1. **ANS:** D	**DIF:** Average	**OBJ:** Reading Strategy
2. **ANS:** B	**DIF:** Average	**OBJ:** Reading Strategy
3. **ANS:** A	**DIF:** Challenging	**OBJ:** Comprehension
4. **ANS:** A	**DIF:** Average	**OBJ:** Literary Analysis
5. **ANS:** D	**DIF:** Challenging	**OBJ:** Literary Analysis
6. **ANS:** B	**DIF:** Average	**OBJ:** Interpretation
7. **ANS:** C	**DIF:** Challenging	**OBJ:** Interpretation
8. **ANS:** A	**DIF:** Average	**OBJ:** Interpretation
9. **ANS:** D	**DIF:** Average	**OBJ:** Reading Strategy
10. **ANS:** C	**DIF:** Easy	**OBJ:** Interpretation
11. **ANS:** C	**DIF:** Average	**OBJ:** Comprehension
12. **ANS:** B	**DIF:** Challenging	**OBJ:** Literary Analysis
13. **ANS:** D	**DIF:** Average	**OBJ:** Reading Strategy
14. **ANS:** A	**DIF:** Challenging	**OBJ:** Reading Strategy

Vocabulary

15. **ANS:** B	**DIF:** Easy	**OBJ:** Vocabulary
16. **ANS:** B	**DIF:** Average	**OBJ:** Vocabulary
17. **ANS:** C	**DIF:** Average	**OBJ:** Vocabulary

Essay

18. Students should recognize that by moving to the woods, Thoreau was able to simplify his life, thereby allowing himself to concentrate on what he considered the important things involving the human spirit; he also lived closer to nature and gained a keener appreciation of its beauty and power. Among the details students may cite are the details about the poet appreciating a farm more than a farmer does; the descriptions of the Hollowell farm; the paragraph beginning "I went to the woods because I wished to live deliberately"; all the elaboration, in the next paragraph, on the idea of "Simplicity, simplicity, simplicity!"; and the details in the paragraph beginning "However mean your life is, meet it and live it."

    Difficulty: *Easy*

    Objective: *Essay*

19. Students should recognize that by taking action, Thoreau does not mean that people need to be busy, but that they need to contemplate the essentials of nature and the human spirit. Students may suggest that taking action can involve expressing one's opinion, refusing to go along with the rest of society, and/or dedicating oneself to a simple life experiencing nature and the human spirit. The many references to time stress Thoreau's idea that life is precious. It seems Thoreau is urging people to take action immediately, not to wait.

    Difficulty: *Challenging*

    Objective: *Essay*

20. In *Walden*, Thoreau explains his motives for wanting to retreat into a small cabin in the woods for an extended period: "I wanted to live deep and suck out all the marrow of life, to live so sturdily and Spartanlike as to put to rout all that was not life." He felt that he had to do this because a life in society is "frittered away by detail," by the unnecessary and maddening complications of day-to-day life; his motto was "Simplify, simplify." By this example and outlook he hoped to inspire people to examine their inner lives more closely, undistracted by the pressures of normal careers and superficial social attachments. "Civil Disobedience" preaches a similar

message, but on a less personal, more political and social level: He advises people that they should deliberately refuse to obey laws that violate their personal principles. On a personal and political level, Thoreau tries to reshape society by urging people to pay less attention to external pressures and more to their inner spirit.

Difficulty: *Average*

Objective: *Essay*

Benchmark Test 3, p. 149

MULTIPLE CHOICE

1. ANS: C
2. ANS: B
3. ANS: A
4. ANS: D
5. ANS: D
6. ANS: A
7. ANS: C
8. ANS: B
9. ANS: A
10. ANS: C
11. ANS: D
12. ANS: A
13. ANS: D
14. ANS: A
15. ANS: B
16. ANS: B
17. ANS: A
18. ANS: D
19. ANS: D
20. ANS: C
21. ANS: C
22. ANS: A
23. ANS: D
24. ANS: B
25. ANS: C
26. ANS: A
27. ANS: B
28. ANS: B
29. ANS: C
30. ANS: D
31. ANS: D

Essay

32. Students should describe a time when they made a difference in someone's life. Essays should describe the impact and importance of the experience both to the recipient and to themselves.

33. Essays should begin with a summary of the story. Then students should explain what they like and do not like about the story. Explanations should be supported by details from the work.

34. Character studies should include a detailed description of the character that includes physical attributes and character traits. Students should explain why they find the character memorable. Explanations should be supported by details from the work.

Emily Dickinson's Poetry

Vocabulary Warm-up Exercises, p. 156

A. 1. leisure
2. absorb
3. portion
4. assignable
5. keepsakes
6. quivering
7. onset
8. wrung

B. Sample Answers

1. Two setbacks <u>befell</u> James, but he dealt with them well.
2. Because our resources are <u>finite</u>, we must limit our pledge of money for that cause.
3. The <u>immortality</u> of the Greek gods was one way in which they differed from humans.
4. The election was close, and the winner received a very small <u>majority</u> of votes.
5. In all his undertakings, Tom <u>strove</u> hard, putting in maximum effort.
6. Willing to use an educated guess, Phil <u>surmised</u> the ending from hints in the story.
7. In favor of exhibiting the new painting, the museum director prepared to <u>unveil</u> it.
8. <u>Valves</u> are used to regulate the flow of water in those pipes.

Reading Warm-up A, p. 157

Sample Answers

1. <u>often finished her homework early . . . she had an hour or two of . . . before dinner</u>; When Rita had *leisure*, she enjoyed reading Victorian novels.
2. (fairy tales that left Betsy . . . with delight); *shaking*
3. <u>reserved a . . . of each journal page . . . fill this section</u>; *part*
4. (accumulated); *assimilate, take in, incorporate*
5. (each fictional character . . . to a poem . . . she might use the character in a story poem . . . lyric poem using the character as the speaker); *assign, assignment*
6. <u>late fall, with the . . . of winter not far off</u>; *approach, beginning*
7. (had survived and were treasured in the family); I treasured the *keepsakes* that Grandpa had left me in his will.

8. a difficult time when Hetty had . . . beautiful verse out of the challenge of her life experience; *squeezed, compressed*

Reading Warm-up B, p. 158

Sample Answers

1. to create a distinctive style . . . in this effort; Spending hours at the piano daily, Ian *strove* to refine his technique.
2. (it is the use of surprise . . . there are very few Dickinson poems); A *minority* voted for the bill.
3. inferred; *guessed*
4. surprising word choices . . . suggests mechanical devices, as if the soul had water spigots or faucets . . .
5. (we learn that death . . . the speaker before the poem opens); *happened to*
6. the perspective of someone approaching the threshold of . . .; After his long illness, his death was expected.
7. limited; *restricted, bounded, limited*
8. (reveal); *hide, conceal*

Literary Analysis: Rhyme and Paradox, p. 159

A. 1. see/me, exact; 2. chill/Tulle, slant; 3. Despair/Air, exact; 4. I, Fly, internal

B. The paradox is that the speaker refers to two deaths that preceded her final death. This seems impossible until you consider that she might be talking about the death of her heart, or having her heart broken so badly that life had no meaning after that.

Reading Strategy: Rereading to Monitor and Repair Comprehension, p. 160

Sample Answers

1. It has been centuries since then, yet it feels shorter than the day I first thought the horses were heading in the direction of eternity.
2. The brain is deeper than the sea, for if you hold them side by side, the brain will be able to absorb, or understand, the sea, just as sponges can absorb the water in buckets.
3. Space, the sea, and death are types of solitude, but they will really seem like society

Vocabulary Builder, p. 161

A. Sample Answers

1. to limit a word to a particular meaning; to provide the limits of a word's meaning
2. to redo the outer limits, or outside, of something (such as a piece of furniture)
3. ending (as of a piece of music)

B. 1. surmised; 2. infinity; 3. eternity; 4. finite; 5. ample; 6. affliction 7. interposed

C. 1. C; 2. D; 3. B; 4. B

Enrichment: Art, p. 163

Students should demonstrate understanding of the images in the poems and the way in which the paintings relate to Dickinson's messages and themes.

Open-Book Test, p. 164

Short Answer

1. Sample answers: away/civility; chill/tulle; day/eternity
   Difficulty: *Easy* **Objective:** *Literary Analysis*
2. The paradox is the suggestion that all the centuries that the poet has been dead have seemed a shorter time than the day she died. The truth is that the realization that she was dying seemed to last forever on the day it happened.
   Difficulty: *Challenging* **Objective:** *Literary Analysis*
3. Sample answers: I first *guessed* the Horses Heads; I first *predicted* the Horses Heads; I first *realized* the Horses Heads.
   Difficulty: *Average* **Objective:** *Vocabulary*
4. It indicates that the speaker is aware of the natural world even as she is dying. It suggests that one's senses remain alert up to the moment of death.
   Difficulty: *Average* **Objective:** *Reading Strategy*
5. The image is the afternoon slant of light, which the poet suggests is a reminder to people that as each day dies, they will eventually die, too.
   Difficulty: *Average* **Objective:** *Interpretation*
6. She means that parting, even though it leads to heaven, is also very painful for human beings.
   Difficulty: *Challenging* **Objective:** *Reading Strategy*
7. Sample Answers: Slant Rhymes: Gate/Mat, one/stone, nation/attention

   Exact Rhymes: society/majority, door/more

   Students may suggest that a poet uses slant rhymes to focus the reader's attention on her ideas or on the way words sound.
   Difficulty: *Average* **Objective:** *Literary Analysis*
8. The Brain - is wider than the Sky - ; The Brain is deeper than the sea - ; The Brain is just the weight of God -." The paradox is that the brain can be held in one's hand, while the sky, sea, and God are so much larger. The truth is that the brain has the power to interpret, explore, and understand many things that are larger than its own material self.
   Difficulty: *Challenging* **Objective:** *Literary Analysis*
9. She suggests that the privacy and solitude of the soul, and therefore its depths, are much greater than the depths we associate with space, sea, and death. She implies that the soul is endless and limitless by comparing it to the most unlimited concepts we know. She says because it is limitless, the soul should be valued highly.
   Difficulty: *Challenging* **Objective:** *Interpretation*

10. She suggests that we learn about a specific element of life through meeting its opposite, water by thirst, land by oceans, and so forth.

Difficulty: *Easy*   **Objective:** *Interpretation*

Essay

11. "Because I could not stop for Death"

Students' essays may address any three of the following images: the Carriage that holds Immortality; the poet has put away the things of her life - labor and leisure; the Carriage passes the Setting Sun; the Carriage pauses in a cemetery, before a grave or a mausoleum; the Horses are headed toward Eternity.

"I heard a fly buzz - when I died"

Students' essays should note that the life experience is that of the poet dying in a room with family and friends around her. They have been crying and she has made her will. Then, suddenly, as she dies, she hears a fly buzzing, her last conscious connection with the world of her senses.

Difficulty: *Easy*   **Objective:** *Essay*

12. "There's a certain Slant of light"

Students' essays should note that the poet's view of the afternoon light is a somber one. The light is not bright and cheerful, but heavy and oppressive. It is even hurtful and causes despair. In this description of the last light of the day, Dickinson is comparing the end of the day to the end of a life, or death.

"The Soul selects her own Society"

Students' essays should note that Dickinson's soul, and by association her person, is very selective about whom it allows into its space. It rejects famous people and chooses one very special guest. The poem suggests that the approval of the world and personal popularity are not worth courting or having.

Difficulty: *Average*   **Objective:** *Essay*

13. Students' essays might address any of the following: (1) her focus on Death, found in almost all the poems, perhaps related to her own ill health and the death of her father; (2) her belief in solitude and privacy as a necessity for her creativity, found in "The Soul selects her own society," and "There is a solitude," perhaps related to her small circle of beloved friends and family; (3) her attention to the ordinary events of life, which she turned into poetic images, such as the buzzing fly, the children playing in the schoolyard, the way the sun looks and feels in the late afternoon; etc. Students may suggest other connections that are justified by the biographical information and the poetry

Difficulty: *Challenging*   **Objective:** *Essay*

14. Students should recognize that Dickinson explores serious, complex ideas in poems that on the surface have an almost childlike simplicity. The poems are like brief jingles with their short lines and stanzas and their singsong rhythms and rhymes—though probe deeper and the breathy dashes and slant rhymes make the poems far more jarring than any jingle. Like the Puritans, Dickinson uses generally simple language and makes plain, direct statements of abstract ideas—though, again, such statements can be jarring and unpoetic, as, for example, in "I heard a Fly buzz—when I died." Dickinson's imagery is vivid and carefully chosen, but it usually comes from everyday experience.

Difficulty: *Average*   **Objective:** *Essay*

Oral Response

15. Oral responses should be clear, well organized, and well supported by appropriate examples from the selections.

Difficulty: *Average*   **Objective:** *Oral Interpretation*

Selection Test A, p. 167

Critical Reading

1. **ANS:** D	**DIF:** Easy	**OBJ:** Comprehension
2. **ANS:** C	**DIF:** Easy	**OBJ:** Comprehension
3. **ANS:** D	**DIF:** Easy	**OBJ:** Literary Analysis
4. **ANS:** B	**DIF:** Easy	**OBJ:** Interpretation
5. **ANS:** C	**DIF:** Easy	**OBJ:** Literary Analysis
6. **ANS:** C	**DIF:** Easy	**OBJ:** Literary Analysis
7. **ANS:** C	**DIF:** Easy	**OBJ:** Literary Analysis
8. **ANS:** A	**DIF:** Easy	**OBJ:** Reading Strategy

Vocabulary

9. **ANS:** A	**DIF:** Easy	**OBJ:** Vocabulary
10. **ANS:** A	**DIF:** Easy	**OBJ:** Vocabulary

Essay

11. Students' essays should note that stanza one uses exact rhyme in *door/more* and slant rhyme in *Society/Majority*. Stanza two uses only slant rhyme: *pausing/kneeling; Gate/Mat.* Stanza three uses only slant rhyme: *nation/attention; One/Stone.* The unexpected slant rhyme in lines 6/8 draws attention to the idea that even if a king arrives at her gate and kneels upon her mat, she remains unmoved. Slant rhyme in lines 10/12 emphasizes especially the final word, *Stone*, which shows that she is completely unmoved.

Difficulty: *Easy*

Objective: *Essay*

12. Accept any poem that uses opposites in a paradoxical way, as they are used in Dickinson's poems.

Difficulty: *Easy*

Objective: *Essay*

13. Students should recognize that the poems stress Dickinson's belief in solitude and privacy as a necessity for her creativity. They should cite images and other details from the poems—the shutting door in "The Soul selects her own Society," for example, and the contrast between the soul and society in both poems—to support

their general statements about the individualism and need for privacy that each poem conveys. Students may also discuss the style of the two poems—the quirky use of dashes, for instance, and the abrupt, jarring images and slant rhymes—as further illustrations of Dickinson's individualism.

Difficulty: *Easy*

Objective: *Essay*

Selection Test B, p. 170

Critical Reading

1. ANS: C	DIF: Average	OBJ: Comprehension
2. ANS: B	DIF: Easy	OBJ: Literary Analysis
3. ANS: A	DIF: Easy	OBJ: Reading Strategy
4. ANS: A	DIF: Average	OBJ: Interpretation
5. ANS: C	DIF: Challenging	OBJ: Interpretation
6. ANS: C	DIF: Challenging	OBJ: Literary Analysis
7. ANS: C	DIF: Average	OBJ: Comprehension
8. ANS: A	DIF: Challenging	OBJ: Literary Analysis
9. ANS: B	DIF: Challenging	OBJ: Comprehension
10. ANS: B	DIF: Average	OBJ: Literary Analysis
11. ANS: A	DIF: Easy	OBJ: Literary Analysis
12. ANS: C	DIF: Challenging	OBJ: Reading Strategy
13. ANS: D	DIF: Average	OBJ: Interpretation

Vocabulary

14. ANS: A	DIF: Easy	OBJ: Vocabulary
15. ANS: B	DIF: Easy	OBJ: Vocabulary
16. ANS: D	DIF: Average	OBJ: Vocabulary
17. ANS: B	DIF: Average	OBJ: Vocabulary

Essay

18. Students should recognize that Dickinson does not seem to fear death, but that she realizes it is impossible to predict what happens to a person after death. She also recognizes that death means parting with the people one is close to in life. Dickinson seems to believe in an immortal soul and to expect that immortality will accompany death. In "Because I could not stop for Death—," she speculates that after death, centuries may pass very quickly (presumably until Judgment Day). Some students may note that Dickinson seems to think that people are fundamentally alone and that the soul may in fact be more isolated in life than it is after death.

Difficulty: *Average*

Objective: *Essay*

19. Students should recognize that the teachers in the poem often seem to teach their opposites; for example, thirst teaches water, the oceans teach the land, battles teach peace, and death teaches love. The lessons are more often positive (water, peace, love), while the teachers are more often negative and involve human suffering (thirst, battles, death). Dickinson's message thus might be that we appreciate joy only after suffering, or that we need both the good and the bad in life because negative experiences or the absence of something helps define its meaning. Some students may note that love and death and birds and snow are not precisely opposites, but that love may fear death and birds clearly fear, or at least want to avoid, the coming of snow. These students may suggest that Dickinson's message is that we learn the most from the things and experiences that we most fear.

Difficulty: *Challenging*

Objective: *Essay*

20. Students should recognize that Dickinson explores serious, complex ideas in poem that on the surface have an almost childlike simplicity. The poems are like brief jingles with their short lines and stanzas and their singsong rhymes and rhymes—though probe deeper and the breathy dashes and slant rhymes make the poems far more jarring than any jingle. Like the Puritans, Dickinson uses generally simple language and makes plain, direct statements of abstract ideas—though, again, such statements can be jarring and unpoetic, as, for example, in "I heard a Fly buzz—when I died." Dickinson's imagery is vivid and carefully chosen, but it usually comes from everyday experience.

Difficulty: *Average*

Objective: *Essay*

Walt Whitman's Poetry

Vocabulary Warm-up Exercises, p. 174

A. 1. astronomer
2. venturing
3. mechanics
4. moist
5. lectured
6. intermission
7. measureless
8. applause

B. Sample Answers
1. T; *Abeyance* is a temporary suspension.
2. F; A *filament* would be thin or slender.
3. T; *Gossamer* implies transparency.
4. T; *Isolated* people may be acutely conscious of solitude or loneliness.
5. T; *Melodious* means "tuneful."
6. F; A *promontory* would normally be located high up, on a crag or cliff.
7. F; An *unaccountable* explanation would not be logical, and it would probably not be credible.
8. T; All the rooms would be occupied.

Reading Warm-up A, p. 175

Sample Answers

1. he felt he would be nervous; People *venturing* to climb high mountains should be well prepared and in good physical condition.
2. (explaining the movements of the planets and stars); *astronomical*
3. a bunch of objects to be tinkered with; When they worked on my car engine, the *mechanics* found that the carburetor needed to be replaced.
4. (the breath of a few hundred people); I left my wet shoes in the sun until they were dry.
5. (unable to voice an opinion, as the astronomer . . . the crowd); *addressed, delivered a talk*
6. when they could leave the auditorium for a few minutes of fresh air; *pause, break*
7. (they might clap a little); At the end of the concert, the violinist received thunderous *applause* from the audience.
8. its mystery and . . . size; *endless, boundless, infinite, unlimited*

Reading Warm-up B, p. 176

Sample Answers

1. never really finished . . . held in . . . subject to periodic revision; Since Thelma was not yet ready to start up her own business, she held her plans in *abeyance*.
2. (a long and winding thread); The writer uses the word *like* to compare the book to a long thread that parallels and records the poet's development.
3. focusing only on one priority; *solitary, lonely, alone*
4. chaos, confusion, and misery; *explicable, logical, comprehensible*
5. (. . . at the end of the medical middle ages . . . knowledge was . . . -thin); figuratively
6. two thousand wounded men a day were pouring into Washington hospitals, and the beds in them were never vacant; The seats on the bus were fully *occupied*.
7. tuneful; *musical*
8. (or rocky outcropping)

Literary Analysis: American Epic Poetry, p. 177

Sample Answers

1. This passage expresses Whitman's belief in the interconnectedness of all humanity. He felt that each person was a part of every other person's life.
2. This passage shows the connections between generations, with each generation having the same value.
3. This passage lists various kinds of workers, giving each one the same degree of dignity and worth.
4. In this passage, the speaker is feeling a kinship with all the soldiers who are sleeping in the tents.
5. This passage puts all the mentioned workers on an even plane, each one singing a different song, all equally inspiring.

Reading Strategy: Adjust Reading Rate, p. 178

Students should select passages that they had to read slowly, explain why they slowed down, and explain the meaning of the passage.

Sample Answers

Passage: "A noiseless patient spider, / I mark'd where on a little promontory it stood isolated . . ."

Why I Slowed Down: The word order is unusual, I wasn't sure of the meaning of the multiple-meaning word *mark'd*, and I had to look up the word *promontory*.

Meaning of Passage: I watched a little spider where it stood alone on a high point of land.

Vocabulary Builder, p. 179

A. 1. C; 2. A; 3. B; 4. D

B.
1. I depart as air, I shake my white locks at the runaway sun, I *pour out* my flesh in eddies, and drift it in lacy jags.
2. Creeds and school in *temporary suspension*, retiring back a while sufficed at what they are, but never forgotten.
3. In the history of earth hitherto the largest and most *active* appear tame and orderly to their ampler largeness and stir.
4. I *hand down* myself to the dirt to grow from the grass I love . . .
5. . . . as I lift my eyes they seem to be *secretively* watching me.
6. . . .at night the party of young fellows, *healthy*, friendly, Singing with open mouths their strong melodious songs.

Enrichment: Science, p. 181

Sample Answers

1. "When I Heard the Learn'd Astronomer":
   How soon unaccountable *I became tired and sick*,
   In the *mystical* moist night air
   Look'd up *in perfect silence* at the stars.
   "A Noiseless Patient Spider":
   A noiseless *patient* spider
   And you *O my soul*
   in *measureless oceans* of space,
   Ceaselessly musing, venturing, throwing, *seeking* the spheres to connect them
   Till the gossamer thread you fling catch somewhere,
   O my soul.
2. Yes. Like a scientist, Whitman emphasizes observation of the natural world.
3. Students may mention that a scientist would want to know the exact locations of stars, which are stars and which are planets, what kind of star each is, how the locations of stars as seen from Earth change with the seasons and time of the night, and so on.

4. Students may mention that a scientist would want to know what kind of spider this is, where it lives, what it eats, how long its lifespan is, and so on.

5. Students' poems may emphasize objective facts and measurements, and should avoid anthropomorphizing the stars or spider.

Open-Book Test, p. 182

Short Answer

1. Whitman says that American accepts the lessons of the past and moves on to "new forms." He suggests that the forms of the past, which were appropriate to that time, are now ready to pass on their lessons to their "heir," or new forms and insights.

   Difficulty: *Challenging* **Objective:** *Literary Analysis*

2. A slow reading rate would be better than a faster one. The sentence contains many ideas that need to be connected with one another, and reading the passage quickly might cause the reader to lose understanding.

   Difficulty: *Easy* **Objective:** *Reading Strategy*

3. Sample answer: fullest, greatest, largest, largeness, teeming, magnificently, vast, tremendous, crampless, prolific, extravagance

   Difficulty: *Easy* **Objective:** *Interpretation*

4. Line 11 suggests that while Whitman studied creeds and schoolwork a while back (line 10), he has now retired from such study. He has moved on to other things, and the creeds and schoolwork are no longer part of his life. *Abeyance* probably means "no longer in effect."

   Difficulty: *Average* **Objective:** *Vocabulary*

5. Whitman creates a short exchange between himself and a child. The child asks a question and Whitman cannot answer it. This natural occurrence is common in ordinary conversation.

   Difficulty: *Average* **Objective:** *Literary Analysis*

6. Sample answer: Whitman celebrates his unity with and empathy with his fellow man. He celebrates their common ground and shared understanding. Students may cite such details as "These are really the thoughts of all men"; "they are not original with me"; and "this is the common air that bathes the globe" or other details that support their answer.

   Difficulty: *Challenging* **Objective:** *Interpretation*

7. Whitman criticizes the astronomer for using charts and diagrams instead of taking his audience out into the night and having everyone look at the stars.

   Difficulty: *Average* **Objective:** *Interpretation*

8. The mood is slow and full of the end-of-day tasks of tired soldiers. Whitman uses phrases such as "solemn and sweet and slow" and "A Solemn and slow procession" that suggest a slow reading pace.

   Difficulty: *Average* **Objective:** *Reading Strategy*

9. Sample answers: mechanic, carpenter, mason
   boatman, deckhand, shoemaker
   hatter, wood-cutter, ploughboy

   mother, young wife, washing girl
   The workers are all involved in physical occupations that take place either outdoors or in a home, not in an office. They are rural and housekeeping occupations.

   Difficulty: *Easy* **Objective:** *Literary Analysis*

10. A spider needs to spin a thread to connect itself from place to place. Whitman feels that his soul must search for truth in the same way, throwing out "threads" that connect him with truths and experiences.

    Difficulty: *Average* **Objective:** *Interpretation*

Essay

11. Sample answers: *Leaves of Grass*: Students' essays may focus on one or more of the following: a nation of largeness; a nation of many kinds of people (forms of poetry); hospitality; pioneers; audacity; riches of the seasons, etc. Students may cite other examples.

    "I Hear America Singing": Students' essays may suggest that Whitman focuses on many of the people who built the country - the laborers in all kinds of occupations, from building, to repairing, to transporting, as well as the women and girls who keep the homes running.

    Difficulty: *Easy* **Objective:** *Essay*

12. "Song of Myself": Students' essays should note that Whitman shows no fear of death and thinks it may be very different from what people think. Lines 10 and 14 in Section 6 are particularly revealing. Students may also cite the the final eight lines in Section 52 as Whitman's playful view of death.

    Nature: Students' essays should note that Whitman revels in the natural world and loves all kinds of animals. The honk of the gander seems to be an invitation to him in Section 14 of "Song of Myself," and he goes on to list all the animals with whom he feels connected, from the house cat to the turkey hen. In Section 52, Whitman notes that a swooping hawk seems to judge him for his laziness. Students may also note that the entire poem "A Noiseless Patient Spider" is a comparison of the strivings of a small creature with the strivings of a man—Whitman.

    Difficulty: *Average* **Objective:** *Essay*

13. Sample answers: *Leaves of Grass*: Students' essays should identify the anaphora as the word *Here*. They should recognize that *Here* refers in each case to America and what characteristics one can find in the America of his time. Students may feel that repetition of the *Here* adds emphasis and power to Whitman's writing.

    "When I Heard the Learn'd Astronomer": Students' essays should identify the anaphora as *When*, and in three cases *When I*. They should recognize that Whitman uses *When*, a word that represents time, to suggest that the astronomer is wasting Whitman's and the audience's time showing charts and diagrams instead of showing them real stars.

    Difficulty: *Challenging* **Objective:** *Essay*

14. Whitman's poetry shows that he values American democracy and takes joy in a nation with such diversity of ethnic background, occupation, income level, region, and so on. His poetry also shows his deep admiration for the average person and his view, gleaned in traveling through the United States, that Americans of all sorts are admirable and interesting. Students should recognize that Whitman's long catalogs support his expansive view of America and that his free verse celebrates the freedom of America. Students are likely to cite details from "I Hear America Singing" as well as other poems and the introduction to *Leaves of Grass* to support statements about Whitman's view.

Difficulty: *Average* **Objective:** *Essay*

Oral Response

15. Oral responses should be clear, well organized, and well supported by appropriate examples from the selections.

Difficulty: *Average* **Objective:** *Oral Interpretation*

Selection Test A, p. 185

Critical Reading

1. ANS: C	DIF: Easy	OBJ: Literary Analysis
2. ANS: C	DIF: Easy	OBJ: Literary Analysis
3. ANS: C	DIF: Easy	OBJ: Literary Analysis
4. ANS: B	DIF: Easy	OBJ: Literary Analysis
5. ANS: C	DIF: Easy	OBJ: Reading Strategy
6. ANS: C	DIF: Easy	OBJ: Interpretation
7. ANS: D	DIF: Easy	OBJ: Interpretation
8. ANS: B	DIF: Easy	OBJ: Comprehension

Vocabulary

9. ANS: B	DIF: Easy	OBJ: Vocabulary
10. ANS: C	DIF: Easy	OBJ: Vocabulary

Essay

11. Students may say that Americans still feel that immigrants make the nation stronger, by bringing new energy and ideas to the country. Accept responses that show examples of the contributions of diverse groups to the nation.

Difficulty: *Easy*

Objective: *Essay*

12. Students' essays should reflect that much of Whitman's poetry was positive about nature, work, life, democracy, and the variety of experiences that were available to people in nineteenth-century America. Students might use a variety of examples from the poetry as evidence.

Difficulty: *Easy*

Objective: *Essay*

13. Whitman's poetry shows that he values America's democracy and its diversity of ethnic backgrounds, occupation, income level, region, and so on. It also

shows his deep admiration for the average person and his view that Americans of all kinds are admirable and interesting. Students may cite details from "I Hear America Singing" as well as other poems and the introduction to *Leaves of Grass* to support statements about Whitman's views.

Difficulty: *Easy*

Objective: *Essay*

Selection Test B, p. 188

Critical Reading

1. ANS: A	DIF: Average	OBJ: Comprehension
2. ANS: D	DIF: Challenging	OBJ: Interpretation
3. ANS: D	DIF: Easy	OBJ: Literary Analysis
4. ANS: D	DIF: Challenging	OBJ: Reading Strategy
5. ANS: B	DIF: Average	OBJ: Interpretation
6. ANS: C	DIF: Easy	OBJ: Literary Analysis
7. ANS: A	DIF: Average	OBJ: Interpretation
8. ANS: D	DIF: Challenging	OBJ: Comprehension
9. ANS: B	DIF: Average	OBJ: Literary Analysis
10. ANS: B	DIF: Average	OBJ: Reading Strategy
11. ANS: C	DIF: Challenging	OBJ: Literary Analysis
12. ANS: C	DIF: Challenging	OBJ: Interpretation
13. ANS: D	DIF: Average	OBJ: Literary Analysis
14. ANS: D	DIF: Average	OBJ: Interpretation

Vocabulary

15. ANS: B	DIF: Average	OBJ: Vocabulary
16. ANS: C	DIF: Average	OBJ: Vocabulary

Essay

17. Students should recognize that Whitman admired the average person and was more likely to write about jobs that involved physical work, such as carpentry or mechanics, than about jobs that involve a lot of education, such as practicing law or medicine. They should also realize that America is bigger and includes more occupations than it did in Whitman's day. Students may wish to include some fairly recent occupations, such as computer programmer or astronaut.

Difficulty: *Easy*

Objective: *Essay*

18. Whitman seems to feel that death is not an unhappy event but rather one that he accepts as part of nature. By observing nature, Whitman learns about death. Some students may quote lines such as the following: "The smallest sprout shows there is really no death," and "to die is different from what anyone supposed, and luckier."

Difficulty: *Average*

Objective: *Essay*

19. Students' essay should note that Whitman revels in the natural world and feels wonder at the details of nature. They may note all the specific birds and other animals he mentions in the selection from "Song of Myself" and may discuss his careful observation of the spider in "A Noiseless Patient Spider." They may interpret the central message of "When I Heard the Learn'd Astronomer" as one that criticizes science and reason and instead urges direct emotional experience with the natural world. Students should note that in "Song of Myself," Whitman associates himself with the grass of his book's title and may say that the grass represents imaginative rebirth or poetic wonder as well as the simple wonder of nature.

    Difficulty: *Challenging*

    Objective: *Essay*

20. Whitman's poetry shows that he values America's democracy and its diversity of ethnic background, occupation, income level, region, and so on. It also shows his deep admiration for the average person and his view, gleamed in traveling through the United States, that Americans of all sorts are admirable and interesting. Students should recognize that Whitman's long catalogs support his expansive view of America and free verse celebrates the freedom of America. Students are likely to cite details from " I Hear America Singing" as well as other poems and the introduction to Leaves of Grass to support statements about Whitman's views.

    Difficulty: *Average*

    Objective: *Essay*

Writing Workshop—Unit 2

Narration: Reflective Essay, p. 192

Students should provide answers with varied sentence beginnings, such as the following:

1. I heard the wind howling. Then the door suddenly slammed, and the windows rattled.

2. Making choices is hard, but it is an important part of growing up.

3. My big sister is my best friend because she really listens to me. When I ask her for advice, she gives it, but usually she lets me make my own decisions

Unit 2 Vocabulary Workshop, p. 194

A. Sample Answers

1. constitution

    Prefix: *con-* (together)

    Root: *statuere* (set up)

    Suffix: *-tion* (act or thing)

    A *constitution* is a thing set up when elements come together.

2. unanimous

    Prefix: *un-* (one)

    Root: *anima* (mind)

    Suffix: *-ous* (having)

    In a *unanimous* vote, all the voters have one mind.

3. demographics

    Prefix: none

    Root: *demos* (people)

    Suffix: *-graphics* (writing)

    Demographics means writing about statistics of populations.

4. politics

    Prefix: none

    Root: *polis* (city)

    Suffix: *-ics* (art, science, study)

    Politics is the study of how to govern a city, state, or nation.

B. Sample Answers

1. meritocracy: rule by people who have merit and intellect

2. nationalism: quality or practice of intense devotion to a nation

3. convention: thing that results when people come together

4. expedition: act of going out, putting foot *(pes)* out *(ex-)*